The Daughter's Way

The Daughter's Way

Canadian Women's Paternal Elegies

Tanis MacDonald

WLU PRESS
WILFRID LAURIER
UNIVERSITY PRESS

This book has been published with the help of a grant from the Canadian Federation for the Humanities and Social Sciences, through the Aid to Scholarly Publications Programme, using funds provided by the Social Sciences and Humanities Research Council of Canada. Wilfrid Laurier University Press acknowledges the support of the Canada Council for the Arts for our publishing program. We acknowledge the financial support of the Government of Canada through the Canada Book Fund for our publishing activities.

Library and Archives Canada Cataloguing in Publication

MacDonald, Tanis, 1962–
The daughter's way : Canadian women's paternal elegies / Tanis MacDonald.

Includes bibliographical references and index.
Issued in print and electronic formats.
ISBN 978-1-55458-362-1 (hardcover).—ISBN 978-1-55458-521-2 (softcover)
ISBN 978-1-55458-401-7 (PDF).—ISBN 978-1-55458-402-4 (EPUB)

1. Elegiac poetry, Canadian (English)—History and criticism. 2. Feminist poetry, Canadian (English)—History and criticism. 3. Canadian poetry (English)—Women authors—History and criticism. 4. Canadian poetry (English)—20th century—History and criticism. 5. Death in literature. 6. Fathers in literature. 7. Loss (Psychology) in literature. 8. Grief in literature. 9. Mourning customs in literature. 10. Fathers and daughters in literature. 11. Paternalism in literature. I. Title.

PS8145.E4M32 2012 C811'.54093548 C2012-900185-6
C2012-900186-4

Waterloo, Ontario, Canada
www.wlupress.wlu.ca

First paperback printing 2018

Cover design by Blakeley Words+Pictures. Front-cover image by Erica Grimm Vance: *Whatever you hear from the water remember* (2006), encaustic and steel on board (42″ x 30″). The artist's work can be seen at www.egrimmvance.com. Cover photo by Mike Rathjen. Text design by Daiva Villa, Chris Rowat Design.

"Jove's Daughter" and a portion of "Self-Portrait" reprinted from *Archive for Our Times: Previously Uncollected and Unpublished Poems of Dorothy Livesay*, edited by Dean Irvine (Arsenal Pulp Press, 1998), with permission of the publisher.

"No Man's Nightingale," "Absence, Havoc," "The Love-Song of Jenny Lear," "Love-Song II of Jenny Lear," and portions of "A Winter," "The Beauty of Job's Daughters," "Some Ghost & Some Ghouls," and "Playing" reprinted from *Poems Twice Told: The Boatman and Welcoming Disaster*, by Jay Macpherson (Oxford University Press, 1981), with permission of the publisher.

This book is printed on FSC recycled paper and is certified Ecologo. It is made from 100% post-consumer fibre, processed chlorine free, and manufactured using biogas energy.

Printed in Canada

RECYCLED
Paper made from recycled material
FSC® C103567

Contents

Acknowledgements

The work of turning a series of questions into a book requires the attention and good will of many people over a numbers of years, and I must thank those who provided me with their assistance, scholarly and personal, during the years that I thought about, researched, composed, and revised this book.

I owe a debt of thanks and acknowledgement to the many generous conversations I had with various scholars over the years this book was in development. Some of these conversations were limited to the page as I read the work of scholars of contemporary elegy whose books were so important to the generation and sustenance of my ideas. The works of Jahan Ramazani, W. David Shaw, and Melissa F. Zeiger were instrumental to this book, and I recommend their works to all readers who are interested in reading more about the dynamics and difficulties of the contemporary elegy.

Initial research into the paternal elegy as written by Canadian female poets was supported by a doctoral fellowship from the Social Sciences and Humanities Research Council in 2003–2004. Further research into Dorothy Livesay's paternal elegies in the Archives at the University of Manitoba was funded by a Research Grant from Wilfrid Laurier University in 2007. Wilfrid Laurier University also supported me with a Book Preparation Grant in 2012. I thank the people in the WLU Research Office and the University of Manitoba Archives for their assistance, as well as Paul Tiessen for our many conversations about Livesay. Cailen Swain at Oxford University Press and Brian Lam at Arsenal Pulp Press supplied prompt assistance in securing permission for me to republish portions of work by Jay Macpherson and Dorothy Livesay. Everyone at Wilfrid Laurier University Press was tremendously helpful, and I especially wish to thank Lisa Quinn for her calm, cool, and collected advice, and Leslie Macredie for leading me to the paintings of Erica Grimm-Vance, whose art adorns the cover of this book.

For her supervision and application of perspicacious logic during my doctoral study, I thank Smaro Kamboureli. Jamie Dopp was the longest-standing member of my committee, and I thank him for his kindly eye and for his consistency. Misao Dean leaped to my rescue and onto my committee on short notice. Ingrid Holmberg of the Department of Greek and Roman Studies at the University of Victoria was marvellously willing to read poetry and quiz me on Ovid and Homer. Thanks also to Lynnette Hunter, Professor of Rhetoric and Performance in the Department of Theatre and Dance at the University of California, Davis for serving as external examiner for my dissertation defence.

Thanks are also due to scholars whose discussions and recommendations were so valuable in the early days of my research. I thank Eric Miller for all our discussions about Anne Carson's work, Dianne Chisholm for telling me about *Zero Hour*, and Iain Higgins for his patience and generosity. The students in my graduate seminars on the Canadian elegy, taught at Wilfrid Laurier University in the winter sessions of 2007 and 2009, kept me thinking about these texts, and their thoughtfulness and curiosity went a long way to convincing me of the resilience of my ideas. Special thanks to David Bentley at the University of Western Ontario for his work with modernist poetry, his editorship of the journal *Canadian Poetry*, and for smiling the first time I said the word "elegy" to him.

Parts of this book were presented and discussed at numerous conferences and seminars, most frequently at the annual meeting of the Association of Canadian College and University Teachers of English, but also at University of British Columbia in 2002, and at the "Poetics and Public Culture" conference in honour of Frank Davey at the University of Western Ontario in 2005. I'd like to thank Ian Rae for his support of my work with Anne Carson's texts, and the organizers, recommending readers, and audience members of all of these conferences for their support.

Parts of the book are revised versions of previously published essays, and I wish to thank the editors and anonymous readers of those publications for their roles in encouraging this work at an early stage of its development. Early versions of some of these chapters appeared first in the following scholarly journals and I thank the editors of these publications for their interest and support: Chapter Two as "'The Battle Done': Reading the Military Father in the Poems of P. K. Page" in *Canadian Poetry* 53 (2003): 71–86; Chapter Three as "Absence, Havoc: Gothic Mourning and Daughterly Duty in Jay Macpherson's *Welcoming Disaster*" in *Studies in Canadian Literature* 34.1 (2009): 58–80; Chapter Six as "The Pilgrim and the Riddle:

Father–Daughter Kinship in Anne Carson's 'The Anthropology of Water'" in *Canadian Literature* 176 (2003): 67–81; and Chapter Seven as "Gateway Politics: West Meets West in Kristjana Gunnars's *Zero Hour*" on pages 25–40 in the anthology *The Last Best West: An Examination of Myth, Identity and Quality of Life in Western Canada*, edited by Anne Gagnon, W. F. Garrett-Petts, and James Hoffman, and published in 2009 in Vancouver by New Star Books.

Because every idea has such deep roots in the texts and arguments that preceded it, I also owe a debt of gratitude to the professors who taught me as an undergraduate student, those stalwart scholars who showed no signs of being daunted by my ignorance, or perhaps more dauntingly, by my zeal. The late Dr. Clement Wyck, in whose Milton seminar at the University of Winnipeg I first read "Lycidas," deserves special praise for his calm demeanour and unshakable belief that my mind would rise to meet his expectations. Neil Besner, Keith Louise Fulton, Dawne McCance, Dennis Cooley, and Mavis Reimer taught me how to ask questions. Brenda Austin-Smith rolled up her sleeves and taught me how to sustain an argument.

Finally, I am grateful for my friends and family: Frances Sprout, Chris Fox, and Karina Vernon who made everything fun during the Victoria years; my mother for always displaying my books on her coffee table; and my father for teaching me to have eclectic reading tastes. I am lucky that my partner, John Roscoe, has an unflappable nature and the proven ability to convince me that a walk in the woods is good for the brain.

Part One

The Daughter's Way

Introduction

Who Could Not Sing
Elegy and Its (Female) Discontents

> For Lycidas is dead, dead ere his prime,
> Young Lycidas, and hath not left his peer.
> Who would not sing for Lycidas? He knew
> Himself to sing, and build the lofty rhyme
> . . . .
> Begin, then, Sisters of the sacred well,
> That from beneath the seat of Jove doth spring,
> Begin and somewhat loudly sweep the string.
> — John Milton, "Lycidas"

"To Build the Lofty Rhyme": Muses, Nightingales, and Female Elegists

I blame it on Milton. And given the opportunity, who would not?

More specifically, I credit an early encounter with Milton's "Lycidas" with awakening my questions about consolation as a possibility and the elegy as a genre, and for eventually nudging me towards thornier questions about female elegists, literary mourning, and father–daughter kinship. There may be irony to be found in this kind of beginning—a very homosocial elegy written by one young man for another young man in the seventeenth century as the spark for feminist questions about the political energy of melancholia in late-twentieth-century elegy—but sometimes the question that will not go away is the question that can be followed like a ball of string through the labyrinth of literary history.

Milton's poem, with the epigraph "the Author bewails a learned Friend, unfortunately drown'd . . . on the Irish Sea, 1637," has become an important example of the endurance of elegiac convention in the Western canon despite the fact that it is an immature work compared to almost all of Milton's other poetry and certainly has neither the scope nor the poetic power of *Paradise Lost*. In fact, Milton's use of elegiac convention in "Lycidas" has been deemed so stylized that "its inherent improbability always forces dissatisfaction on the mind," as Dr. Johnson famously declared as early as 1790 in his *Lives of the Most Eminent English Poets* (226), but even so, these conventions have retained a remarkable hold upon the contemporary imagination. "Lycidas" is considered by elegy theorists to be the gold standard, a kind of precedent text that demands attention for its crystallization of the poetic command to which all subsequent elegists must listen: sing for your dead, if you are human. Mourning in this poem is an imperative underscored by a question that rings with incredulity: who would *not* sing for the dead? This uncomfortably necessary question has become indispensable to the rhetoric of elegy for the way, among other things, that it does not let the reader off the hook. The implicit answer is that no listener, no bystander, no callow young reader would dare to dishonour the dead by refusing to sing, or by extension, refusing to acknowledge the importance of singing for the dead. This injunction carries weight even in the classroom where "Lycidas" is often encountered as assigned reading. While it would not be accurate to say that the injunction necessarily inspires mourning, it can and does inspire a resistance to mourning that connotes the need for the question itself. Part of the poem's strange appeal is its demanding, almost accusatory, tone, and its influence on contemporary elegy lies in its appeal to affect and its still resonating inquiry into the demands of mourning.

I was young—a very naïve twenty—when I first read these lines. Despite my confusion over the copious classical allusions that loomed in the latter half of the poem, Milton's resonant prosody combined with the skill of the professor—the generous and patient Dr. Clement Wyke at the University of Winnipeg—made it nearly impossible for me to squirm away from the uncomfortable demands of "Lycidas." (I had also agreed to lead a seminar on it in an effort to keep my head above water in a course in which I was the youngest and least experienced student. "Do this poem," my older and wiser fellow seminar participants said when the sign-up sheet came around. "It's short." Dr. Wyke said nothing, though now many years later, I imagine that he must have laughed, inwardly at least. Short? It was *Milton*.) Who would be hard-hearted enough, arrogant enough *not* to sing either a dirge or a hymn of praise for someone so emphatically "dead, dead ere his prime"? The question dared me to resist at the same time that it promised that resistance would usher in the darkest of fates. Trapped between the command to sing and the intimation of a dire fate bereft of human consciousness if I did not sing, I could not help but be aware of the rhetorical force of these lines as they reinforced social and philosophical injunctions to mourn immediately, plangently, and properly. Affect may have been the initiatory force, but social obedience was the currency. Though I chafed against its rigours, I could not fully extricate myself from the elegiac contract: the lyrical assertion that those who hear of death may not ignore the necessity for mourning, even if they do not enter into it themselves. Such an elegiac contract lurks on in contemporary expressions of the command to mourning, such as Arthur Miller's in *Death of a Salesman*: "attention must be paid" (56).

But back in my Milton course, even after I accepted the necessity of observing the rituals of mourning and of engaging with the poem's insistence and inquiry, Milton trapped me again by introducing the problem of gender a mere handful of lines later with the lines about the Muses' role in mourning. These "Sisters of the sacred well," spiritual embodiments of the font of inspiration, the daughters of Jove and Mnemosyne, the goddess of memory, were powerful female figures of artistic inspiration; they played their instruments and inspired song from the lips of humans, but did they sing for Lycidas? Did Milton's command to "Begin" refer to the sweeping of the string alone or also to their singing, those unheard female songs? Was this then a matter of who "would not sing" or a matter of who *could* not sing? Was it even a case of not hearing what was being sung? How else to think about the role that these female figures played in the dynamic of mourning?

More than a decade passed after that course before I read Jay Macpherson's "No Man's Nightingale," the lyric sestet that serves as the epigraph to her Governor General's Award–winning collection *The Boatman*, published in 1957. Macpherson's nightingale suggests a reply to Keats' "Ode to a Nightingale" as well as to Milton's designation of the nightingale as "Sweet bird that shunn'st the noise of folly / Most musical, most melancholy!" in 1645's "Il Penseroso." Macpherson's nightingale as a kind of female mourner is complicated by her reference to the Greek myth of Procne and Philomel as it intersects with the bird as "shrouded in secret" yet "singing and thriving," not quite Coleridge's "merry nightingale" but something akin to it. This was another piece of the puzzle about women's mourning songs and their complex relationship with elegiac convention. If Macpherson's bird, who announces herself as "no man's nightingale," is a symbol of a female elegiac mode, it prompts as many questions as it initially appears to answer. Here is the poem in its entirety:

Sir, no man's nightingale, your foolish bird,
I sing and thrive, by Angel finger fed,
And when I turn to rest, an Angel's word
Exalts an air of trees above my head,
Shrouds me in secret where no single thing
May envy no-man's-nightingale her spring.

Macpherson's impersonation of a nightingale in this tiny dramatic monologue adds another piece to the puzzle of women's voices in the elegiac mode. Both poet and nightingale do sing: no ambiguity there. Macpherson's bird also leaves no question about her spiritual allegiance. She is "no man's nightingale": fed by the Angels themselves, a touch of divinity is granted to her voice, beyond male—or human—intervention. Where Milton's Muses inspire the male voice only to accompany it, Macpherson's nightingale "sings and thrives," fed by Angelic divinity and protected from worldly envy by a leafy canopy spread by a single mysterious Angelic word.

The mystery deepens when set against Macpherson's classical allusion. Procne's weeping song (the traditional nightingale's "sob") signifies grief over the rape of her sister and the betrayal by her husband, as well as acting as a warning to men about the power of sisterhood. However, there is a degree to which Procne—as "man's nightingale"—is a cautionary figure who mourns in male service, regretting the end of her marriage, the death of her son, and her own foolishness in believing in Tereus's fidelity. What is the difference here between grief and remorse? The lightness of Macpherson's tone in "No Man's Nightingale" disguises its serious intent and double meaning. Macpherson embraces the nightingale's song as female, but refuses the notion that the nightingale sings for the ears of men. For what, then, does Macpherson's "no-man's-nightingale" mourn, and why must "an Angel's word / shroud [her] in secret?" What, for instance, are the consequences of being "envied" against which this nightingale has been safeguarded?

The questions raised by this short lyric articulate the conundrum encountered by the female elegist as both privileged and tied to an unenviable task, touched by the ineffable and shrouded by difficulty. The ambiguities and paradoxes of Macpherson's poem suggest that to "sing and thrive" as a female elegist requires a complex series of lyric, linguistic, and social negotiations. Macpherson's poem does not suggest that female access to the elegiac tradition is easy; indeed, it will take an act of appropriation to "loudly sweep the string" and build the lofty rhyme in female terms. In fact, the nightingale's (and, putatively, Macpherson's own) address to "Sir" ironizes claims of independent feminist power that the poem might imply.

But certainly in having the bird/poet speak back to Keats, who in "Ode to a Nightingale" envies the bird her forest, and even suggests that forgetfulness, rather than relentless obdurate memory, is her milieu, Macpherson is speaking back to centuries of male elegiac tradition as it has been drawn from poems like Milton's "Lycidas."

Milton's poem and Macpherson's were published more than three centuries apart: Milton's elegy for his Cambridge fellow student Edward King in 1638, and Macpherson's lyric in 1957. In placing them alongside each other here, I am aware of a number of disjunctions that the comparison invites: the authors are separated not only by time, but also by geography, by gender, and by genre. But do such differences draw razor-sharp distinctions between the works, or do they, as I think, exist as voices in a debate about the functions of elegiac convention and appropriation? Seventeenth-century England appears to be a long way from Canada's modernist period until we think about Macpherson's British childhood and her career as a Romance literature specialist; add to that Macpherson's acknowledgement in *University of Toronto Quarterly* that "Lycidas" was a poem that obsessed her from an early age, and the distance—historical and geographical—between the two poets seems a little smaller. In terms of readership, Milton's widely studied elegy has the weight of hundreds of years of scholarship behind it, while the lack of attention given Macpherson's poetry since the 1960s makes it an exemplar of Canadian literary neglect. Then there is the question of genre: can we even call Macpherson's "No Man's Nightingale" an elegy, and if so, in whose terms? For whom or what could this nightingale mourn? While the Angel may be protecting the nightingale from the wrath of men, it is equally possible that the Angel may be protecting the world from the song of the nightingale. She sings (or "sobs" as Auden writes of his nightingales as prostitutes doing in "Song of the Master and Boatswain") and "thrives" as Macpherson maintains, but how should we read her femininity, her grief, and her robust song together?

Part of the aim of this book is to consider such questions about the female elegiac mode as they appear in Canadian poetry written by women. This volume will focus on how Canadian contemporary female elegists refuse to be the "foolish bird" dwelling within and promoting the masculine tradition of mourning, and instead produce elegies that assert a variety of feminist positions that are negotiated within and beyond the parameters of the male elegiac tradition. To begin, we must consider the influence of Milton's "Lycidas" as the example through which women's adoption and adaptation of elegiac tradition may be read against the long-held literary investment in a profoundly male homosocial dynamic within the elegy.

Between Men: Elegiac Homosociality

"Lycidas" is by no means the only or—some would argue—even the best elegy in the British literary tradition, but it presents a starting point from which a stream of profoundly homosocial elegies has issued, each becoming canonized in turn. Elegiac production in the nineteenth century deserves a special mention for it produced, among others, Percy Bysshe Shelley's "Adonais" in 1821 for John Keats. Similarities between Milton's elegy and Shelley's are numerous and have been explored elsewhere, but the youth of both elegized men is worth noting, as is Shelley's prominent exhortation "O, weep for Adonais, he is dead," a command that bypasses Milton's inquiry entirely to instruct the reader in a rather aggressive manner. Alfred Lord Tennyson's "In Memoriam A. H. H." written in 1850 for Arthur Henry Hallam also elegizes a young man, Tennyson's close friend and "brother of my love," fellow poet and Cambridge scholar Hallam. Matthew Arnold's "Thyrsis" (1865) for Arthur Hugh Clough also sets up a brotherly relationship between poet and elegiac object and demonstrates Arnold's debt to "Lycidas" in his use of the pastoral elegiac convention. The poet and the lost friend appear in "Thyrsis" in the personae of two shepherds, Thyrsis and Corydon respectively, who compete in a singing contest, a competition that underlines the elegiac injunction to sing of the lost friend after his death. Algernon Charles Swinburne's "Ave Atque Vale" (1868) for Charles Baudelaire also addresses the elegized man as "brother" and even alludes in its title to Catullus's Poem 101, an elegy for Catullus's brother killed on the battlefield.

The homosocial and determinedly fraternal dynamic of these poems underscore the position of the elegy in the nineteenth century as the literary offering of one young man's lament for the untimely and unjust death of another young man. Female elegists existed prior to the twentieth century; how could they not given that women's mourning work is so profoundly tied to the care and cleaning of the dead? But with the exception of the Puritan poet Anne Bradstreet, the work of female elegists who wrote prior to the twentieth century has been given comparatively little scholarly attention. Even in the twentieth century, critical ideas, such as Harold Bloom's "anxiety of influence," reinforce homosociality as absolutely necessary to the elegy, asserting a father–son dynamic in which a young writer makes himself over into a "strong poet" by explicitly or implicitly elegizing his mentor (5). The elegy between men traditionally moves through a declaration of personal grief to angry political statement to philosophic/spiritual declaration, relying heavily upon the truths discovered through melancholic profundity to complete the elegiac discovery of the self through the media of art and philosophy. There can be little doubt, as Bloom himself asserts, that this movement is careerist, but Bloom also excuses such careerism as a rite of passage that every strong poet must pass through in order to assert his individual genius in the tide of tradition.

Bloom's reading of the ephebe's claim of mastery as a cultural and literary tradition reminds us that no discussion of politics in the elegy, feminist or otherwise, should begin without first considering how mourning becomes a rhetorical claim in poetry. Ronald Schleifer, in *Rhetoric and Death*, asserts that the rhetoric of mourning is itself a work of mourning, and while this statement seems impossible to refute, it is important to distinguish the rhetoric of mourning as work as an idea unto itself and not necessarily subservient to Sigmund Freud's conception of the "work of mourning": that is, a work that strives for, and is often guided towards, a psychological completion or curative effect. Schleifer's suggestion that the rhetoric of mourning takes as its task the "recovery of voice in the face of death" (221) seems appropriate to consider in terms of the elegy as a literary artifact of mourning, but on the other hand, the "recovery of voice" suggests an initial pathological loss of voice that sits ironically beside the voluble narrators of the canonical elegies just discussed, and seems specifically aimed at the elegies by the movement towards confessional lyric popularized in mid-twentieth century American poetry. Although much good feminist work has been done in the last thirty years to re-appropriate the female voice in literature, this book will concentrate less on recovery of voice and more upon the female voice's contribution to debates about death, power, and subjectivity that drive the elegy.

Despite its initial dependence upon annotating affective grief, inquiry—such as Milton's "Who would not sing?"—lends the elegy a peculiar but unmistakable vitality. Abbie Findlay Potts, in her 1964 study *The Elegiac Mode*, makes an eloquent and mischievous argument for what she calls "the elegiac imagination" and its boundless questing energy: "Restless and challenging, [the elegiac imagination] makes and unmakes ethical codes, ritual, and liturgy. It rearranges even as it disturbs the patterns of civil government and ecclesiastical hierarchy. Although its themes are the puzzles of life and the riddle of death, it settles down neither in the tavern nor in the churchyard" (2). Potts's emphasis on the play of order and chaos is important to understanding the inquisitive energy of the elegy, and her terms are unmistakably equivocal. An elegy "makes and unmakes" ways of reading and regarding death; it "rearranges" (i.e., creates order of various degrees) "even as it disturbs" civic and liturgical law. The meta-conceptual challenge to elegiac convention itself constitutes an elegiac convention. In the mid-twentieth century, Potts reads nineteenth-century elegies as less sorrowful than "skeptical," more concerned with "revelation" than with affective closure (2). The "Sisters of the sacred well" invoked by Milton's swain in "Lycidas" take on new life in Potts's reading as she playfully names the muse of elegy "Elegeia," and claims that Elegeia imbues the human elegist with an unflagging energy for the performance of "sorrowing, challenging, questioning" (11). Drawing from Aristotle's *Poetics*, Potts pinpoints the discovery, or anagnorisis, of the elegy as the poem's most necessary feature, noting that this revelation can be read "through the display of feelings aroused by memory, by reason or inference, fictitiously by false reference or intended deceit or—best of all—out of the nature of previous events or antecedent discoveries" (37). Using Potts's elegant theorem, we might say that the revelatory energy that drives the female-authored elegy in the twentieth century comments on the "previous event" of male elegiac history and the "antecedent discovery" of the difference between refusing to sing and having song refused for reasons of gender.

Loosened Tongues and Antecedent Discoveries: Contexts for Female Elegies

> Why does a woman's plaint (lament), as we shall see with *Hamlet*'s Ophelia and Freud's "conscientious" women, typically come across as mere chatter and thus less dignified than the ranting of a Hamletian nobleman (or Tassian poet), whose maddened vituperations are attended to and readily given a status of truth? And why aren't there more women speaking out this "truth" then, and why is it that when a melancholic woman speaks, her loosened tongue is not granted the same extraordinary virtue and wisdom as a man's?
> —Juliana Schiesari, *The Gendering of Melancholia*

Feminist theory teaches us that literary history is never apolitical, and the history of the elegy is no exception. Juliana Schiesari's important study on the "gendering of melancholia" in Renaissance literature and culture asks the question that remains largely unanswered in contemporary elegy studies: What can we make of the cultural importance and literary place of a female work of mourning? Schiesari's question about the value and cultural negation of "melancholic" female speech is a concern as germane to contemporary feminist poetics as it is to *Hamlet*. Although Schiesari refers to literary characters rather than elegists or their speaking personae, her tart indictment of a sexist elegiac history resonates in the twenty-first century, rhetorically and politically. British culture, and by extension, the British-influenced settler cultures in the United States and Canada, have long considered Schiesari's "melancholic woman's ... loosened tongue" as so much "chatter" rather than a source of philosophic and spiritual truth. Schiesari's identification of the "extraordinary virtue and wisdom" granted to melancholic men and summarily denied to mourning women in Renaissance literature demands contemporary application. Schiesari affirms the need to define melancholia as potentially creative rather than pathological: "to become melancholic one would need some access to cultural production, that is, what [Luce] Irigaray calls 'access to a signifying economy'" (65) in order to "create out of the feeling of loss some valid way to articulate that loss, that 'painful dejection,' meanfully" (66). The elegy is, among other things, such a method of cultural production, and I adopt Schiesari's question in order to contend that virtue and wisdom can be granted to the female elegist who speaks through productive melancholia.

Recent elegy studies have positioned Anne Bradstreet, Phillis Wheatley, Sylvia Plath, Anne Sexton, Adrienne Rich, Marilyn Hacker, Audre Lorde, Amy Clampitt, Margaret Atwood, and Lola Lemire Tostevin as poets who have served as elegists for people passed and for worlds vanished. However, the history of elegy has, in part, been a non-history of its female discontents, as the discovery of the kinds of feminisms or proto-feminisms that can be read in women's elegiac writing is still new territory. After Potts's sly inference about the muse of elegy in 1964, Celeste Schenck articulated the challenges of the feminine elegiac mode in her 1986 article, "Feminism and Deconstruction: Re-constructing the Elegy," first published in *Tulsa Studies in Women's Literature*. Schenck suggests the serviceability of a "methodological compatibility of feminism and deconstruction" (14) to reclaim the intellectual and affective force of the elegiac contract. Melissa F. Zeiger's *Beyond Consolation* (1997) responds to and reconfigures Schenck's theory in order to challenge the Orphean assumptions of the elegiac mode in her examination of Rich, Hacker, and Lorde as American female elegists whose literary work of mourning is steeped in political exigency. Zeiger's study is groundbreaking not only for elegy studies, but also for feminist studies and illness discourse. She begins with a feminist refusal of consolation, situating the "ongoing affectionate relations with the dead" established by women's elegies as a vital step towards "recognizing affinity, disarming suspicion and engaging in a strategic dialogue" about misogyny and tradition that in Zeiger's terms "can barely be said to have started" (25).

Zeiger's view of the elegy as a "strategic dialogue" between the living and the dead and, indeed, between two (or more) states of mind available to the elegist herself is intriguing for its suggestion that the elegy performs affect with a healthy dose of intellect. Like love poetry, the elegy examines the extremities of common experience in order to direct the force of its attention to the "uncommon"—in that it cannot be anticipated or predicted—combinations of affect that the experience of loss reveals. The elegy, as a genre, is driven by the multiple ways the ineffable lurks in the experience of loss, and herein lies its quizzical poetic project steeped in the tension between opposites. The elegist invokes the divine in order to address earthly taboos, writes of the achingly absent as painfully present, finds consolation in inconsolability, and questions the meaning of existence by searching the parameters of non-existence. There can be no surprise then that— to better perform these tasks of affect and inquiry—the elegy is structured by conventional devices that serve literary tradition. Like the funereal rituals that require mourners to act out grief in order to access mourning, the elegy performs the function of questioning the ineffable from the wasteland of mourning, making conscious the inquiry that grief awakens but may have initially hidden. The elegiac dynamic in poetry has a corollary to that of tragedy in drama; just as tragedy provides catharsis through its invocation of pity and fear, the elegy provides a mourning ritual through its inquiry into the boundaries of consolation. As a literary display of mourning that "has persisted," as Sandra Gilbert phrases it in *Inventions of Farewell*, "through massive cultural and theological turmoil" (25), the elegy engages affect by yoking the twin energies of inquiry and discovery.

Contemporary elegies are as suffused with numinous pleasures as they are with painful recall. Among the pleasures, we can count the epiphanic moment, the invocation of the muse of mourning, both the relief and the refusal of consolation, the effusiveness of encomium (the act of heaping praise upon the dead even to the point of hyperbole), and, perhaps the most damning and the most poignant pleasure, that of being alive—being the elegist and not the elegized. This last pleasure leads readers of the elegy straight to its central, rather queasy, tension: the ways in which an elegy performs a speech act about the dead in which the speech act is supported by elegant and elaborate poetic conventions that stylize illness, accident, and death. Similarly troublesome aspects of elegiac convention are the many ways mourning masks (or seems to mask) melancholia and perhaps madness, as well as a social history that designates some bodies as more worthy of mourning than others, and a parallel history that differentiates between gender, race, age, and class to determine whose work of mourning may be considered worthy of literary posterity. If we consider the elegy not as a spontaneous outpouring of grief, but, rather, as a designed artifact of mourning that is created primarily to testify to the presence of a passed entity and the memory of a living entity, then it becomes clear that any study of the contemporary elegy must have one foot in the past and the other in the future— a compromising position, perhaps, but one that speaks to the present with a good deal of political urgency.

The concern with loss and melancholia in recent European critical theory, led by Jacques Derrida, Roland Barthes, and Julia Kristeva and practised by many other thinkers, grapples with the social and cultural violence that defined the twentieth century and produces a sometimes problematic emphasis upon affect complicated by the pathology of aestheticized or immured melancholia. This trend loads the contemporary elegy with expectations that, as Derrida asserts about mourning in "Mnemosyne," are both "impossible and necessary." Derrida is by no means the only critic to locate such contradictory energies at the core of mourning, and the elegy's relationship to the rhetoric of mourning makes it subject to paradox, so much so that the elegy as a poetic genre may be defined by its inherent contradictions. W. David Shaw, in his excellent 1994 study *Elegy and Paradox*, asserts "to commemorate death rightly is also to magnify the life and love that make death terrible" to the point that the reader may be "hard pressed to say whether so much strange ordinariness—or ordinary strangeness—is heartbreaking or consoling" (6). Calling the contemporary elegy "a spur for rethinking the vexed experience of grief in the modern world" in *Poetry of Mourning* (also published in 1994), Jahan Ramazani notes that the contemporary elegy emerges from a social history of mourning as a genre that "can hold up to the acid suspicions" of modern thought (x–xi). Between Ramazani's location of the role of anger in the elegy and Shaw's conflation of love and terror in the commemorative project, readers would be right to conclude that the contemporary elegy is emerging as a genre that is defined by its sense of discontent and by its resistance to being reduced either to pure affect or to pure philosophy.

Parent Material: Canadian Elegiac Ground

To frame the kind of signifying economy in which elegies articulate loss in a Canadian context, it is necessary to think about the elegy not only as a national literary project, but also—as befits the elegy's paradoxical tensions—as a national blind spot. Grieving the nation, after all, has been a national literary sport for decades, perhaps most exemplified by George Grant's mourning for the sacrifice of Canada to American imperialism in *Lament for a Nation* (1965) that proclaims *The Defeat of Canadian Nationalism* in its lugubrious subtitle. Whether or not readers—and Canadian citizens in the main—subscribe to Grant's anti-modernist beliefs in a martyred Canadian nationalism, it cannot be denied that such beliefs defined (and some say, limited) Canadian studies as an academic discipline from the 1960s until well into the 1990s. Grieving for the nation's losses, as well as for its bartered sovereignty, became something of a Canadian literary commonplace in this period, and such a legacy—or habit, depending on your point of view—is not easily shaken off. While it would be precipitous to claim large and immutable differences between literary artifacts of mourning in Canada, the United States, and Britain at this point in literary history, Jonathan Kertzer's admonition in *Worrying the Nation* that Canadian literature and history thrives on a combination of anxiety and obstreperousness suggests that the Canadian literary project of "worrying" all inherited genres, including the elegy, is unavoidable. Thankfully, the elegy—so obstreperous *and* so flexible—resists all attempts at thematic paraphrase, though it seems that the elegy, as a genre, is perfectly satisfied with its ability to worry its own conventions and its own consolatory powers.

Until the publication of Priscila Uppal's *We Are What We Mourn: The Contemporary English-Canadian Elegy* in 2008, little critical work had been produced concerning the place of elegy in Canadian literature. A greater emphasis on fiction than poetry was evident in Canadian elegiac studies, as well as a marked interest in casting elegiac fiction as a literary version of Freud's "work of mourning." Karen E. Smythe's 1992 study on the elegiac mode, *Figuring Grief: Gallant, Munro and the Poetics of Elegy*, works with the short stories of Mavis Gallant and Alice Munro as a style of "fiction-elegy" concerning "a quest for knowledge and self-identity (undertaken after a loss is experienced) which is accomplished by remembering the past and then telling it in a narrativized work of mourning" (5). In a similar vein, Christian Riegel's 2003 volume, *Writing Grief: Margaret Laurence and the Work of Mourning*, takes a Freudian perspective on Laurence's prose fiction and suggests that Laurence's work of mourning is part of a Canadian tradition of "explorations of mourning" that Riegel also locates in Robert Kroetsch's *Badlands*, Joy Kogawa's *Obasan*, Nino Ricci's *In a Glass House*, and SKY Lee's *Disappearing Moon Café*, as well as other works by Munro, Gallant, Jane Urquhart, Aritha van Herk, and Kristjana Gunnars (Riegel 4, cf. 151). The essay anthology *The Heart Does Break: Canadian Writers on Grief and Mourning*, compiled and edited by Jean Baird and George Bowering and published by Random House Canada in 2009, is another indication that literary works on grief and mourning have become culturally and critically central in recent years.

Nevertheless, despite the proliferation of elegiac fiction and essays in Canadian literature since 1980, a surge in the production and publication of elegiac poetry has laid its own claim to Canada as a "mourning territory" in the latter half of the twentieth century, and there is no escaping the fact that poetry and poetics are fundamental to elegy studies, both outside of and within a national context. It is undeniably felicitous that in 1995, Margaret Atwood, a novelist and a poet with considerable experience in writing poetic elegies as well as "fiction-elegy," claimed the elegy to be "a natural Canadian form" ("Dire Things" 29). However, her statement invites examination, not the least because of her problematic implication that the elegy, as a poetic form, retains the naturalism of affect. The highly constructed, self-conscious elegy is distinctly and designedly unnatural, as is any genre that must obey the rules of such literary conventions, at least in part. Be that as it may, Atwood cannot be blamed for pointing out the cultural space that the elegy has begun to occupy in Canadian literature. The elegiac output in Canadian poetry since 1980 has been truly prodigious, and Uppal's note in *We Are What We Mourn* that elegies by twentieth-century English-Canadian poets number in the thousands is evidence of the space that elegies have carved out in the Canadian literary landscape.

Uppal's ambitious and elegant exploration of the Canadian elegy pinpoints the need for a wider study of the elegy in Canadian literature, "not merely to correct its critical omission but also to supplement existing studies by providing an examination of its relation to the English language elegy tradition as a whole as well as to the tradition of English literature" (5). Examining no fewer than twenty poets who have devoted themselves to the elegiac project since 1967, Canada's anniversary of Confederation, Uppal's concentration on elegies of place and "elegies of cultural losses and displacements" (v) emphasizes nation over gender just as this volume will emphasize gender over nation. While Uppal notes a trend towards elegies for parents in Canadian literature in her chapter, "The Burned House: Parental Elegies and the Reconstruction of the Family after Death" (38–112), she focuses upon the "elegiac conceits of language and landscape as consolatory metaphors for reconnection between the living and the dead" (25). For Uppal, these consolatory metaphors function not only to recall the past in the forms of dead parents, lost places, and displaced culture and communities, but also to perform a "corrective" function in Canada's national literature: "to memorialize and revitalize those sources of identity that have been shunned, ignored or even suppressed" (Uppal 264).

While this volume shares with Uppal's book a concern with suppressed categories of identity in the elegiac tradition, my aim with this book is to focus on gender in the Canadian elegy, and I will do so by suggesting that feminist and proto-feminist elegies are less concerned with identity and consolation than they are with subjectivity and inquiry. Memorialization plays a role here—in some elegies more than others, undoubtedly—but the encomiastic imperative in the female-written elegy tends to refuse resolution rather than invite it. This book will focus not so much on a corrective function as on an inquisitive gesture that a woman's elegy for her father makes in Canadian women's literature. Such a gesture combines cultural expectation, spiritual force, and political energy, and produces enduring questions about how the politics and rhetoric of the elegy designedly and persistently trouble concepts of gender and consolation as they appear under the aegis of a nation. The action of inquiry is full of energetic equivocation that resists the potential consolation of a corrective gesture, and, instead, the elegies under examination in this volume return again and again to the shape of female literary subjectivity.

Uppal's emphasis on nation as context is important and the difficulty of defining a Canadian national elegiac mode should not dissuade us from inquiring into it as a frame for a particular kind of feminist poetics. Gender and geography do not align in simple ways, but they certainly influence each other. For instance, let us return to Atwood's comment about the "naturalness" of the elegiac form. The context of Atwood's statement is important because it emphasizes that the national culture of elegy is rigorously contested along gender lines. Atwood made the comment in an interview with Mark Abley, published in *Poetry Canada Review* in 1995, shortly after the publication of Atwood's *Morning in the Burned House*. Responding to Abley's question about the autobiographical elements of elegies written for her father, Carl Atwood, Atwood asked if the interviewer was trying to "wring some emotion" from her, and then asserted the elegy's place in Canadian literature. While in many cases autobiography is the starting place for elegy, it is presumptuous to assume that personal affect is the only force at work in the elegy, or that an autobiographical beginning remains unadulterated by the elegy's inherent tensions. In the competing claims to "naturalness" in the interview—Abley's assumption that autobiographical affect was "natural" to Atwood's elegies, and Atwood's vehement assertion that elegiac is more nationally "natural" than the assumption of autobiography—the tensions of the elegy in Canada are laid out. Additionally, Atwood's response to Abley's question about emotion in her poems displays her awareness of the historical intolerance of female sentimentalism, and her assertion that the poems are elegiac (i.e., traditional) and a "natural" part of a national aesthetic emphasizes Atwood's choice to emphasize the rectitude of national literary culture over a social judgment of gender.

Misleading cultural equations of sorrow with sentimentality have led to the misappropriation of the elegiac mode as one of hyperbolic sensibility, as practised, perhaps, by F. R. Scott's "virgins of sixty who still write of passion" even as they "percolate self-unction" in 1927's "The Canadian Authors Meet." Mark Twain, as early as 1885, spoofed the brisk traffic in sentimentality with the character of the adolescent poetess of elegiac "tributes," Emmeline Grangerford, in *Adventures of Huckleberry Finn*. Emmeline dies for her art, pining away to nothing after being unable to find a rhyme for "Whistler." It is significant that these examples of would-be elegists are female and silly in indefensible ways, as is Paul Hiebert's wholly Canadian Sarah Binks, the "Sweet Songstress of the Saskatchewan" who puts her prolific pen to elegizing livestock. Such bathetic targets are intended as comic figures, but I cannot help wondering if the gender choice that each of these male writers made for their fictional "bad elegists" does not say everything about the challenge that women faced as elegists publishing in the twentieth century.

So not only does Atwood defend herself against (albeit unspoken) charges of female sentimentalism, but in the same interview, she also speaks about her right to write the dying body of the father, an issue that crops up for all of the female elegists of this study. If we find Atwood a little prickly about the subject in 1995, she comes by it honestly, for despite the proliferation of paternal elegies in the past two decades, the subject of father–daughter kinship remains a cultural and political minefield, an urgent feminist project that grew in part from the emphasis in feminist writing of the 1980s and 1990s on "writing the mother." In Daphne Marlatt's 1983 book-length maternal elegy, *How Hug a Stone*, the narrator travels around England, searching for traces of her dead mother's former life in that country. Marlatt questions the need to understand the whole of her family's history, and examines a corresponding urge to make something of what she discovers. Her pun about the dredging up of family histories suggests not only the material uses of these histories, but also their textual uses: "What is parent material? And how long do we need it?" (141). Marlatt's use of the words "parent material," a term used in soil science to refer to the bedrock or drifted mineral deposits that make up a soil horizon, connotes that which physically lies beneath the earth (in *How Hug a Stone*, the buried body of the mother) as well as that which dwells beneath consciousness (traces of lost language, the syntax of mourning). However, Marlatt's reference to the shared etymological roots of "parent" and "*parcae*, the Fates, who allot what you get" (141), is arresting, particularly when considered with the fateful presence of her mother's sister "spinning and cutting . . . in the family room" (141). It is no accident that Marlatt emphasizes the "distaff" side of her family through the metaphor of the spindle; this is, after all, her mother's family, and it is her "mother's trace" for which she is searching. But the father, who does not appear as a character in *How Hug a Stone*, slips into Marlatt's text as the unmentioned (and perhaps unmentionable) figure included in the term "parent material."

In a feminist text, the absence of a father figure is not especially unusual, but the trace of the father as "parent material" seems veiled and even surreptitious. If she were to address the death of her father openly, what would a feminist poet have to say about her father, and how she would say it?

When the elegy is guided by the dynamics of father–daughter kinship rather than by the dynamics of male filiation or fraternization, the elegist engages a triangle of possibilities: consolation, refusal, and the possibility of elegiac discovery. Each of the poetic sequences in this book pursues a way to illuminate or interrogate consolation that does not sacrifice the daughter to silence, madness, or sentimentality, but instead grants her subjectivity outside the bounds of paternal authority.

In addition to its reference to the family of origin, the term "parent material" points to a strain of literary autochthony that is useful in considering questions about the feminist elegy within Canada, and although the national historical concern with land is not explicitly acted out in these Canadian women's paternal elegies, the metaphor of parent material suggests that junctures between the family and the nation should not be ignored. Ultimately, considering the Canada literary aesthetic as one form of "parent material" for these elegies—a national critical bedrock that grounds the poetics—can be useful for situating these elegies in relationship to major movements and emerging trends in British and American elegy studies.

Such categorizations defy all attempts to simplify, and as well they might. The declaration of anything as "Canadian national" is doomed to dissatisfy, particularly when funnelled through pan-global, post-industrial, post-colonial, and post-modern theories and politics. Nevertheless, if we consider the contemporary elegy as a burgeoning genre, the time taken to regard the nationalist or anti-nationalist politics of such a phenomenon may be time well spent. It may help to locate the ways in which the urgency of the twentieth-century elegiac intersects with contemporary feminist poetics in Canada, as Zeiger and Ramazani have claimed space for female elegists in American elegiac studies. Ramazani's caveat that the contemporary elegy may contain more "fractured speech" than outright lyricism and more "memorable puzzlings" than consolation suggests that the suspicions of cynical citizenry may also show up in the elegy as a distillation of sexual and national politics (x).

In the twentieth century, the elegy is most often discussed as a literary artifact that charts Freud's "work of mourning," a theory that is attractive for its promise of completed mourning, but remains problematic for the same reason. There is a reductive tendency for the late-twentieth-century elegy to enact a slavish obedience to the letter of completed mourning, but also to remain distant from any revelatory experience, ignoring the anagnorisis that is axiomatic to the elegiac mode. Elegies that fall into this genre trap become merely conventional, rather than thoughtfully entwined with and resistant to convention; Max Cavitch calls these elegies "literary journeywork for the industriously maudlin" (1). Cavitch's 2006 study *American Elegy: The Poetry of Mourning from the Puritans to Whitman* offers an elegant reading of American history through eighteenth- and nineteenth-century elegies, and Cavitch begins by warning those who would historicize the elegy as a nationalist force that the elegy in the United States of America "has been left behind in the attempt to narrate the very history it helped to make" (2). But even while noting that the "consolidating force of elegiac tradition became increasingly attenuated under countervailing pressures of migration and encounter, pluralization and secularization, war and independence" (2), Cavitch discusses elegies that situate the energy of grief as an important force that pushes against the historic rise of capitalism in the United States as it undergoes a transformation into a consumer society, crumpling "older Calvinist modes of introspection" (5). With respect for Cavitch's reading of the social history and material production of the elegy in colonial America, it is his phrase for the elegy's most enduring project in the New World that suggests the need for Canadian attention to elegiac production. Cavitch asserts the elegy persists through political and ideological shifts as "a highly adaptive discursive resource, not just for mourning the dead but for communicating and managing anxieties in contexts of survival" (3). To paraphrase Robert Frost's "Mending Wall," as the metaphor may be an appropriate one across which we can consider the differences between Canadian and American literatures, something there is—in the elegy—that does not love a completed narrative, and Cavitch's observation that the elegy creates history but is ironically absent from its narrativization is intriguingly apt. The persistence of the elegiac genre through shifts in ideology has depended upon its ability to comprise the discourse of anxiety, and such a concept is relevant to reading feminist elegy in twentieth-century Canada. While Cavitch's invocation of national historical "contexts of survival" has resounding echoes of Atwood's take on thematic criticism from this side of the 49th parallel, a return to Marlatt's "parent material" metaphor ought to remind us that tracing the terms, material conditions, and politics of any act of survival is perhaps more useful in a feminist context than a national one. To return to Marlatt's geological metaphor, if we use the female-written elegy as a sieve through which to sift a soil sample of Canadian literary history, we will get not a complete narrativized history, but a history of genre, a history of feminisms, and a residue of Canadian politics as it impacts upon those particularized histories. For much of Canadian feminist poetics, these are the "parent materials" that make up the foundations of our aesthetics.

Elegiac Daughteronomies: Fathers and Other Questions

It cannot, and should not, be denied that the metaphor of "parent material" also gestures towards family narrative as a resonant and sometimes problematic structure for an elegy. In *Poetry of Mourning*, Ramazani's examination of "the American family elegy" tells a tale of a subgenre in which confessional ethics are predicated largely upon postwar oppression of affect and sexuality and the legacy of violence, misogyny, and explosive language in mid-century America. Canada was not exempt from such cultural movements following the Second World War, but neither was Canada subjected to the extreme tensions between liberal and conservative politics in the same way as were the United States in the 1950s and 1960s. Ramazani claims that "the personal act of mourning the father is politically charged, and the politics of resistance begins at home" (264), noting that female poets who have written the American family elegy from mid-century onwards have "been more than willing to use the genre to exorcize, slough, divorce, defame, even annihilate the dead" (263). Though Ramazani concludes that contemporary American female elegists write parental elegies in order to "rethink the daughter's position within the family romance" (294), paternal elegies by Canadian women tend to resist merely rethinking the daughter's position in favour of using the elegy as a literary microscope through which the "family romance" may be examined, reconfigured, and sometimes discarded. In doing so, these poets suggest possibilities for a more efficacious theory of female mourning that regards paternal power with a certain skepticism. Distinct from the postwar American trend in elegies that "articulate an aggression toward the dead" (Ramazani 241), the Canadian female elegists of this volume inquire into the mythical implications and political possibilities that emerge when a female poet explores the death of her father, whether he is her biological progenitor or a representative of patriarchal power.

The project of speaking back to centuries of elegiac tradition puts the contemporary elegy in a position that may be considered postcolonial in tone, if not always in substance. Canadian women's elegies speak back against elegiac convention—not coincidentally, against the British tradition as an elegiac "fatherland"—but it is important to note that what these elegies are unraveling is not affect itself but that which succeeds affect: the constitutive place of the elegiac in the rhetoric of mourning. This is not to suggest that the poems do not have an emotive base; they certainly do. However, each of the poets turns to—and turns upon—a rigorous examination of language as a tool to dismantle prescriptive models of mourning. Anger is not absent from these poems, but curiosity about the feminist negotiations of elegiac convention is a more consistent concern. Is it possible to create an elegy that not only records emotive pain, but also considers the passing of a particular kind of daughterly subjectivity that presages the forging of a feminist subjectivity? What might be Canadian about this kind of rhetorical curiosity that overrides anger? Many of these poets refuse, and are sometimes even wryly amused by, the family romance even as they reach towards more complex formulations of relationship; there is more at stake here than reconsidering the role that the daughter plays in the family romance. These Canadian women's elegies lean markedly upon self-reflexive language that questions the persona and poetic function of the mourner. Instead of venting unadulterated fury or debilitating grief, the mourning persona explores the poem as a fulcrum for launching a subjectivity that exists beyond the father, one that comes partially through inheritance, partially through resistance.

As a feminist project, the examination of women's paternal elegies is haunted by questions about maternal force and its influence on poetic and political feminisms. Should not the business of the female-written elegy involve mourning for the lost mother figure and inquiring into reclaiming and legitimizing the maternal force? This, too, is literary daughterhood as it has been explored by Canadian feminist poets such as Marlatt in *How Hug a Stone*, Nicole Brossard in *These Our Mothers*, Betsy Warland in *Bloodroot*, and Di Brandt in *mother, not mother* (and many other works). These examples of the maternal elegiac force in Canadian literature locate the body of the mother in the gap in elegiac discourse, and suggest that the unspeakable corporeality of the lost mother becomes a touchstone for feminist inquiries into the language of loss. I am sympathetic with this persuasive point of view, particularly with the way that maternal elegies underscore various ways in which cultural elision can masquerade as family dynamics, and the ways that elision becomes lauded as literary tradition. Undeniably, the idea of the mother hovers near the paternal elegy, sometimes informing it by her absence, sometimes inviting comparisons between maternal and paternal love. However, the paucity of discourse about the complexities of father–daughter kinship is startling, especially when considered against the avalanche of material available on father–son kinship, and the growing body of feminist studies on mother–daughter kinship. The gap is so significant that it appears to function as a literary/critical imitation of the incest taboo, but even asserting that supports the inherent misogyny of such an assumption, for to attribute women's paternal mourning solely as a demonstration of repressed desire and/or sexual guilt is reductive in the extreme, and in its own way, such an assumption out-Freuds Freud. But such extremities have their uses. One of the reasons that these paternal elegies have become such urgent points of study is because so much criticism has dismissed the idea of father–daughter kinship as insignificant to feminist thought or as simply pathological.

Against this tide of history, literary tradition, generic expectation, and the weight of psychoanalysis, how does a woman write her father's death? The twentieth century saw a proliferation of female-written paternal elegies, suggesting that feminism had pried open the floodgates that barred a daughter's poetic gaze upon, and poetic speech about, the father's moribund body. However, while the appearance of female-written paternal elegies may be considered a literary manifestation of a social phenomenon, the frequency with which these elegies have appeared and the way the poets position themselves as critical mourners make it quite clear that these elegies are doing more than merely appropriating a homosocial literary genre as a feminist exercise. The rough nub of the elegiac mode is an image as enduring as it is problematic: the male body as the martyred object of praise, as the political lynchpin for his filially designated successor, and as the basis for profound and epiphanic insight into the price of being alive. If a female poet chooses to perform as "no-man's-nightingale," must she engage in a literary gender switch, taking on the role of the inheriting son to do so? Though women have distinct and valuable roles in public rituals of mourning in many societies, from keening to preparing the body for burial, the literary project of the elegy leaves behind an artifact, a made object of mourning that oral expression and performance of ritual cannot.

The issue is one of inheritance, both familial and literary. "The right to mourn was from the earliest times legally connected to the right to inherit," writes Peter Sacks in *The English Elegy* (37), and given this, Bloom's "anxiety of influence" that favours elegiac homosociality as a vehicle to produce and reproduce literary genius seems very much the literary equivalent of filial piety filtered through a bold coming of age. If we consider the right of inheritance as it is powered by the elegy, we could do worse than recall that Jacques Derrida, in *Specters of Marx*, calls such inheritance not a passive acceptance but the very stuff of ontology: "Inheritance is never a *given*, it is always a task.... All questions on the subject of being or of what it means to be (or not to be) are questions of inheritance" (54; emphasis in original). Indeed, how women are to be—as bodies, as artists, and as elegists—is predicated on their ability to memorialize and inherit, whether or not they are invited to do so by tradition.

"I Sing and Thrive": Poetic Economies of Discontent

Discovering Canadian poems in which female poets addressed the moribund body and eventual deaths of father figures from the modernist period onwards was something of a melancholy joy. To consider the elegy as a genre with a weighted cultural and literary tradition is one challenge; to regard the role that gender plays in elegiac production is another. This book examines elegies written from the mid-1940s to the 1990s by Canadian women poets who deliberately appropriate the elegiac mode to write about the death of their fathers, or, in some cases, the death of significant father figures. From some perspectives, particularly in branches of feminist literary study, this book's focus on the father as an elegiac object could be interpreted as retrograde. Set against a background of feminist theory that has emphasized the reclamation of the mother figure in the final decades of the twentieth century, an emphasis upon the woman writer's relationship with the paternal figure may seem to recall the kind of "literary daughteronomy" that Sandra Gilbert discusses in her 1985 article, "Life's Empty Pack: Notes Toward a Literary Daughteronomy": the daughter whose gendered disinheritance assures her desperate alliance with the father figure. Indeed, the shadow of this kind of spiritual or literary "paternity" through which women's writing has been legitimized, by financial, editorial, and familial support, is in evidence as a tension for the modernist poets in this volume: Dorothy Livesay, P. K. Page, and Jay Macpherson. But there is a world of critical and poetic difference between acknowledging the social injunctions of a society that expects daughteronomy and negotiating poems that undermine such expectations.

The tension between a physically absent but psychically present father as elegiac object and mourning daughter-poet as elegiac subject make the written father and the writing daughter personae into actors in the literary-familial drama of the paternal elegy, and launches a dynamic that can illuminate the multiple layers of emotion and subjectivities percolating in these poems. The emphasis on father–daughter kinship in this book means that the notion of patriarchal privilege with all its attendant political and familial snares is never far from the discussion of how elegiac convention works in these female-written poems. Fathers are not intrinsically more worthy elegiac objects by virtue of their gender than are mothers, siblings, spouses, friends, or children, but female-written paternal elegies are consistently foregrounded by a cultural discomfort with their gendered authorship as well as with their chosen elegiac object. My discussion would be remiss if I did not acknowledge the difficulty of discerning the Lacanian symbolic Father from the biological, familial father, and doubly remiss to treat "Father" and "father" as easy equivalencies. Along with the daughter's cultural duty to serve the father and the elegist's charge to memorialize him, the feminist's determination to interrogate the symbolic Father complicates these elegies.

Macpherson's assertion that the nightingale's sobbing song belongs to "no man" but to the angels and the nightingale herself informs a poetics of discontent throughout this study. The first chapter of this book, "Elegy and

Authority: The Daughter's Way," examines the elegy's pull towards forms of authority as dictated by nation, by family, by theory, and by pathology as elegiac forces. The discussion in this chapter includes but is not limited to psychoanalytical readings of grief, mourning, and melancholia, and considers how to extricate the daughter's way of writing the paternal elegy from the quagmire of assumptions surrounding the Freudian family romance and seduction theory. Following models of mourning and melancholia as discussed by Jacques Derrida, Judith Butler, George Steiner, and Gillian Rose, this chapter examines the urgency of defining a politically productive melancholia that emerges from the shadow of psychoanalysis in the final decades of the twentieth century.

The next section of the book, titled "Daughters of Jove, Daughters of Job: Canadian Modernism's Bloody-Minded Women," discusses three female paternal elegists—Dorothy Livesay, P. K. Page, and Jay Macpherson—who all began publishing during the Canadian modernist era and continued to do so for several decades. This section charts the ways that all three poets, moving from young womanhood to more advanced age, reconsider their positions as daughter figures as decades pass. Livesay, Page, and Macpherson present problematized portraits of the masculine authority figure as both ideation and reality, and situate the project of politicized mourning for the father alongside the struggle to maintain a feminist ethic in the postwar rush towards cultural and personal re-feminization. The appellation "bloody-minded" comes from Atwood's reading of Macpherson's poems, but the epithet may be applied with equal interest to the poems of Livesay and Page. The task of being "bloody-minded," with that phrase's metaphoric conjunction of corporeality and intellect, as well as its connotations of feminine refusal and literary determination, captures the political and epistemological position of these female modernists who debate the force of paternal authority on female speech prior to the boom in feminist critical theory.

Dorothy Livesay's decades-long struggle to situate the rebellious daughter as a good mourner for her spiritually nurturing but socially conservative father, co-founder of Canadian Press J. F. B. Livesay, negotiates the distance between being a "Daddy's girl" and "Jove's shrew," the two terms that Livesay uses in her 1979 poem "Jove's Daughter." Chapter Two examines three groups of Livesay's poems: the "immediate" elegies of the late 1940s (written in the years immediately following her father's death) in which Livesay explores the necessities and limitations of daughterly mourning duty; the "inheritance" elegies of the 1950s into the 1970s, in which the poet resituates herself as an inheritor of the Livesay line and reconnects which Sacks' idea that "the right to mourn was from the earliest times legally connected to the right to inherit" (37); and, finally, the emergence of the "Minerva" elegies of the late 1970s in which Livesay considers the terms of power and gender as a feminist legacy against her psychoanalytical inheritance of a Lacanian Father. Livesay's playful attitude towards the confessional mode combines with the political exigency of her socialism to problematize her earlier elegies, including her much-anthologized 1946 poem, "Lament," against her more ambivalent work of the 1970s. Livesay's poems from the 1940s appear to reproduce the modernist postwar elegy, but the wry perspective of her later poetry, up to and including 1979's "Jove's Daughter," suggests strongly that Livesay's attempt to define daughterly duty paralleled career-long tensions in her discursive and poetic choices. This chapter charts the stylistic and political movement of Livesay's elegiac work from a restrained and grateful modernist "daughteronomy" to a feminist re-visioning of the daughter's mourning self as a political entity.

Exploring the father as a metaphor for a cultural authority through a series of militarized metaphors, the third chapter presents the paternal elegy as an ongoing project in P. K. Page's poetry. Page explores a shadowy father figure as a body and psyche traumatized by bellicosity and rendered vulnerable by the gaze of his silent daughter. These poems, written over three decades, move from the mythical father to the individual father, as Page herself strays (albeit temporarily) from her high modernist dependence upon the Eliotean objective correlative to attempt poems that traffic in autobiography. The negotiations of power in these poems, from early attempts to figure the heroic father to later attempts to negotiate the daughter as the father's inheritor, are funnelled through the poet's watching daughter persona. In *Gynesis: Configurations of Women and Modernity*, Alice A. Jardine reminds us that the "woman-in-effect" (48) emerges from patriarchal tropes, and she cannot always be freed from the system that she criticizes. Neither Page nor Macpherson is immune to the kind of miming and rejecting of inherited patriarchal structures that Jardine emphasizes, but they begin to situate melancholia as a creative position rather than a pathological one.

After Page's configuration of the demanding mourner as "spokesman and... axeman" in her poem "Father" from the sequence "Melanie's Nite-Book," the daughter figures of Macpherson's *The Boatman and Other Poems* and *Welcoming Disaster* may be identified as melancholically subversive figures that both embrace and refuse abjection. Macpherson's adamant mourners search for a mourning practice that challenges the symbology of the Bible and of Romance literature. The potential violence of the systems of authority against which both Page and Macpherson write suggests that the authority of the (literary) state is formidable, and both poets create defiant daughter-speakers who enact a rigorous search for subjectivity outside the proscribed patriarchal belief in transcendence. Macpherson's paternal alchemist figure in *Welcoming Disaster* predicts the failure of the Orphean journey for the grieving daughter. The daughter's position as a stubbornly abject mourner reinforces her potential as a Kristevan subject-in-process and Macpherson's position in Canadian literary history as Northrop Frye's protegée cannot be ignored as part of her struggle for poetic subjectivity. Macpherson's poetry regards her partial consolation in the failure of mythology as a Freudian compromise mixed with a hope for subjectivity born from the lessons of abjection.

Turning to paternal elegiacs of the late twentieth century, the book's third section—"Nation and Nowhere: The Mourner's Journey"—discusses Atwood's *Morning in the Burned House*, Kristjana Gunnars's *Zero Hour*, and Anne Carson's long prose poem "The Anthropology of Water," with particular emphasis on how the texts engage the dynamics of writing the "elegy before death," as Edna St. Vincent Millay has termed it in her 1921 poem of the same name. By emphasizing the act of mourning the still-living body, the works put pressure on the question of daughterly inheritance, troubling both the rights of mourning and the rituals of elegy. The nation, too, becomes a palimpsest for mourning in these works, a quasi-paternal body that both promises consolation in national identity and denies an easy subjectivity of nationality.

Atwood's chronological and political position as the lynchpin between modernists and poststructuralist literary feminists should not be ignored, particularly considering Macpherson's influence on Atwood's poetic production early in the younger poet's career. *Morning in the Burned House* does not refuse consolation outright, but, rather, negotiates provisional consolation, as does Judith Butler in *The Psychic Life of Power* when she suggests that in cases "where there is no public recognition or discourse through which such a loss might be named and mourned, then melancholia takes on cultural dimensions of contemporary consequence" (139). Atwood, searching for such a "contemporary consequence," suggests ways in which these elegies meditate upon the observable paternal body, returning to the daughter as a watching figure as Atwood explores the void of melancholia as a geographic and epistemological space. Her ironic inquiry into the limitations of the body moves towards a belief in transformation that replaces consolation as the elegist's prime consideration, and the text seeks ways for mourning to turn into "morning," as Gillian Rose has suggested. Atwood does not give up her career-long fascination with Jungian archetype for this elegiac project, and her creation of another self that mourns while her speaker refuses is suggestive of the kind of doubling that is not only psychological but subjective.

The mourner's journey in Kristjana Gunnars's *Zero Hour* offers a look at the nation's role in defining contemporary paternal mourning as part of a diasporic post-prairie elegy. A marked resistance to closure in *Zero Hour* aligns the personal affect of mourning alongside the political implications of historical violence. Such explorations are not unknown in Canadian elegiac work, with Dennis Lee's *Civil Elegies* and Fred Wah's *Waiting for Saskatchewan* as two examples of long poetic sequences that fold the mourner's grief into troubled revelations of governmental policies of racism and war. However, resistance to closure, and perhaps to consolation itself, is also a vital component of what Gunnars calls her "poetry of belligerence" in her essay "Avoidance and Confrontation: Excerpts from Notes on a Longpoem Poetics" (183). Asserting that writers of her generation inherited "the post-war language of crisis that comes with the nuclear age," Gunnars describes her struggle to write two kinds of psychological and linguistic estrangement as "the 'permanent' alienation" of modernism and a post-Hiroshima 'social alienation' from 'the company of the living'" (180). Written with the intergeneric allusiveness that Gunnars claims to be characteristic of the "short book" ("On Writing" 81), *Zero Hour* presents social and geographical estrangement through two central metaphors: grief as the emotional equivalent of a nuclear winter, and the mythological West as a paradise that lies beyond consolation.

No study of the female-written elegy would be complete without a text that questions the Antigonal imperative for the daughter to sacrifice herself in order to legitimate her mourning. Anne Carson's "The Anthropology of Water" proposes the pursuit of knowledge as a displacement of daughterly sacrifice. Carson, who is also a well-known classics scholar, proves herself to be more Sophoclean than Freudian when she rewrites the Antigone myth to repudiate the demands of daughterly duty. Emphasizing the poetics of philosophical inquiry as it comments upon the vicissitudes of daughterly devotion, Carson employs the metaphor of a pilgrimage in order to test the tension between melancholia and consolation in a daughter's paternal elegy. The narrator's puckish riddles keep consolation at bay, despite her hard-won elegiac subjectivity. Even as Carson uses the metaphor of the pilgrimage to suggest a strong connection between epistemology and mourning, this prose poem struggles with Derrida's contention that a willing acceptance of the incomprehension of corporeal death relinquishes one's responsibility for sorrow. "The Anthropology of Water" is perhaps the most overtly sorrowful of the elegiac texts offered by this study, for the consolation that Carson's narrating persona pursues is not merely elusive, but jeopardized by the narrating daughter's willingness to ask questions but not answer them.

The book's final section, "Furies and Filles de la Sagesse: Language and Difference at Century's End," considers two texts by theory-based language poets who position their work firmly and defiantly in feminist space. These two chapters explore the influence of the father as a haunting presence in Canadian poetry that traces and defies traditional elegiac motifs of sacrificial mourning and paternal power. This section reads Lola Lemire Tostevin's *Cartouches* and Erin Mouré's *Furious* as melancholic texts according to Butler's concept of the melancholic: she who regards the past with strict and careful attention in order to structure a future freed from the errors of the past, so that, paradoxically, "melancholia produces the possibility for the representation of psychic life" (*Psychic* 177).

In *Cartouches*, Tostevin negotiates the terms of female consolation by rejecting both the Orphean descent pattern and Derrida's "unbearable paradox of fidelity" ("By Force of Mourning" 159). Both poets resist the completion of mourning in order to question the daughterly duty of the female elegist, in a self-conscious inquiry into the elegy as both celebratory and transformative. Tostevin rewrites consolation as transformation by considering the responsibilities of the wise daughter as a resurrective figure. Tostevin moves from mourning an individual father to debating Derrida as the symbolic father, and engages in a debate over the ability of the daughter to inherit "the body of her name" as a feminist gesture that challenges both filiation and the Lacanian symbolic order.

Elegiac convention as a patriarchal construct clashes with the "furious" bid for feminist subjectivity made by Erin Mouré's poetry. Mouré's Governor General's Award–winning collection, *Furious*, is not strictly an elegiac sequence in the manner of the other texts of this study. The father upon whom the Fury of the text vents her anger is largely symbolic, though Mouré writes him into several human incarnations. However, his patriarchal stance is not mythic, as is Macpherson's symbolic father, but, rather, Mouré's father figure exists in the politicized power of language, most clearly designated as the keeper of "the civic house of memory" ("The Acts 7") into which the narrator is refused entry. Throughout *Furious*, the father figure is marked by his absence as a literary character and his overwhelming presence as a social and literary structure. That absence may be read as a force of oppression: a metaphoric masculinity behind the poetic structures of defiance. Mouré uses *Furious* to probe the absence that surrounds questions of female citizenship and sorrow, and, ultimately, to spur textual challenges to the tradition of sacrificial mourning. Exploring feminist possibilities that denaturalize the written body in order to challenge the assumed subjectivity of the male body, she points out elegiac convention as an oppressive rhetoric that dispossesses sorrow. Reading Mouré's *Furious* through Rose's "perennial anxiety" (36) suggests that politically disobedient melancholia can, in fact, reinvigorate the political life of a community.

The assumption of autobiography presents a problem for much of women's literature and for women's paternal elegies in particular. Beginning with the understanding that the elegist offers a self-consciously constructed mourner by offering the narrative "I" in an elegy, the reader must also understand that elegiac convention irrevocably, and intentionally, ruins autobiographical fidelity in order to explore the place of mourning in the world. Poetry, even poetry of affect, does not always serve as autobiography; the significance of these poems, as with most elegies, is not that they record an individual death, but rather, that the death has ushered in a radical shift in the poet's faith, philosophy, or politics. When appropriate, I will offer some biographical facts that pertain to the poems, but even these "facts" should be considered historiographic beginnings, full of the emphases and elisions that characterize the literary rendering of the factual. In other words, I treat the biographical bases for these poems much as the poets themselves do: as a site of generation but not an end in themselves. Part of the intricate balancing act of the contemporary elegy includes the proposition that "truth" is a literary device that is painstakingly constructed. This proposition was a given in the classical elegy, played out through the mourner's persona as a naïve-wise swain or shepherd. The contemporary elegy adapts that convention, and studies of the elegy that assume a purely confessional (or rigidly psychoanalytical) motive in the poem miss the literary vitality of elegiac convention and the political potential of elegiac inquiry.

It is the task of the poets themselves to worry the distinctions between individual man and representational authority, and to chip away at history's discomfort with father–daughter kinship and its accompanying modes of mourning. Acknowledgement that individual feminisms and individual readers will engage with such conflations or discernments with varying degrees of skepticism or acceptance seems to be one more manifestation of elegiac paradox: perhaps a paradox of kinship. By focusing first on the father as family member, the poets question the mourning of a particular death within the historical and cultural matrix of paternal authority. Each of these poets then tangles with the traditions of elegy as a literary manifestation of cultural oppression, positioning the dead paternal body as an authority that demands daughterly obedience even as it denies her consolation. By challenging and even flouting elegiac convention, these daughterly elegies arrive at anagnorisis, discovering a feminist subjectivity through inquiring into the terms of melancholia and inheritance. A paradox of refusal: discontent enlivens.

1

Elegy and Authority
The Daughter's Way

De mortuis nil nisi bonum.
Of the dead say nothing but good.
— Chilo of Sparta, quoted by Diogenes Laertius, *The Lives and Opinions of Eminent Philosophers*

What is socially peripheral is often symbolically central, and if we ignore or minimize inversion and other forms of cultural negation, we often fail to understand the dynamics of symbolic processes generally.
— Barbara A. Babcock, *The Reversible World*

Risk Management: Kinship and Elegy

The elegy's ongoing negotiations in the twentieth century make the poetry of mourning a contentious literary space, even more so when the tensions of gender and nationalism are factored into this rich literary mixture of affect and authority. Luckily, elegies are constitutionally audacious; the act of elegizing is, to a greater or lesser degree, an act of authorization, and such authority can be as critical as it is conventional. Suggesting in *Elegy and Paradox* that the subgenre of the elegy functions as the container for difficult inquiry, W. David Shaw contends that the elegy's energy of resistance is fundamental to its efficacy as a genre. He asserts that in the twentieth-century elegy it is not unusual for "the uneasy peace of a paradox" to "break down into an open war of opposites: an insurrection of the self, a civil strife" (5). Shaw's use of bellicose metaphor is particularly apt when applied to female-written paternal elegies, for the daughter-elegist is as likely to quarrel with herself in the elegy as she is to argue against the cultural authority of the dead or dying father, or, often, against the power structures that estrange her from him. In *Poetry of Mourning*, Jahan Ramazani suggests that the vexatious quality of the twentieth-century elegy springs from its position as a modernist work of art that has been consciously stripped of centuries of mourning ritual and now is charged with the task of remaking grief in the cold light of a technological age. Ramazani's designation of the elegy as poetry that engages "the vexed experience of grief in the modern world" (x) comes to the fore in female-written paternal elegies, as the vexed quality emerges from the daughter's search for a way to elegize the father without falling into the desperate daughteronomy of hyperbolized praise and to think critically about the dynamics of daughterhood. The ancient injunction to "say nothing but good" of the dead haunts the modern elegy, part of that "vexed experience" of elegiac duty.

Although Ramazani is addressing the special tensions of the modern elegy, certainly father–daughter kinship has been recorded as a vexed experience for centuries. From the Book of Judges, in which Jephthah sacrifices his daughter to fulfill a vow to God, to the Greek tragedies of *Antigone* and *Electra*, through early modern drama in *King Lear*, *The Winter's Tale*, and *Hamlet*, and Victorian novels such as *Silas Marner*, *Little Dorrit*, and *The Mayor of Casterbridge*, such examples of relationships fraught by death, duty, and sacrifice—all predicated on the strength of a daughter's devotion to her father—are so abundant in Western literature that these canonical texts—among others—have formed indispensable cornerstones of what has become literary tradition. From such evidence, we ought to be able to say that father–daughter kinship presents a series of issues that occupies the forefront of the conscious mind, that cultural theorists by the hundreds are focused on parsing father–daughter kinship for its cultural significance, and that public discourse turns up discussion about this enduring issue again and again. However, despite the literary ubiquity of father–daughter kinship and its entanglement with questions of love and grief, duty and betrayal, critical examinations of father–daughter kinship are disturbingly under-represented in theoretical discourse. The quotation from Barbara A. Babcock's *The Reversible World* which begins this chapter contains an explicit and intriguing warning against assuming that symbolism and cultural approbation are equivalent, and her contention that an inverse relationship between symbolic centrality and social centrality rules literature is stubbornly true. Literature functions as a repository for questions that shock, persist, or dumbfound, and the preservation and exploration of such questions are poetry's special province.

So, while the image of a daughter grieving for and often sacrificing herself for her father is symbolically central in Western literature to the point of obviousness, it remains socially peripheral to the point of oddness. Among a handful of scholarly texts that addresses the critical or theoretical perspective of the daughter's experience of her father's death, Lynda E. Boose and Betty S. Flowers's 1989 critical anthology *Daughters and Fathers* begins with an introductory essay by Boose and Flowers identifying a "cultural filialogy" (9) that includes daughterly experience and responds with incredulity to the historical silence surrounding father–daughter kinship in literary works: "While the territory of daughter and father is a discourse that stands virtually unmapped, it is hardly a space that could be called unmarked. The relatively dark discursive terrain that this family relationship occupies has been written all over by tacit injunctions that have forbidden its charting" (1). The wry astonishment of this passage by Boose and Flowers reflects the extent of the cultural negation of daughterly mourning. When they point out the centrality of the father–daughter relationship to foundational texts of Western literature, these critics emphasize texts that explicitly position daughters as mourners for doomed father figures.

Working from the terms established in Gayle Rubin's classic article, "The Traffic in Women," Boose asserts in her follow-up essay "The Father's House and the Daughter in It," that a daughter's lack of inheritance and her exchange value as a marital commodity make her a liminal figure in the family: "daughterhood is, in fact, inseparable from absence in the psychoanalytic definition of social development" (21), a condition which places the daughter in the position of a "temporary sojourner within her family, destined to seek legitimation and name outside its boundaries" (33). Canadian scholar and poet Di Brandt revisits this point in her article "The Happiest Reader in the World: David Arnason's Revisionary Stories," in her 2007 collection of essays, *So this is the world and here I am in it*, where she asserts that "the troubled father–daughter nexus" at the heart of the "emotional economics of the traditional patriarchal exchange system" has gone unexamined for too long, and has yielded men who cannot understand their own paternal "broken-heartedness and desperate attempts to avoid loss and betrayal in a system that supposedly privileges" them (58–59). Noting that fathers must give away the daughters that they love, Brandt assesses with equal amounts of asperity and poignancy, "Freud might have read Lear with better care" (59).

With understandable eagerness to address the long-neglected body of the mother, many feminists have postponed answering questions about what they may have inherited from their fathers, and how that relationship influenced their feminism for good or for ill. In an ironic reversal that mirrors Babcock's symbolically central/socially peripheral formulation, the deferral of feminist questions about father–daughter kinship seems to support the patriarchy. In critical terms, discussions of father–daughter relationships have traditionally concerned themselves with daughterly obedience (and its attendant frustrations) or with daughterly victimization (sometimes with a resulting liberation), but very seldom does literary or critical theory examine the range of modalities between these two positions. The psychoanalytical emphasis upon a daughter's infantile and apparently irresolvable erotic desire for her father locks her in a single, not particularly interesting, critical position: forever offering thwarted pathological love and forever rejected as a threat to familial and cultural order. Because her grief over her father's death is symbolically central while it is socially effaced as a legitimate topic of concern, a daughter's love for at her father endures as a deeply subversive topic in literary studies, feminist and otherwise. As long as mourning the father remains disguised as an issue of patriarchal obedience and/or incipient violence, the problem of the father continues to rankle. If women's refusal to regard relationships with their fathers is a critical blind spot, then the patriarchy remains free from hearing women discuss their fathers as influential—and sometimes problematic—forces in their literary and political subjectivity.

The daughter's interrogation of paternal power and her attempts to redefine female filial piety in elegiac form necessarily occur within the bounds of a literary system that favours a daughter's mourning as an iteration of self-sacrifice. The search for a satisfactory mourning practice for the father appears in these poems as a demand for female subjectivity that refuses the ritual self-sacrifice of the daughter as an expiation of her father's death. The primary aim of this book is to examine the daughter's way of mourning while asserting subjectivity through the dynamic of the elegy. But no audacious act, literary or otherwise, is performed without cost. When female elegists venture onto paternal ground, their challenge to normative gender expectations translates into an open confrontation with forms of authority other than the literary: familial, psychoanalytical, and critical authorities.

The study of the female-written elegy, to date, has done little to unravel the theoretical snarls and political consequences of grief in a family setting. Sacks ghettoizes the female elegy in his reading of Amy Clampitt's "Procession at Candlemas" by suggesting that women must necessarily mourn first and ask questions later, effectively separating them from a philosophical melancholic tradition. Certainly in comparison with Sacks's analysis of a single female-written elegy, Ramazani's study of the subgenre of the American family elegy as written by Anne Sexton, Adrienne Rich, and Sylvia Plath is more expansive in its proposition of a profound ambivalence at the core of the female elegy, though Ramazani limits his focus to discussing female anger as part of the daughter's negotiated position in the family dynamic. Female-written paternal elegies can represent viewpoints that are politically more complex than an iteration of feminist anger towards the father as individual and the Father as social authority. Certainly the refusal of consolation that an elegist frequently uses to assert her right to mourn is so conventional that it can create the conditions for a fresher definition of consolation itself—an elegiac tautology that, in the best cases, may serve as an elegiac teleology. Ramazani's identification of anger and ambivalence in the female-written elegy is important, and serves as a springboard for considering a resistance to libidinal family politics in the larger world, and how a daughter's ambivalent grief about her father's death may be explored as other than a literary demonstration of Freudian seduction theory. Shaw's contention that elegies are inherently risky propositions for the reader and the writer offers an intriguing possibility for reading the work of female elegists, and the discovery and exploration of a post-paternal subjectivity in these elegies can be, as Shaw puts it, "inseparable from the satisfaction of being open to adventure and risk, including the fear of dissolution that any enlargement of consciousness might bring in its wake" (6). Such risks and the possibility of dissolution are definitely visited by the elegists of this study, most especially since these works engage with the discovery of a daughter's mourning as inherently and inescapably political, both within and outside of the family dynamic.

Given Derrida's insistence that inheritance is fundamentally ontological, a cultural economy is truly what is at stake in the acknowledgement of women as paternal elegists. As long as a woman's love and grief can be diminished as incestuous, pathological, and aesthetically compromised, the problem of female grief can continue to be limited to ritualized funerary rites that have neither the individualized public approbation nor the literary permanence of the elegy, with the added patriarchal "bonus" that women may be prevented from inheriting from the father. The single feminist act that unites the elegists in this book, as different as they may be from each other, is a defiance of this law of inheritance as it is reflected in British literary tradition. Their engagements with, and resistance to, the demands of elegiac convention emerge as a willingness to debate the definition of female filial piety. The resistance that complicates a woman poet's paternal elegy is inevitably a gendered political resistance, fuelled by the desire to challenge convention in the name of female subjectivity.

Contemporary female poets who take up the task of being paternal elegists demand as much from their generic concerns as from their approach to the subject, and they ask as much from the daughter as elegiac subject as they do from the father as elegiac object.

Whose Seduction?: Psychoanalytic Theory and the Elegy

As much as the contemporary elegy is haunted by convention, it is spurred on by inquiry into modes of mourning in the present day, and such inquiry is exacerbated by shifts both temporal and geographical. Perhaps the two most urgent concerns currently putting pressure on elegiac convention are (1) the reassessment of the role of consolation in an increasingly secular Western society and (2) the challenge to psychoanalytical notions of melancholia as they may appear in the contemporary elegy. These two concerns are causally linked. In the twentieth century, any elegy must deal with the possibility that a Christianized consolation may be puzzling, unappealing, or simply incomprehensible to the reader. This ushers in a second problem: without an understood spiritual tradition of consolation and apotheosis, how does the elegist resist languishing in melancholia, making the elegy itself static and vulnerable to reductive psychoanalytical manipulation?

This is not a small question in our post-Freudian world, and by using the prefix "post," I do not mean that we have advanced beyond the influence of Freud's ideas, but rather, that his ideas have become enculturated in Western society to the degree that they have taken on the trappings of social truisms whether or not we are fully conscious of their influence. The acceptance of Freud's narrative of the family romance has alarming and often annoying implications for women's paternal elegies, as does Freud's obfuscation of the differences between mourning and melancholia. The phenomenon of the shock of expectation—an oxymoron used in this instance to connote the amazed reaction of readers to Freud's oldest ideas (incest, parricide, melancholia), despite the patina of social savvy that many post-Freudian readers adopt—nibbles at the edge of elegiac convention, and contributes to the volatility of the female-authored paternal elegy. How shocking is it to refuse consolation, to minimize encomiastic praise, to speak ill of the dead, or even damn them with faint praise? Michel Foucault's phrase (from volume 1 of *The History of Sexuality*) "we 'other Victorians'" nicely captures this form of sophisticated prurience (4–5). Foucault's use of the first-person plural is a reminder of the impact of that shock of expectation. Reducing every paternal elegy to an overworked or undigested literary manifestation of an Electra complex is as dismissive to elegy studies as it is to feminist literature. In the face of social beliefs that it is moribund to discuss the dead and that it is psychologically aberrant for a woman to explore the political meaning of the father's death, assumptions about women, love, grief and fatherhood are unequivocally political. The most popular example of this shock of expectation and its impact on the reception of a female-written paternal elegy would be the scores of early—and ongoing—critical readings of Sylvia Plath's "Daddy" that reduced that complex poem to an individualized Oedipal mania by ignoring Plath's political challenge to the hegemony of violence, both familial and historical, and emphasizing its confessional aspects. According to such readings, women who write the father must be—by necessity—unbalanced, death-worshipping, self-sacrificial. While psychoanalytical criticism is not necessarily a dragon to be slain in service of the female-written elegy, its pervasive influence and persistent assumptions are exemplary of the kind of cultural influences that have informed against a serious study of the female-written elegy in North American literature.

Convincing readers that a daughter's mourning duty to her father is neither self-sacrificing nor sexually pathological is the formidable task of many female paternal elegists. Freud's belief in a necessarily completed mourning, his focus on melancholia as pathological, and his misapprehension of female sexuality combine to prescribe a prohibition of the female gaze upon the paternal body. In his 1917 article, "Mourning and Melancholia," Freud's differentiation between normative mourning and pathological melancholia designates completed mourning as the only psychologically healthy solution to grief. The "work of mourning," for Freud, requires a "testing of reality" of the loss, in order that the mourner may withdraw all libido attachments from the lost object (144). In order to complete mourning, the mourner must consciously recoup all emotional losses by reappropriating affection from the lost beloved, leaving the mourner's ego "free and uninhibited" at the end of this "work" (145).

"Mourning and Melancholia" remains surprisingly influential on contemporary formulations of "proper" mourning by psychologists and scholars, despite the fact that Freud revised his ideas several times, notably after the deaths of his daughter Sophie in 1920 and her son, four-year-old Heinz Rudolf Halberstadt, in 1923. Freud's emphases on the super-ego's role in a fundamental death drive in *Beyond the Pleasure Principle* (1920) and *The Ego and the Id* (1923) are critically much less popular than the prevailing theory from the comparatively slim article "Mourning and Melancholia." The earlier distinctions between mourning and melancholia endure because the idea of mourning as "work" has captured the literary and symbolic imagination in a way that the concept of mourning as a libidinous engagement with the death-drive has not. While it would be too simple to think of "the work of mourning" as an appeal to Canada's inherited Protestant work ethic, there is something undeniably familiar about Freud's metaphor of mourning as concrete, effortful, executable work that will result in an end product. If only mourning was indeed so measureable, so achievable, and so obedient to formula, which, alas, it is not.

As for melancholia, even though Freud admits freely that "[e]ven in descriptive psychiatry the definition of melancholia is uncertain" (142), he later draws a specific distinction between the two affective states, noting that, unlike the mourner, the melancholic "knows whom he has lost but not *what* it is he has lost in them" (145; emphasis in original). This describes the elegist's dilemma—and drive—exactly, but for a writer, this is less pathological than it is productive; each time Freud refers to the "melancholic," we could easily substitute the word "elegist" and come away at the end of the article with a description not of a psychological anxiety, but of a creative process. By this I do not wish to imply that elegists are ill but just the opposite: that what Freud describes as melancholia is malleable enough to describe a literary tradition rather than a mental condition.

Let me demonstrate. For Freud, melancholia performs a similar type of "inner labour" as mourning does, but the melancholic's work is complicated by the melancholic's puzzlement about the importance of the lost object. This puzzlement leads to a lack of social shame, a propensity for the melancholic's "insistent talking" about herself to the point that she will derive "pleasure in the consequent exposure" (147). Freud sees the melancholic tending towards a kind of exhibitionism in which discussing loss or displaying grief leads to a certain social satisfaction in presenting the self as a spectacle. Publishing a book of elegiac work is certainly one way (although not the only way) of achieving that kind of social satisfaction while displaying a culturally sanctioned version of the self as grieving spectacle. Melancholia, with its apparently self-centred verbosity and its focus on the lost object of affection as a defining feature of the self, is a more likely psychological parallel to the vicissitudes of the elegiac mode than is the prescriptive efficiency of completed mourning. Granted, the initial lyric impulse of most elegies seem to perform the work of mourning in that the poem brings up memories of the lost object in the way Freud describes, "bit by bit, at great expense of time and cathetic energy" (143). However, the elegy almost always engages more fully with melancholia, in that the elegist identifies her grief for that which remains unnameable despite identification of the lost beloved figure. It is this melancholic opacity, this resistance to complete understanding that the elegy takes up as its driving force. Elaine Scarry, in her groundbreaking work, *The Body in Pain*, notes that a poem written after suffering is an artifact of pain that necessarily stands in for ineffable, inexpressible experience. The elegy is such an artifact, in that it records not the completed work of mourning but the problem of the ongoing work of melancholia.

Ultimately, Freud concludes that the process of melancholia either renders the lost object valueless and abandons it, or attains "the satisfaction of acknowledging [the melancholic] as the better of the two, as superior to the object" (160). Certainly this final judgment of "superiority" takes us back to Bloom's careerist young poets proving themselves superior to their literary fathers, but it is even more important to note that the melancholic seems to shuttle between satisfaction and restlessness, neither committed to grief nor pursuing a psychological replacement for the loss. That is, she is not necessarily doomed to a psychic limbo of ego-generated labours that could never be mistaken for spiritual consolation or efficiently completed mourning, but she may be moving towards the creation of an artifact—something very like an elegy.

A willingness to read feminist politics through kinship structures can give us the final piece to this puzzle. Freud notes that mourning and melancholia share similar "distinguishing mental features... a profoundly painful dejection, abrogation of interest in the outside world, loss of the capacity to love, [and] inhibition of all activity," but distinguishes the melancholic condition as beset by "a disturbance in self-regard" (143). If, as I have proposed, the inquisitive female elegist is engaged with writing herself into a new form of subjectivity after the death of the father, can it be any surprise that her "self-regard" is disturbed from its previous state? Freud also theorizes that the melancholic's self-reproaches are sublimated transferences of the sins of the lost beloved, with the result that melancholics "give a great deal of trouble, perpetually taking offence and behaving as if they have been treated with great injustice" (149). In the case of female elegists as political commentators, "giving a great deal of trouble" would be a requirement rather than a problem, and the great injustices that daughterly mourners may have experienced at the hands of the patriarchy may be entirely appropriate subject matter for an elegy.

Though both mourning and melancholia are "complicated by the conflict of ambivalence" (158), Freud points out that "[i]n melancholia, countless single conflicts in which love and hate wrestle together are fought for the object" (159). Father–daughter relationships are indeed characterized by ambivalence and ambiguity, and the elegies that these defiant melancholic daughters produce are political in their stance and scope. As Schiesari observes in *The Gendering of Melancholia*, Freud's admission that melancholia proceeds outside the bounds of normative behaviour implies that melancholia may be construed as "a culturally prestigious condition over and beyond its own shortcomings" (38). Schiesari's study concerns the traditional split between male melancholics, who are culturally exalted as intellectuals and artists, "disagreeable but justified rebel[s]" against social restrictions on affect, and female mourners whose expressions of grief or ontological inquiries are granted no particular cultural power (50). Hypothesizing that current psychological terminology pathologizes female melancholia as clinical depression rather than an aesthetic or philosophical position, Schiesari maintains that such a diagnosis precludes women from being culturally situated, as men can be, as "legitimator[s]" who challenge the status quo "by virtue of [their] overdeveloped conscience" (53).

Elegy theorists have grappled with Freud's formulation of completed mourning for much of the twentieth century with mixed results. For example, in *The English Elegy*, Sacks suggests that the elegy imitates the Oedipal triangle to regulate mourning practice. Sacks's Freudian reading of the dynamics of loss, longing, and substitution proposes the lost object as the absent mother, the mourning subject as the longing child, and the passage of time as the authoritative father who is responsible for separating the mother and child and so introduces the child to loss. In situating the lost object as a maternal source of love and acceptance, Sacks rejects ambivalence out of hand. The mourner's longing after the lost object may describe much of the emotional arc of an elegy, but for such longing to go unchallenged by more equivocal melancholic feelings seems reductive. Sacks's elegiac triangle is also politically objectionable in its designation of the father figure as inexorably and naturally authoritative as time itself, and the characterization of the lost beloved figure as inevitably maternal and defeated. Configuring time as a masculinized, authoritative master plays into the cultural codification of survival as "men's work" steeped in a tradition of heroics.

Working with heterosexist foundational myths, Sacks reiterates Freud's ideas of completing "healthy" mourning through the process of substituting an artifact for the lost object, and finding consolation in the substitution. Citing the Greek myths of Pan and Syrinx, and Apollo and Daphne, Sacks contends that as each male lover is abandoned by his female beloved, he consoles himself with a substitutive device composed of his lost beloved's transformed body: reed pipes for Pan and a laurel wreath for Apollo. This theory has a certain symbolic elegance, but its implications are anything but innocent. While it may be consoling for a male lover to play upon or wear a piece of his transformed lover's body, what does this symbolism say about the cost of such consolation? A woman's body, even when transformed into a reed (Syrinx) or a laurel tree (Daphne), remains a consumable object that a man can bend to his own desires and call enduring. This is creepy, to put it mildly. Sacks elides the fact that, in both of these legends, the female figures are not consensual partners of the men. Both Syrinx and Daphne flee from the men who desire them and beg goddesses to transform them into emblems of nature in order to elude the lust of their pursuers. Seen in this light, Sacks's theory of substitution as consolation is at best a misogynist joke; at worst, it is an elegiac theory based on an ethos of violent rapture. Is the refusal to complete mourning in the female elegy then based upon a lack of faith in the substitutive symbol, or upon a rejection of the violence of substitution, or both?

Sacks's characterization of the father as time is not very distant from Jacques Lacan's concept of the Father as "the effect of a pure signifier" that "religion has taught us to refer to as the Name-of-the-Father" (*Écrits* 199). If the Father is situated as the overriding symbolic function of the mourning triangle, then the Father becomes the force that dictates the terms of the elegy, if not of mourning itself. But Lacan suggests that declaring the Father the supreme victor associates him immediately with profound loss, and asserts that "the appearance of the signifier of the Father" is linked in psychoanalysis to "the creation of the law" and ultimately "with death" (199). The results of this formulation position the father as an object that is inevitably elegiac; as the Father as signifier is speedily linked to the lawmaker and the lost body, the father as human being is foreclosed upon with a kind of bodiless mastery. Patricia Yeager, in her article "The Father's Breasts," calls this notion of bodilessness "asomia," noting that such asomia acts as a societal complement to a belief in feminine "somatophobia," or a "fear of the body's fleshiness and mutability" (9).

While Freud's family romance positions the father as the primary object of his daughter's sexual attachment, Lacan does not emphasize any kind of daughterly role. His assertion is that for the son the living father must eventually become the dead Father, a figure who transcends the flesh to exist in perpetuity in his offspring's psyche as a powerful authoritative memory. However, if a son's reception of the dead father's authority is part of inheriting that authority, how then does a daughter receive this word-of-the-dead-Father, particularly as she does not participate in the son's symbolic murder of the Father, an act which "binds himself for life to the Law" (Lacan 199)? Daughterly reception of this authority is at the heart of *Antigone* and *Electra*, tragedies in which young women take on the authority of their formidable fathers to right a social wrong with tragic results. In *Antigone's Claim: Kinship Between Life and Death*, Judith Butler claims that Antigone's self-sacrifice "emblematize[s] a certain heterosexual fatality that remains to be read" (72). Butler's comment is a good reminder of the ways that psychoanalysis has heretofore represented the standing model by which the father–daughter kinship has been discussed in Western culture, and both literature and psychoanalysis have drawn heavily upon the self-sacrificing figure of Antigone as the exemplary familial mourner. George Steiner's book-length study, *Antigones*, is a testament to the popularity of the myth of Antigone as "a work of art nearer to perfection than any other produced by the human spirit" (1), a belief strong in Western philosophy and literary criticism throughout the nineteenth century and into the early twentieth century. Steiner notes that Hegel, Kierkegaard, and Hölderin all produced major treatises that discussed Antigone as the most noble of heroines, and operatic and theatrical productions of the myth were performed frequently to popular and critical acclaim. Steiner also asserts that Freud turned the twentieth century's attention to Oedipus as the foundational myth of human experience. The critical attentions of Lacan in "The Splendor of Antigone" in his *Seminar VII*, Irigaray in "The Eternal Irony of the Community" in *Speculum of the Other Woman*, and Butler in *Antigone's Claim* suggest that the early twenty-first century may have more interest in Antigone as a heroine who emblematizes "the convergence of social prohibition and melancholia," as Butler claims (80). Butler reads the Antigone myth as evidence of a centuries-old "crisis of kinship" that raises questions about a woman's physical and psychic vulnerability in performing mourning duties that have been inextricably linked to ideas of female sacrifice (*Antigone's* 24).

If a sacrifice of the female self is considered proper literary mourning, then melancholia can be interpreted as a deliberate refusal of such a consolatory sacrifice, a rejection of a mourning practice that is too dangerous to complete. Butler also asserts that Antigone's burial of Polynices "at once reflects and institutes the equivocation of brother and father," that through the jointly cursed deaths, Oedipus and Polynices are "already interchangeable for her" and that her act can only "reinstitute and re-elaborate that interchangeability" (61). Thus, for Butler, Antigone is the ultimate "daughterly" mourner; her determination to mourn Polynices is enlarged by and emerges from Antigone's thwarted attempts to mourn for her father, Oedipus. His mysterious disappearance in *Oedipus at Colonus* denies to her both his body as an object of ritual mourning and his graveside as a site of ritual remembrance.

The limits of psychoanalytical criticism in discussing the dynamics of father–daughter kinship become increasingly evident when exploring how a daughter's duty to her dying father might be influenced by feminist theory. The most immediate result is a textual self-consciousness, as the daughter notes her position in the libidinal politics of the family. Freud's concept of the inner labour of grief is not the only way to think about the "work" performed by the elegy, but his distinctions between mourning and melancholia have become widely socially accepted despite (or perhaps because of) Freud's uncertainties. Ideologically implicit in many Western attitudes towards the affect of grief, Freud's identification of the melancholic's investment in ambivalence and in perceived injustice sits uncomfortably beside Freud's marked tendency to assume sexual dysfunction as the source of all female illness, as well as the source of a good portion of feminine affect. Even seduction theory, as extreme as it seems, remains a powerful force in contemporary beliefs about father–daughter kinship. While there is nothing to be gained—and a great deal of harm that may be done—by denying that father–daughter incest occurs in Western culture, it is equally inaccurate to position incest as the primary way of speaking about father–daughter kinship. Such a position, or such a lack of language, only reinforces Freudian seduction theory and effaces the many other dynamics that may exist between fathers and daughters. Examining elegiac practice and feminist thought about paternal power at the end of the twentieth century emphasizes Shaw's contention that the elegy "stages swift progressions in shock and intimacy" (172), and sometimes what is most shocking about elegies is the discovery of the ways in which elegists are trapped in a web of cultural and literary sanctions against intimate expressions of affect and similarly intimate explorations of political urgency.

Undeniably complicated by Freud's seduction theory, a woman's grief for her father is easily misconstrued as a snarl of obligation and pathology. Too little a display of grief makes the daughter socially monstrous, but too large a display of grief appears to reveal a pathologically sublimated sexual desire for the father. Of course, the mourning daughter could always try to transgender herself in grief: to become the "good son" in order to inherit the father's power and male privilege. Nancy K. Miller, recording her reaction to her father's illness in *Bequest and Betrayal*, gives a good example of how such a negotiation might appeal, and subsequently, appall. Mockingly calling herself "Ms. Oedipus," a daughter who longed to "at last have [her] father to [her]self," (20) Miller realizes to her chagrin that this desire will be flouted. In the debilitated state brought on by his illness, her father cannot be "the good father of [her] childhood: Daddy" (20). Miller writes that caring for her father felt like "a mockery of the maternal," and she chafes against this frame on daughterly duty: "I was sick of Being a Good Daughter (though I of course reveled in it as well)... his constant complaining, the endless tasks of running another household, the white panic at being responsible for another life. Being like a son" (27). Miller's capital letters on "Being a Good Daughter" emphasize her awareness of cultural and social performance. Miller goes on to point out her own gender crisis as she cares for her dying father: the "feminine" nature of the day-to-day domestic care set against the "masculine" responsibility for another life.

Miller's conflation of "son" and "responsibility for another life" suggests that such an inheritance may induce a "white panic," but such responsibility may also encourage consolation, another part of "being like a son." Jane Gallop's take on Freudian seduction theory, *The Daughter's Seduction: Feminism and Psychoanalysis*, suggests that throughout a daughter's life she must step carefully to keep a father's attention without scaring him away with the spectre of desire. Such carefulness can result in silence, in which daughters are forbidden to speak of their fathers to others because a father fears not only his daughter's criticism, but also the possibility of the daughter's love as an emotional, intellectual, or social seduction, if not a sexual one. This condition of daughterhood ventures near to what Derrida calls "the unbearable paradox of fidelity" ("By Force" 159), though the conditions of daughterhood do not necessarily invest in Derrida's incomplete and impossible mourning. Rather, they debate the balance to be maintained between fidelity and distance, the balance that is socially demanded from a daughter as her father's gendered Other.

But if we want to take seriously a situation in which a daughter strives to become closer to her father by occasionally acting the part of a good son, eventually we must ask where and how the mother appears in all of these familial gender negotiations. The daughter's connection with the mother is one social expectation that is openly and sometimes obviously flouted within the paternal elegies discussed in this volume. The absence of mothers in paternal elegies could be part of the generic convention that pits the lonely mourner against the memory of the singular lost beloved, her sorrow unrelieved by the presence of others. Mourning is not always but is often a solitary duty, even when (or especially when) the beloved has been shared with others; while these daughters may culturally inherit mourning practice from a tradition of shared female mourning, they address their grief in their mothers' approbation or censure. Without a doubt, the absence of mothers from these elegies exacerbates the tensions of father–daughter kinship. The daughter's focus narrows to include only her father; her mother can neither mediate nor distract from the tensions produced by father–daughter kinship. Or can she? Gallop maintains that, in the father's eyes, a daughter can never be truly separated from her mother, that despite a daughter's "plea for separateness, its impossibility manifests itself" (114). But even this "impossibility" must recognize the Freudian seductive atmosphere that accompanies many of these poems—a seduction that may be more intellectual than sexual, but one that remains a seduction all the same. Gallop herself suggests that the father's law will turn a blind eye to "a veiled seduction" by the daughter in lieu of a forbidden sexual seduction (70). If, as Gallop suggests, any engagement the daughter has with the father is assumed to be seductive, then the presence of the mother is evidence that a daughter need be actively protected from the father's (seductive) law. This is the vicious circle of seduction of and by the daughter, according to Gallop. When the daughter's otherness proves unsuccessful and unworthy in her father's eyes, the daughter discovers the only way to "avoid scaring the father away, is to please him, and to please him one must submit to his law which proscribes any sexual relation" (71). Of course, even this kind of a submission is sexually encoded as a kind of seduction. In Gallop's title, the seduction by the daughter is proposed as a reversal of the seduction of the daughter, and Gallop grapples with the phantom of incestuous relations that so petrifies Freudian readings of daughterhood. Gallop's suggestion that the daughter's attention frightens the father, and that she must carefully modulate her actions to "avoid scaring" him, is intriguing, and is, perhaps, the key to the mother's absence from these elegies. The mother is not represented in these poems not because she is, as Brandt puts it in *Wild Mother Dancing*, "unspeakable, unrepresentable, unconscious, associated with death, double-handed" or difficult to locate in the "master narrative of Western history" (6), though all of the former may be an accurate description, but because female paternal elegists ask impertinent questions about the family romance that undermine the stark triangulation of father–daughter–death. While Gallop's warning that any feminist politics needs to interrogate the "complex power relations that structure our world" while "avoid[ing] the pitfall of familial thinking" (xv), changing the terms of familial thinking may be the solution to examining this particular set of power relations. These paternal elegies represent a showdown of sorts: father and daughter fixed with a demanding agenda, wherein she has the lexical authority to scare him, interrogate him, praise him, exonerate him, abandon or remake him, all without the mediation of his wife and her mother.

The ambivalent energies of the elegy are most clearly revealed by the genre's investment in paradox, most specifically the double paradox that defines elegy as a practice of memory that presages forgetting and as a practice of forgetting that requires remembrance. Shaw reminds readers that the elegy can be defined by the paradoxes of mourning enacted within the genre: "the best way to forget the dead by giving them a quiet grave is first to remember them. Only a past that has been genuinely recollected can also be forgotten" (216). If the elegy is the mechanism by which mourners "recollect"—to remember and to gather together—then the elegy acts as an artifact in Scarry's terminology: an object that has the power to "make and unmake the world" (22). The elegiac artifact recalls mourning as a practice in which the dead are genuinely recollected and sincerely forgotten, and in doing so, Shaw argues that elegy has a tendency to make myth from the force of its assertion: "By the end of the elegy, the vagueness of a mere memory has been replaced by the defining details of an authentic recollection" (215). But "authentic recollection" favours a fictive or mythic mode rather than a demotic confession; for Shaw, and for the poets discussed in this volume, elegiac memory is almost always filtered through a fictive modality. The poems in this volume may begin with an autobiographical impulse, but they quickly move beyond the merely personal to consider the dynamics of mourning and daughterhood in the twentieth century. If "mere memory" can lead the mourner through Freud's "healthy" mourning, then perhaps the workings of Shaw's ironic designation of "authentic recollection" could lead the elegist through a productive melancholia to a reformed subjectivity.

Impossible Mourning, Inaugural Mourning: Critical Theory and the Elegy

The elegiac mode has in the past relied upon the mourner's declaration of inconsolability to begin the poem and to sustain the mourning arc of the poetic narrative. The movement towards consolation traditionally signals a poetic conclusion that is written as an emotional resolution. The inconsolability of grief fuels the poem until the mourner discovers a reason, sometimes beyond the reaches of quotidian logic, to be consoled or at least to admit the possibility of consolation.

In contemporary critical theory, perhaps no one has debated issues of consolation and mourning as exhaustively as has Jacques Derrida. In his essay "Mnemosyne," dedicated to the memory of Paul de Man, Derrida proposes that all writing about mourning reproduces the central paradox of mourning because the remembering "I" chafes against a "tendency to accept incomprehension," and so refutes the completion of mourning according to the Freudian model (31). Derrida declares mourning to be equally "impossible" and "necessary," and the mourner to be inevitably trapped in a way that both creates and consumes sorrowful incomprehension. Mourning, in this model, simultaneously demands and denies a conscious observation of the interiorized image of the dead, and so privileges a permanently unresolved but affectionate mourning, with the mourner caught forever between the release of mourning and the maintenance work of memory. Such a pattern seems to describe Freudian melancholia, even though Derrida insists that the movement between impossible and necessary mourning puts into order "the whole rhetoric of mourning, and describes the essence of memory" (34). While Derrida's resistance to a simple resolution of mourning seems encouragingly unlike Freud's "free and uninhibited" ego, his choice of imagery to describe the interiorized image of the dead person is distinctly problematic. Focusing upon the interiorized dead as a kind of fetus—"we grieve for him and bear him in us, like an *unborn child*, like a future"—Derrida describes a refusal of memory as "an *aborted* interiorization" that functions as "a sort of tender rejection, a movement of renunciation which leaves the other alone, outside, over there, in his death, outside of us" (35; emphases added). Derrida is quick to note that these formulations, too, are part of the paradox of mourning. The fetus of memory, ambiguously "unborn," functions as a representative of both future and past, and the refusal of this fetal burden casts the mourner as a rejecting or annihilating mother. Derrida's choice to gloss mourning as a pregnancy is paradoxical given his discourse on male filiation in mourning, though his choice of abortion as a metaphor to describe a refusal to mourn cannot help but place interiorization under the stress of an imagined but no less problematic religious and civil conception of Law.

Between the choices of bearing the beloved dead forward into the future and rejecting the beloved dead (however "tenderly"), Derrida emphasizes that the mourner cannot choose, and so is left with only the "trace of the other" that perpetuates mourning (31). But in "By Force of Mourning," his essay in memory of Louis Marin, included in 2001's *The Work of Mourning*, Derrida advances his metaphor of the interiorized image from a fragile doomed fetus to a commanding father figure. Writing about the dead forces the elegist to enact an "unbearable paradox of fidelity" to an interiorized image of the dead that maintains agency through the mourner's grief:

> When we say "in us," when we speak so easily and so painfully of inside and outside, we are naming space, we are speaking of a visibility of the body, a geometry of gazes, an orientation of perspectives. *We are speaking of images.* What is only *in us* seems to be reducible to images, which might be memories or monuments, but which are reducible in any case to a memory that consists of visible scenes that are no longer anything but *images.* (159; emphasis in original)

This "naming space" returns to the metaphor of pregnancy, that which is "in us" and outside us at once. However, by staying focused upon "memories or monuments," Derrida sidesteps the corporeal problem to "speak of images" instead of space. He chooses to discuss visibility instead of the tactile sensation of interiority, and, in effect, to reiterate the Lacanian conception of the dead Father rather than to return to his own fetal mourning trope. According to Derrida, the inevitable reduction of the lost beloved figure to a series of images cannot help but result in a posthumous infidelity to the deceased. Such infidelity not only flouts the elegist's obligation to serve the dead faithfully, but all those who write or speak of the dead should be warned that this interiorized image "sees more than it is seen. The image looks at us" ("By Force" 160). Derrida invokes this interiorized gaze of the dead as a reminder of the responsibility of speaking of the dead. From a female paternal elegist's perspective, this metaphoric gaze is a problematic replay of the male gaze, now interiorized and imbued with the authority of the dead Father.

Far from inheriting the power of her dead father's gaze to emerge as the subject of her own narrative, the daughter-elegist remains the object of the (fatherly) male gaze, now interiorized within her. Is this the gaze of Lacan's authoritative dead Father, watching to assure that her regard is properly filial? Derrida's fidelity to an image of the dead becomes highly complex for female elegists, for, if they are caught in a male gaze from beyond the grave, can their elegies assert any kind of female subjectivity or are they inevitably subordinate to a haunting male authority, a kind of perpetual Father? Such formulations constitute an unbearable paradox for female elegists, not because, as Derrida suggests, the paradox of fidelity is potentially infinite, but rather because of the patriarchal imperative that such an interiorization serves. Derrida cites fidelity to the dead as the most important responsibility in writing about mourning, but Shaw's ironic assertion about "authentic recollection" that usurps "mere memory" should not be forgotten. At what point does fidelity become fidelity to a memory that no longer represents the lost beloved and, in addition, sacrifices the subjectivity of mourner? If the truth about mourning is caught between necessity and impossibility, how can this cycle of irresolvable mourning—a mourning that comes suspiciously close to Freudian melancholia—be broken? The answer may lie in the introduction of a third term to the dynamics of mourning.

In *Mourning Becomes the Law*, Gillian Rose proposes that the Derridean cycle of irresolvable mourning is not only an inaccurate description of the mourning dynamic, but further, that Derrida's insoluble binary represents an unethical model of "postmodern" mourning, or, as Rose terms it, a "despairing rationalism without reason" (7). Rose deflates Derrida's ironic aphorism "I mourn, therefore I am" as a statement that is indicative of a "static condition between desire for presence and acceptance of absence," something Derrida would not deny (11). She declares that Derrida's paradox of impossible yet necessary mourning offers little beyond a bid for tragic drama, reiterating the dynamic of the *Trauerspiel*. Working with Walter Benjamin's *The Origin of German Tragic Drama*, Rose emphasizes that the *Trauerspiel* represents "interminable mourning play and lament" rather than productive work, and so reproduces a dynamic that concentrates upon the "pathos of concept in the place of its logos" (64). Rose loses no opportunity to gloss the German *Trauerspiel* as literally "mourning play" and contrasts this play to her interpretation of Freud's "work of mourning." She is adamant that mourning requires a "combination of self-knowledge and action which will not blanch before its complicities in power" (121). For Rose, the danger of the *Trauerspiel* dynamic lies in its unethical presentation of "death without determination" that presupposes "life without reason" (137). Rose calls this "aberrated" mourning, an irresolute stasis that was labelled melancholia in another era (as Schiesari points out), accompanied by a guarded attitude of intellectual despair (7). Rose asserts that mourning is necessary, and she advises an intellectual courage that she finds lacking in postmodern thought and, indeed, she implies that the concept of impossible mourning only inspires people to shirk the duties of the mourner. The unresolved standoff between reason and love may be compelling as drama, but Rose argues that it is a dangerous substitute for actual mourning practice.

Rose cautions that Derrida's image of the mourner as pregnant with the spirit of the dead is not innocent; when "the remains of the dead are incorporated into the soul of the one who cannot mourn," the result is "a death-in-life, revenant evil" (70). Any attempt, metaphorical or theoretical, to incorporate a dead soul in a living body invokes a "baroque melancholia immersed in the world of soulless and unredeemed bodies, which affords a vision that is far more disturbing than the salvific distillation of 'spirit' or 'spectre'" (69–70). Situating the work of mourning as socially productive and culturally necessary work, Rose suggests that mourning women are neither "transgressors" nor ironic counterpoints to patriarchal law, but rather women who "reinvent the political life of the community" with their "delegitimate acts of tending the dead" (35). Rejecting Derrida's concept of a "spectral someone other" (*Specters* 7), Rose proposes "inaugurated mourning" (70), asserting that the mourner's task is not only to transgress the ways in which civic law restricts mourning practices, but also that the performance of the "just act" (103) of mourning will actually become the law that reifies women as civic subjects. Rose emphasizes mourning as that which bears meaning forward; mourning is always active, always becoming. The mourner is one who makes meaning of death, grief, and the loss of the beloved, not only for herself, but for the larger community; the project of making meaning out of mourning finds purchase in the continuing health of the mourner and, by extension, the health of the citizenry.

Rose does not ignore the trope of the mourner as a voyager who is forever altered by the rigours of travel, but she emphasizes the voyager's return to the city—that is, to making meaning of mourning—as part of the "just act." She cautions against resisting the imperative to mourn: "to be deprived of, or to refuse, the work of mourning has *political consequences.* It tempts us to oppose pure, gratuitous love to the injustice of the world; to see ourselves as suffering but good, and the city as evil.... This opposing of our cherished good to public ill denies the third term which gives meaning to both judgments—the just city and the just act, the just man and the just woman" (103; emphasis in original).

It is difficult to discern whether Rose proposes mourning as a function of reason, or whether she believes that mourning is necessarily contiguous to meaning. But for her, as for Freud, the completion of mourning is vital for the maintenance of a civil society, though Rose's civil society is profoundly concerned with political responsibility that may be attained through balancing the demands of reason, ethics, and justice: "Completed mourning acknowledges the creative involvement of action in the configuration of power and law: it does not find itself unequivocally in a closed circuit which exclusively confers logic and power" (11). For Rose, the resistance to a closed circuit of logic and power with the introduction of the concept of mourning as a "just act" is the key to completing the process of mourning and to maintaining a balanced society.

This concept of inaugurated mourning as a political position invokes the dynamic of elegiac anagnorisis; the "just act" is a discovery that has the potential to revitalize the political life of the elegy. The search for consolation and a redefined subjectivity in the female-written paternal elegy must begin with the elegist considering the urgency of her mourning practice. An examination of the elegy as a revelatory artifact must consider not only the power of the elegy's metaphysical devices, but also its ability to function as "protest against arbitrary power" (Rose 26).

But the elegy under Rose's terms is perhaps easier said than done, particularly if part of the approach requires a consideration of the work of melancholia. Like a true Freudian, Rose denies that melancholia has any political agency, even though her concept of mourning as a "just act" describes precisely the kind of "melancholic turn" that Butler links explicitly to the establishment of subjectivity in *The Psychic Life of Power* when she suggests that melancholia precedes and even creates the conditions for mourning (171). For Butler, subjectivity is always a social condition; "The subject who might grieve is implicated in a loss of autonomy that is mandated by linguistic and social life; it can never produce itself autonomously. From the start, this ego is other than itself; what melancholia shows is that only by absorbing the other as oneself does one become something at all" (195–96).

If Rose's theory is correct, the more the elegy-writing daughter pursues mourning as a "just act," the more she may present her paternal elegy as an act of political defiance that situates her as a civic subject. If Butler is correct about melancholia as a source affect for subjectivity, then becoming something in "linguistic and social life" is an inevitability of attachment that may only be thwarted by isolation or social oppression.

Just Acts: Renegotiating Female Filial Piety

The paternal elegy as a daughter's "just act" is negotiated by the daughter's demands on her own subjectivity, as well as by what the work of melancholia demands of the daughter. The chapters that follow concentrate on how individual Canadian female poets risk a redefinition of feminine filial piety by investigating negotiations of female subjectivity in paternal elegies. The focus is on reading the fundamentals of mourning and melancholia through the poems with an emphasis on how each poet challenges the genre to mourn the father without being afraid of subjecting to scrutiny the terms under which love is defined.

As the daughter figures of each poem become more demanding of themselves as subjects, they become less defined by the object of mourning, suggesting that the efficacy of the daughter's paternal elegy is predicated on its definition of consolation and its opportunities for subjectivity. Lynda E. Boose reminds us that father–daughter kinship "is locked in a conflicted text of desire and sanction" that is filtered through a complex blend of "asymmetries of age, authority and gender privilege" (46). The daughter, bereft of both marriage bond and inheritance, is the family outsider in Boose's view, perfectly positioned to consider the various paternal personas available in Western literature and critical theory: Father as Freudian social authority, as Lacanian lawgiver, as Kristevan "imaginary father... simple virtuality, a potential presence," (*Tales* 43), or as a Butlerian Oedipus who demands "promiscuous obedience" from the daughter (*Antigone's* 61–62). In elegizing the father without resorting to encomium, memorializing the father without sacrificing daughterly subjectivity, and thinking critically about daughterhood within the social order of mourning the father as individual and as social structure, each of these daughterly elegists discover an elegiac subjectivity, a way that a female poet can, in Schiesari's terms, represent herself "as a subject who is the subject of her loss" (65). A daughter's elegy may be considered a literary artifact that sets the work of mourning against the libidinal politics of paternal authority, including the daughter-mourner's desire to delineate, and perhaps dismantle, the fidelity demanded by the father's death.

Part Two

Daughters of Jove, Daughters of Job

Canadian Modernism's Bloody-Minded Women

2

Jove's Daughter

Dorothy Livesay's Elegiac Daughteronomy

> Death is a displaced name for a linguistic predicament, and the restoration of mortality by autobiography (the prosopopeia of the voice and the name) deprives and disfigures to the precise extent that it restores. Autobiography veils a defacement of the mind of which it is itself the cause.
>
> — Paul de Man, "Autobiography as De-Facement"

Defacement and the Good Modernist Daughter

Before looking at the paternal elegies that grew out of Dorothy Livesay's struggle with her father's critical and creative influence, I want to consider the autobiographical impulse in poetry and its place in the kind of political elegiac practice that is the subject of this volume. To acknowledge that the assumption of autobiography has often been the bane of women writers is to acknowledge the clingy film of cliché that sometimes causes readers and critics to dismiss elegy as too personal to study or too autobiographical to engage in any kind of political thought. This is indeed a danger that must be considered when reading elegies, and while I am loathe to suggest that any writer's life (or any person's life, for that matter) can or should be reduced to a series of facts, it is important to keep in mind that the movement towards and, subsequently, away from confessional poetry in the twentieth century means that poets, perhaps even more acutely than writers of other genres, are aware of the complexities of writing versions of themselves into their poetry. Biographical criticism alone cannot be sufficient to unpack the power of paternal elegies, but neither should it be ignored. There is a balance to be maintained between assuming that biography is all and pretending that biography has no impact on the poem. The elegy occupies a specific position in this argument, and in this genre the circumstances of a writer's life cannot quite be argued away by relying on Barthesian "death of the author" theories or on older "new critical" approaches that eschew all reference to biography. But the balance is delicate and must be acknowledged.

Paul de Man's discussion of the role of autobiography in poetry in "Autobiography as De-Facement" notes that autobiography reminds poets of their mortality and does so through a "convergence of aesthetics and history" (67). The elegy reworks personal history by turning to the convention of the lost beloved figure even as the invocation of a specific loss suggests individuation. Even more germane to the study of the elegy is de Man's warning that readers should understand that even when poems begin from an autobiographical basis (like the death of a poet's father), we should not expect that poem to reveal an autobiographical "truth," but, rather, to offer an autobiographical "defacement" or significant alteration that is itself "veiled" by the impulse towards the portrayal of the poet's mind. de Man's metaphors of deprivation and disfigurement in poetry, and the role of the veiled version of the self, are particularly pertinent to the ways that Dorothy Livesay positions herself as the elegiac subject or mourning daughter in several short lyric poems that date from 1944 to 1979. In these poems, Livesay works intensely with autobiographical elements that she also explored in fiction, prose essays, and memoir, and my purpose here is less to "unveil" Livesay than to consider how her layers of veils serve her negotiations of inheritance and power through her decades-long elegiac conversation with her father, John Frederick Bligh Livesay (or "JFBL," as his daughter always refers to him in her writing).

So de Man's warning that poetry does not work towards self-knowledge in a therapeutic fashion comes as something of a relief. I would like to encourage readers to think about autobiographical elements in elegy for the ways that they "demonstrate in a striking way the impossibility of closure and totalization (that is the impossibility of coming into being) of all textual systems made up of tropological substitutions" (de Man 71). Substituting the individual father for the lost beloved or substituting the lost beloved for the Lacanian dead Father makes the paternal elegy a site of negotiations of power that exacerbate the elegy's mournful tone. Death, as a "linguistic predicament," may draw an autographical "veil" over a paternal elegy, but it is the responsibility of readers to consider how we invest in such "defacement" as elegiac veridiction or as an acceptable, aestheticized poetic falsehood.

Women's paternal elegies practice a kind of skepticism that often leads to a felicitous infidelity to the Father as Law, and the move towards a critical take on mourning and filial duty begins with the question of how the elegy may serve women's experience of loss. There is no better place to begin this history of the paternal elegy in Canadian literature than with the work of modernist poet and fiction writer Dorothy Livesay. Livesay's writing career spanned more than sixty years; from her first book of poetry, *Green Pitcher* in 1928 to her memoir *Journey With My Selves* in 1991, Livesay made a name for herself as an iconic feminist poet, a political artist, a worker for social justice, and a mentor to many other writers through her production of twenty-six books of poetry, fiction, and memoir. In current scholarship, Livesay remains a figure who is well respected for her early forays into socialist poetry, her investigations into the dimensions of the documentary poem as a Canadian genre, and for her outspokenness about sexual politics.

Livesay has long had a reputation as a wayward modernist and the reasons for this are not difficult to figure out. Various commentators have noted that modernism was slow to catch fire in Canada, and that coat of modernist poetry was tailored to a greater or lesser extent by F. R. Scott and A. J. M. Smith in *The McGill Fortnightly Review*: that is, it was cut to fit a male, Eastern, urban, university-educated figure. Female writers were often mocked out of the public eye by F. R. Scott's disdain for "poetesses" who did not produce poetry with the proper modernist rigour. His poem, "The Canadian Authors Meet," has become standard CanLit shorthand for either championing a particular kind of modernist aesthetic, or for noting the force of canon formation to exclude otherness, depending on the viewpoint of the person reading the poem. From the more removed historical perspective of 1986, David Arnason suggests that modernist poetry is "suspicious of the narrative mode, preferring the lyric," and notes modernism's focus upon the individual image, "the tough intellectual metaphor and...highly charged language" that favours objectivity and irony as defining qualities (6). But while Arnason's description of modernism relies on its aesthetics, feminist critics such as Carole Gerson have emphasized that the male modernist ethic of "detachment, alienated individualism, elitism and formalism over emotion, domesticity, community" influenced Canadian canon formation in the first half of the twentieth century ("The Most Canadian" 91). Gerson also notes that this masculine "valorization of national themes" ("The Canon Between the Wars" 46) extended into more recent decades, casting critical aspersions on stylistic features of nineteenth-century poetry as weak and essentially "feminine": "In addition to the still prevalent modernist critical embargo on 'feminine' concerns and the subsequent demotion of social and domestic issues as 'sentimental' (and not explicitly 'Canadian'), historical and biographical factors conspire against the reputations of women writers" ("The Canon Between the Wars" 46–47). More recently, Gerson has criticized "Canadian modernism's insistence on its own immaculate conception at McGill University in the late 1920s," and suggests a significant suppression of Canadian cultural history may be read in "modernism's treatment of women, natives, and popularity" ("The Most Canadian" 94).

But despite the considerable power of Scott and Smith's canon-shaping rhetoric, Livesay bested the men who would be known as the founders of modernist poetry in Canada at their own game. By 1947, she had published four books of poetry—*Green Pitcher* (1928), *Signpost* (1932), *Day and Night* (1944), and *Poems for People* (1947)—and won the Governor General's Award twice, once for *Day and Night* and once for *Poems for People*. Smith's single book published during the period, 1943's *News of the Phoenix*, also won the Governor General's Award, though Scott's only book published before 1947, *Overture* (1945), did not. How did Livesay manage, with so few female role models and without the approbation of masculinized Canadian modernism, to produce books and generally conduct herself as though the page was hers to explore? Part of the answer may be found in exploring Livesay's relationship with her father, who was a more demanding and critical male muse than any of Livesay's contemporaries could be, particularly because his support of Livesay's writing career was characterized by the extremes of delighted admiration and frank envy.

"Daddy's Girl": Reading Livesay's Psychic Autobiographies

Livesay's paternal elegies emphasize the tangle of loyalties, love, and law that are best discussed through Sandra M. Gilbert's concept of the "daughteronomy": Gilbert's pun conflating the paternal haunting of literary daughterhood with the law-giving Book of Deuteronomy. Pressing Levi-Strauss's concept of the exchange value of women in a family, Gilbert suggests that a text is a literary daughteronomy when a daughter's allegiance to her father is predicated upon her understanding that she will never take the father's place in the way that a son would: "she will never be such a usurper since she is an instrument—rather than an agent—of culture" ("Life's Empty Pack" 361). Gilbert also brings to light the frustrations of the daughter as a literary character who, abandoned by patriarchal and phallocentric culture, is left with "the empty pack of disinheritance" (358) as her paradoxical legacy. Daughteronomy, then, may be thought of as the "book" of obedience: a set of literary and social rules that predict the disinheritance of the daughter following the father's death—but also a text in which the plot, for the daughter, is one of desperate alliance with the father, especially after his death: "since the daughter has inherited an empty pack and cannot *be* a father, she has no choice but to be *for* the father—to be his treasure, his land, his voice" (364; emphasis in original).

Although the three metaphors of daughter-as-instrument—treasure, land, voice—were chosen to refer to the daughter's specific function in the George Eliot and Edith Wharton novels of Gilbert's study, her reading of the daughter as an instrument of patrimony rather than its agent is remarkably pertinent to Dorothy Livesay's own paternal elegiacs. Livesay spent decades discussing her relationship with her father in poetry, fiction, memoirs, personal essays, and interviews. Indeed, in "Daddy's Girl: Dorothy Livesay's Correspondence with Her Father," Pamela Banting writes that Livesay was "absorbed by the attempt to understand, to come to terms with, and even to exorcise, the influence her parents have had upon her" (10), with special emphasis on her father's literary ambitions for Livesay's career. Working with the correspondence between Livesay and her father from 1928 to the date of his death in 1944, Banting notes the "web of written tissue that binds father and daughter together in a mutual complicity and somewhat overblown intimacy" (13) was a profound and sometimes (for Dorothy Livesay) bewildering allegiance. Banting also suggests that the father's "displacement from his wife onto his daughter of an unusually intense emotional attachment" led to Livesay's uncomfortable understanding that "her immediate future as a writer was governed to a frightening extent by her father," which created "a potentially volatile situation for the young poet and her family" (17).

Livesay's lifelong devotion to her father and her corresponding fascination with her father's influential role in her life appears to position her psychoanalytically and perhaps even pathologically as a "daddy's girl": a sacrificing subject acting out her role in the Freudian family romance in a manner that suggests a violent subjugation to heteronormativity. However, Livesay's strong sense of political exigency demonstrated that Canadian female poets often met resistance in the private sphere of the family as well as in the public sphere of publications such as *The McGill Fortnightly Review*. We must recall Livesay's poems for and about her father as sites of political negotiation that emphasize her shifting subjectivity and her evolving feminism over three decades. Livesay's elegies for her father explore the political shift in the elegiac mode beginning with Gilbert's "literary daughteronomy," using the loss of the father as a springboard into feminist poetics.

The wealth of archival and published material left by Livesay reveals a welter of revisions that are given poignancy by Livesay's argument with P. K. Page about how and when to revise already published work. Multiple versions of poems can present a maze of contradictions if our purpose in reading the elegies is firmly attached to an investment in inalterable "truth" rather than the author's veil of defacement. Livesay, like any writer, revised and re-revised her work, and her interest in her family of origin yielded hundreds of poems, essays, novels, and fictional pieces. Scholarly interlocutors do not always agree on what is autobiographical and what is not. Arguments about poetic practice and the impulse towards veridiction could be made about many of Livesay's poems; although she frequently, in interviews and personal essays, aligned herself autobiographically with elegies such as "Page One," "Lament," and "Inheritance," Livesay also argued for a multiplicity of speaking selves throughout her career, perhaps best expressed by the pluralized title of her 1991 memoir, *Journey With My Selves*. Which of Livesay's "selves" speaks throughout these elegies, and to which version of the "truth" do the elegies subscribe?

Livesay's elegiac work presents an intriguing mix of the personal and the political. It is not unusual to see aging poets lean into elegy as they themselves age, especially as poets who live to be elderly may compose elegies out of a practical sense of inevitability as their friends and peers pass away. Livesay certainly did so, to the point of designating an entire section in her volume of selected poems, *The Self-Completing Tree*, to poems written for and dedicated to writers and artists that Livesay admired. But as devoted to elegy and memorialization as this section—simply titled "The Poetry"—may arguably be, it contains none of Livesay's elegiac poems for her parents, and also omits all but one of the elegies ("The Incendiary") that Livesay wrote for her husband, Duncan Macnair, who predeceased her by several decades. The bulk of the elegies for Macnair, and for Livesay's parents—poet and translator Florence Randal Livesay and journalist John Frederick Bligh Livesay—appear instead in the section titled "Rites of Passage." Livesay's interest in the family of origin as a crucible for feminist thought should come as no surprise given that Livesay cites Friedrich Engels's *The Origin of the Family, Private Property and the State* as an early influential text, writing that her friend Gina Watts introduced Livesay to the text when both young women were eighteen, and the text "just shook us to death" as both Watts and Livesay became "completely mesmerized" by the ideas (*Right Hand* 22).

The political implications of the family dynamic became more pressing as Livesay married and bore children, then endured the deaths of her father (in 1944), her mother (in 1953), and her husband (in 1956): three significant deaths in little more than a decade. In interviews and personal essays, Livesay is not reticent in discussing the autobiographical impulse from which much of her poetry and fiction emerges. She declares a considerable portion of her body of work to be "a psychic if not a literal autobiography" (v) in her Foreword to 1972's *Collected Poems: The Two Seasons*, a rhetorical gesture she repeats in 1977's *Right Hand, Left Hand*, her multi-genre anthology of her socialist writings. Pamela Banting's 1988 article proposes that Livesay's "preoccupation with her antecedents and their influence on her is especially pronounced" to the point where "the body of her collected poems" may be read as "one life-long autobiographical poem" (10). In her second volume of collected works, *The Self-Completing Tree*, Livesay writes that she has refused the "strictly chronological" method of setting the poems in the order in which they were written or published, choosing instead thematized groupings that mimic a biographical narrative. The result is that *The Self-Completing Tree* resists a compositional chronology but favours a lived chronology, including sections titled "The Childhoods," "Rites of Passage," "The Unquiet Bed," and "At the Finish" (*Self-Completing* 3).

Reading Livesay's poetry as an eventual autobiography, complete with the self as a veiled subject, is an important consideration when regarding Livesay's shifting sense of feminism. The changes in elegiac approach that Livesay makes over a period of more than thirty years are considerable. One of the repeated motifs in Livesay's paternal elegies is the ways that personal strength emerges from an embrace of or a resistance to her parental inheritance, a supporting structure of her "life-long autobiographical poem." In the repeated poetic return to the deaths and legacies of her parents, Livesay makes a lifelong project of digging at her autobiography in order to question the terms of elegiac representation and gendered inheritance.

As the opening chapter of this book describes, the daughter's elegy has the tensile strength wrought from the struggle to address personal affect in political terms. In several interviews and two personal essays written in the 1970s, Livesay portrays her father as a man who was both brilliant and difficult to please, especially because he encouraged her to be independent but believed that she should do so only under the terms that he chose. In "The Squire of Woodlot," Livesay describes life with her father as "a tremendously educative—if painful experience... any father who is himself so knowledgeable, so resourceful, so ambitious—and withal, so dogmatic—is bound to have a frustrating effect at times on a young personality trying to find itself." In an unpublished prospectus for a manuscript tentatively titled "Do Not Go Gentle"—an allusion to Dylan Thomas's famous paternal villanelle—Livesay includes this dedication: "This book is not in praise of women—it is in praise of men: those rare men who understand and seek to further woman's role in society and who affirm her right to be a creative person. (My father sought to be such a one—but he did not always succeed)." To note that a beloved parent, mentor, or confidante has a contradictory personality is perhaps commonplace; to observe a resourceful and dogmatic manner, a tender and sarcastic nature, and "unsuccessful" feminist leanings in a single person who served as parent, mentor, and confidante, and to articulate these tendencies in three separate documents makes these characterizations of JFBL by his prolific daughter more than mere casual observances. Livesay's father demanded her attention when he was alive, and his death turned him into a lost beloved to whom she attended in her poetry for over three decades.

Pamela Banting's phrase for Livesay, "Daddy's girl," seems like an epithet or at least an accusation; the phrase offers an ironic counterpoint to Livesay's socially progressive politics. In her archival work with the correspondence between Livesay and her father, Banting emphasizes the sometimes coy intimacy between this father and daughter as well as the intensity of their disagreements. Accordingly, Banting's use of the phrase "Daddy's Girl" originates in the title of a Livesay poem that was not anthologized until after Livesay's death in 1996. According to the archival document, the poem "Daddy's Girl" was drafted in 1979, the year Livesay turned seventy; her father had been dead for thirty-five years or for exactly half of her life. Livesay changed the title of "Daddy's Girl" to the more politically robust "Jove's Daughter" upon the poem's publication in 1981 in the feminist literary magazine *Fireweed*. Whether that title change preceded the poem's submission for publication, or whether the magazine's editors requested a title change is not clear from the archival document. But however it came about, the title change from "Daddy's Girl" to "Jove's Daughter" describes a moment in the arc of Livesay's elegiac anagnorisis. What initially appears to be a poet's autobiographical impulse to memorialize a stubborn parent is unveiled as an impulse to use the inquiry of the elegiac mode to argue with a rhetorical figure, the kind of "ongoing affectionate relations with the dead" that Zeiger identifies as a major component of women's elegies in *Beyond Consolation* (63).

Using a kind of fictive autobiography that explores the problems of the "empty pack" of daughteronomy creates also a poetic subjectivity in Livesay's elegiac persona that reconfigures the limitations and pleasures of father–daughter kinship. Livesay's career, tailored to her father's interests and tastes, flourished despite—or perhaps because of—his open admissions of envy about her literary abilities and success. It is possible to discern three distinct elegiac movements in Livesay's poems for and about her father: elegies that were written in the handful of years following the death of Livesay's father in 1944, later poems that question the terms of Livesay's inheritance from her father, and, finally, the very wry Minervan elegies. These poems spring from an autobiographical impulse even as they refuse strictly autobiographical privations. Exacerbated and enlivened by Livesay's relationship with her father, they chart Livesay's evolving definition of herself as a rebellious daughter engaged in a political mourning practice.

Her oscillation between obedience and an ironically negotiated rebellion begins with the elegies written in the years immediately following JFBL's death in 1944. These first paternal elegies show Livesay taking up the obedient but ultimately frustrating position of the good modernist daughter, in which Livesay's encomia for her father can never entirely escape the grasp of his disapproval. These elegies are "immediate" in terms both temporal—in that they were composed soon after her father's death—and attitudinal—in that Livesay appears to be seeking an immediate literary solution to the contradictions of her life with her father. In these poems, Livesay herself is still enough of an Edwardian that she reaches for consolation, but she is also sufficiently modernist in that she ends bitterly with the realization that no resolution to grief can be found. The immediate elegies are starkly composed, structurally sound, but palpably desperate to please. But at whom is this desperate desire to please being aimed—at the lost beloved or the imagined reader? More accommodating and more rhetorically rich are the "inheritance" poems composed between the 1950s and the 1970s, in which the poet positions herself as an heir to the Livesay line. This is a questing period, in which the poems feature the daughter unearthing evidence of kinship in graveyards, mementos, and even her own face and body, and inquires into what it means to belong to a family: genetically, socially, and genealogically. At the end of her writing career, in the late 1970s and early 1980s, Livesay wrote "Jove's Daughter," an elegy that is truly a rebellious daughter poem, in which she considers the father's power as a feminist legacy. Because of the poem's connection to the daughter as powerful in alliance with and in defiance of the father, and because of Livesay's wry use of the figure of Jove to represent paternity, I call this poem an example of Livesay's "Minervan elegies." Paternal elegies are always negotiations of literary and personal subjectivity, and neither devotion nor defiance can be left by the wayside.

JFBL's influence over his daughter began with mutual agreement about literary value, but soon developed into a complex exchange of admiration and envy between father and daughter. Lynda E. Boose, in her article "The Father's House and the Daughter in It," reminds us that unlike the father–son dynamic, "the daughter's struggle with her father is one of separation, not displacement" (33). In Livesay's case, the struggle for separation was complicated by her financial ties to her father as well as her professional ties to his influence. That he also presented a figure against which Livesay could define herself is important, and it was a task that she took on with trepidation and a certain relish. Even though her early poetry, particularly the short lyrics of *Signpost*, suggests a defiant glee in rebelling against a wish to please, it is Livesay's much-discussed "break" from her father during a shared trip to London in 1930 that she emphasizes as the turning point of their relationship.

According to Livesay in *Journey With My Selves*, she and JFBL disagreed violently over Livesay's opportunity to meet George Bernard Shaw at a dinner party on the same day that her father had booked a trip to Portsmouth to visit his sister Ina. Perhaps unsurprisingly for an ambitious young writer, Livesay preferred to meet Shaw rather than an elderly relative, but her father insisted that she refuse the invitation to meet Shaw. In anger or defiance, she left the hotel and spent the day walking alone around London. Her father called the police to look for her, and when she returned to the hotel that evening, she met her father "hatless: a small worried man. Shock set in when he hugged me fiercely.... There was nothing to say. After, we both knew why. I had taken my first steps towards independence. There would be more to come. Perhaps none so painful" (117–18). In interviews, Livesay was explicit about what she saw as a bone of contention between herself and her father, and claimed that rebellion against her father was the catalyst for her poetic exploration of androgyny: "he admired creative women tremendously, but at the same time he wanted me to be submissive. So I guess I was torn; by age twenty I came to be very *anti* everything he stood for, and soon I became independent as a social worker and as an activist" ("An Interview" 14; emphasis in original).

However, Livesay's childhood friend Gina Watts Lawson sees the friction between father and daughter much differently, to the point of refuting Livesay's take on this first step towards independence. According to Lawson, what Livesay calls a rebellion against her father's wishes merely marked a shift from the childhood relationship to an adult relationship of equal intensity. Lawson, in an interview given in 1967, calls JFBL "quite a neurotic character, with a rather marked speech impediment. But a very brilliant man" (Livesay, *Right Hand* 45). Lawson scoffs at the idea of Livesay's rebellion against her father saying that JFBL was also "a born iconoclast" who had to maintain a politically conservative front and so could not join the Communist Party himself but otherwise, "he completely approved of her activities" (45). Lawson's opinion is important here, if only for the perspective that she provides on a relationship that Livesay has written and rewritten multiple times. This is not to suggest that Livesay's assessment of the father–daughter relationship was inaccurate, but rather to consider that the relationship was complex and hard to categorize even by those who were involved in it. We should consider, at least provisionally, that what Livesay called a conflict may have sometimes been in the nature of a violent agreement.

Elegiac Moment I: "The Hand Still Speaks"

The similarities or disparities in disposition between Livesay and JFBL take on particular significance as we regard the first elegies that Livesay wrote for JFBL. The paternal elegies that Livesay wrote in the 1940s and the early 1950s are finely wrought in their use of elegiac encomium; their effusive praise is written for the father in every sense. The much-anthologized poems "Lament," "Inheritance," and "Of Mourners" are testaments to JFBL's influence as father-confessor and patron to his talented daughter, and perhaps not surprisingly, these elegies demonstrate the kind of intensely wrought imagism for which Livesay's early work was been much praised. In "Lament," Livesay begins and ends the poem with the image of her father's hand, still seemingly so alive in her hand in the moment after his physical death. The poem's resemblance to the central conceit of Keats's "This Living Hand" is worth noting, and it is no coincidence that Livesay struggles with the Romantic gesture of memorializing virtue while striving for stark modernist imagism. "Lament" offers a kind of elegiac blazon, listing the abilities and characteristics of the "dead hand" that still "stirs" like a bird in the speaker's hand. This paradoxical image bookends a long lyrical list of qualities, attributes, talents, and biographical details, and suggests Livesay's difficulties in capturing—and managing—the lived contradictions of her father's life: his professional authority contrasted with his social shyness; his free-thinking attitude towards women's artistic abilities against his conservative expectations of women's domesticity; his admiration of his daughter's independence against his insistence that she obey him. "Lament" demonstrates the daughter's duty to honour even as it suggests her efforts at negotiating paternal contradiction.

In miniature, this elegy conveys some of Livesay's own awkwardness in insisting upon her father's accomplishment and erudition while implying the criticism of his temper and judgment. The list of skills that are attributed to the hand offer an inarguable list of accomplishments, a series of gestures to the worthiness of the dead man in good elegiac fashion. But Livesay's complicated relationship with her father surfaces here, for while the list may impress with its evidence of an accomplished life, her phrase "the way your hand held life" suggests the elegiac paradox of the absent present as well as implying a paternal force—a "held life" of restraint and judgment that colours each of these accomplishments. In using the hand as a metonym, Livesay introduces the tension between JFBL's public and private personas, rendered in imperious masculine imagery of manual dexterity as Livesay recounts her father's mastery of carpentry, carving a roast, driving cars and teams of horses, and crewing a sailboat. But the encomiastic tendencies show the strain under which this paternal elegy labours. "Lament" also extols the skill of the father's hand in performing the feminized social skills of "cutting bread" and "pour[ing] a purring cup of tea." Considering JFBL's British roots, and thinking about the British colloquialism that refers to whomever pours the tea as "Mother" (as in the phrase "Shall I be Mother?"), this could be read as a cross-gendered performance; though JFBL is Livesay's father, he can also act as "mother." The rhetorical movement of "Lament" suggests a twentieth-century Renaissance man, someone who could turn his hand to any task.

But the poem also implies that the dutiful daughter has noted the father's violence as well as his skill, and the final lines of the stanza offer a sober postscript to the standard masculinities enumerated earlier:

> The hand so neat and nimble
> Could make a tennis partner tremble,
> Write a resounding round
> Of sonorous verbs and nouns—
> Hand that would not strike a child, and yet
> Could ring a bell and send a man to his doom.
>
> And now unmoving in this Spartan room
> The hand still speaks:

The "neat and nimble" hand and the activity of tennis seem to imply athleticism and sportsmanship, but "tremble," whether chosen for its rhyme with "nimble" or even for potentially satiric purposes, also implies the darker side of gamesmanship that began with the masterful performances in chess and cards in the previous stanza. Over whom is this mastery being held? Who is trembling before his prowess in the tennis game? In the heartbreaking "Ballad of Me"—the poem that immediately precedes "Lament" in the "Rites of Passage" section of *The Self-Completing Tree*—Livesay calls herself "Misbegotten / born clumsy," and near-sighted: "Was it the eyes' fault / seeing the tennis net / in two places?" In "Ballad of Me," the indictment is not long in coming: "*Butterfingers* / father called it" (emphasis in original) she continues, citing her inability to catch a thrown ball. So in "Lament," the ability of the "neat and nimble" hand to "make a tennis partner tremble" may connote admiration of athletic ability, but arriving on the heels of the hyperbolic mastery of the previous stanza, that trembling seems to be the result of bullying rather than awe.

Livesay's next two lines move from the father's comparative athletic prowess over his daughter to a comparison that seems incredible given Livesay's remarkable career and her father's unfulfilled artistic ambitions. Livesay drapes the mantle of the true artist over her father, despite the fact that he did not publish a single piece of literary work in his lifetime. Her diction masculinizes the act of writing, as the assonance echoes the boom of a father's authoritative speech; the choice of the words "resounding round" is indeed "sonorous" as a rumble and as a command. The resonant words of the father's artistic talent—which are hard not to read as ironic given Livesay's poetic prowess—literally re-sound in the daughter's ears as she pays her elegiac duty to him. The final two lines of the stanza seal the image of the father as Lacanian Lawmaker by way of the Old Testament. Though the hand "would not strike a child," the line introduces the possibility of such violence, particularly with the enjambed "and yet" at the end of the line. The hand "would not strike a child, and yet"—might it do so if the child "deserved" it? The equivocation of the next line—"Could ring a bell and send a man to his doom"—is chillingly grandiose; it shows the father's hand wielding the traditional masculine power of the law over life and death, and eerily suggests the child's doom in the pairing of the lines. Though every other activity that Livesay attributes to JFBL appears to have biographical foundation, it is difficult to read this last line of the stanza as anything more than hyperbolic encomium. JFBL was a newspaperman, not a judge, and his ability to hire and fire at Canadian Press was not on a par with life and death, though perhaps, during the Great Depression of the 1930s, his powers seemed to be exactly that widespread and terrible. In "Lament," the father is a king whose benevolence is matched by his arrogance and complicated by the suggestion of intolerance and violence.

Livesay appears to place here father well in line with the Lacanian "dead Father" when she moves to the next stanza, noting that "the hand still speaks" despite the fact that it is "unmoving in this Spartan room." The poetic conceit that the hand-as-Father continues to speak, in images of the father's abilities, is certainly appropriate to Livesay's elegiac tone, and implies that encomium and duty govern the limits to which a daughter as the elegiac subject can speak of her father. However, though the penultimate stanza of "Lament" appears to reinforce paternal encomium with a return to the elegiac oxymoron of life-in-death, the diction supports a discomfiting image of righteously practised Victorian masculinity behind the elegiac praise. Livesay's use of "Spartan" as an adjective, though undoubtedly chosen for its connotation of spareness and functionality, operates as a reminder of Spartan militarism, including the refusal to admit to pain even while dying. Though "the brain was fogged / And the tight lips tighter shut" by pain and death, the hand still "demands the whole, establishes the strife." What can it mean that strife outlives the body? And is this strife for the father or for the observing daughter? The father's "shy, appraising eyes" exchange their bold masculine fire for the Orphean "sea's green gaze": the eyes of the Lycidean drowned poet surface in that quiet room.

"Lament" ends by returning once more to "what moved me," repeating the images of the breathing bird and the clear-running stream from the first stanza as metaphors for the hand, moving away from the metonymic hand-as-Father. After revealing the ambiguous tyranny of paternal mastery in the guise of encomium, Livesay's return to the diction and imagery of the first stanza may be read as a consciously chosen return to the mask of the dutiful daughter. However, perhaps it is also a subversive iteration of previous imagery in order to emphasize the poem's implicit criticism. Such forays into daughterly rebellion are, in some ways, well disguised by Livesay's encomium in the elegies that were written in the years immediately following her father's death; in other ways, these poems shout their frustration at the limited language available to write the complex politics of father–daughter kinship. "Lament" strains to capture the elegiac mode outside of the homosocial tradition, but the speaking voice of the "immediate" elegies grows more aware of the Antigonal imperative of daughterly mourning as it exists alongside the Freudian injunction against melancholic extremities of grief. "Lament" remains Livesay's most anthologized elegy, perhaps because of its implied rebellion.

Although "Lament" is better known than "Inheritance," the latter poem, according to Livesay in *Journey With My Selves*, was her first paternal elegy, composed in the days following her father's funeral (181). "Inheritance" offers the same polarities to the father's personality at which Livesay hints in "Lament," and once again reveals contradictions between her father's public and private personae, as he "pace[s] ... in the rooms of [her] mind." The poem reads as a study in contrasts, remarkable for so short a lyric. Livesay's juxtaposition of the father figure's shyness and fieriness is again apparent in "Inheritance," as is the implied violence of the father's "blustering" temper, his ferocity burning like the sun, and the power of his "acid" speech. Again, Livesay chooses to frame her elegiac mode in motifs of movement, beginning and ending with the image of the father moving through rooms, though the first stanza notes that they are "rooms of my mind" and the last shifts the affective locale to "rooms of my heart." The "sad parent" gains momentum and intensity as an affective object. He is at first a melancholy sacrificial figure whose "thorned" head implies, rather grandly, that he endures the suffering of Christ, even though Heraclitean fire consumes and sustains him by the poem's end. This typical elegiac shift from memory to affect—from the speaker's mind where the lost beloved figure "paces" to her heart in which he "races"—implies not only inconsolability, but a breakdown between elegiac subject and elegiac object that is characteristic of the twentieth-century elegy. The poem's characterization of the father as a misunderstood man dominates the third stanza, and the "agony" of being "stretched between" professional bluster and private shyness seems to be one of the wounds that the father bears. Ironically, no one understood better the complications inherent in seeing that the "grass grew green / Where acid words has lately been" than did his adored and much-criticized daughter.

Livesay's punctuation and syntax in the final stanza is curious. To whose consciousness does the last line's "quiet mind" refer? Does the penultimate phrase, "who yet will face / The day, the dark," refer to the father's "burdened brood," or does the semicolon indicate that the "you," the "fiery father of us," is the subject of the sentence? If the mourning kin are the subjects, then the implication is consolatory; the mourners will learn to face both day and night without the father's "fierce assertion" and in turn will "house" the "fiery father" in the "quiet mind" of his "kind"—a triple pun here on children, relationality, and the assumption of a gentler sensibility. The other possibility—that the father is the subject of the sentence—suggests that death will bring the father peace and the ability to "face / The day, the dark" only when he ceases racing through the rooms of the elegist's heart and instead takes up residence in the "quiet mind." In both readings, the eventual peace of consolation is at issue, but the first possibility suggests that the survivors need consolation, while the second traffics in the gothic assumption that the restless dead can only be appeased by the mourning actions of the survivors.

Elegiac Moment II: "Inevitable Nearness"

An unpublished version of a Livesay poem, "Unwritten Letter," marks a shift from her encomium-filled early paternal elegies to her mid-career poems that question the terms of inheritance. It is difficult to tell for certain whether Livesay reused or recycled the title of this poem, as she often did throughout her long career, or indeed whether the poem that was published first in *The Phases of Love* (1983) and eventually in *The Self-Completing Tree* (1986) with the title "Unwritten Letter" represents a revised version of the archived document that is hand-dated 1949. The two versions, or the two poems, have some superficial resemblances including references to the lost beloved as a skilful gardener, the garden as the space of memory, and the speaker's wish to see the beloved once again. However, in the version of "Unwritten Letter" that appears in *The Phases of Love*, the remembered beloved is an unidentified lover figure; in the 1949 archival version of the poem, the lost beloved is more reminiscent of the father figure of the paternal elegies of the late 1940s and early 1950s. The 1949 date that is handwritten on the archival document situates the poem's composition somewhere between "Inheritance" (composed in the week after JFBL's 1944 death) and "Lament," which *The Self-Completing Tree* cites as having been written in 1953, though it did not appear in a Livesay book until 1955's *New Poems*. This poem—if read as a paternal elegy and as an unsendable letter to Livesay's father—hints at her use of the paternal elegy to forge a redefined subjectivity for her writerly self. If Livesay revised her 1949 "Unwritten Letter" into the 1983 version, she removed the tension of the paternal elegy from the poem to render the elegiac object more general and to make the poem itself less problematically concerned with the power of intellectual companionship linked with the experience of being halved by a parental death. The text of the unpublished poem from 1949 is as follows:

It never was a shock to see you come
Along the walk, stooping to touch a rose;
Your coming was as natural as the sun,
As rain in winter falls, consistently,
Breathed in and out like sadness or a song.
I took you so for granted! Loved you for
The inevitable nearness of your mind,
The eager echoes of your voice, so clear
Even though absence often came between.
Departure is the shock: as if the day
Decided not to break, the night to fall;
As if the rose lay blistered on the ground—
Your going leaves a gap too sudden to replace.
I move with half myself, lacking your face.

Appended by the handwritten note "1949, rejected by *Chatelaine*," Livesay's "Unwritten Letter" rewrites the elegiac tradition by fashioning grief as an unsent letter. While the autobiographical basis for a poem should contribute to but not override the poem's constitutive claim to art, any consideration of this poem as a paternal elegy means factoring in Livesay's daughterly obedience with her dynamics of subjectivity in "Unwritten

Letter." The setting—a rose garden—is a site of pure encomium, rendered pastoral and paternal; JFBL's skill as a gardener is praised in this poem as his other skills are lauded in "Lament." Note, too, the reference to the beloved as the sun, so frequently used to characterize powerful father figures in Livesay's oeuvre. The shocking departure of the lost beloved echoes Livesay's father's sudden heart failure. In "Unwritten Letter," Livesay even echoes the opening story of her unpublished manuscript for the memoir *Her Father's House*, which was revised extensively to be published as *A Winnipeg Childhood* by Peguis Press in 1973. But the opening story of the father's return home and communion with his roses appears only in the first chapter of the manuscript for *Her Father's House* and not in *A Winnipeg Childhood*. The father's arrival home from work, "com[ing] / Along the walk" past the rose garden, was an event so quotidian in Livesay's memory of her father that she begins "Chapter One: The Transplanted" with a description of JFBL's fictional alter ego, "Jeffery Langstaffe," as he arrives home. Like JFBL, Jeffery Langstaffe has a "soft stammer" and "altogether too dapper an appearance to belong to an artist or writer," as well as a "jaunty uncertainty" in his gait as he stoops to examine his prized roses ("The Transplanted" 4–5). "Unwritten Letter," with its unidentified second-person figure, echoes this rose garden walk, this consistent and expected arrival—"natural as the sun"—and contrasts it to the suddenness of the "departure" (i.e., the death) that was a "shock" as the person's regular arrival "never was."

But all biographical evidence would be merely circumstantial if not for the similarities of relationship between the speaker and the addressee of the letter poem. While the biographical reasons for considering 1949's "Unwritten Letter" to be a father-haunted poem may be compelling, the literary evidence is stronger. The unwritten letter of the title may reflect Livesay's voluminous written correspondence with her father, and her desire to appeal to his aesthetic sense, that companionable and perhaps uncomfortable "inevitable nearness of [his] mind" that was so much a part of his support for her career. The correspondence shows that Livesay's father frequently raised the idea that Livesay "took for granted" his financial support, and the appearance of this phrase in the poem has an echo of justification hidden among Livesay's encomiastic praise. Though his financial assistance seemed quite open-handed in one way, JFBL required regular and specific acknowledgement from his daughter for every kindness he tendered to her. Livesay's intellectually intimate relationship with her father is also one entangled in the state of being beholden: an "inevitable nearness" indeed.

Undeniably, Livesay writes that "inevitable nearness" as equal parts comfort and curse as the elegies that she wrote shortly after his death yield to another kind of paternal elegiac exploration in Livesay's oeuvre. One discernible result of Livesay's struggle with the homosocial elegiac tradition can be found in the proliferation of her "inheritance" poems from the 1950s to the 1970s, a series of poems with which she reconfigures her elegiac impulse in terms of a paternal genealogical, intellectual, and spiritual legacy. For these poems, she obeys the elegiac contract, but moves away from the strict examination of mourning to focus instead on familial connection as a method of remembrance and recognition. Inquiries about female subjectivity and political agency are explicitly linked to issues of female inheritance in the poems "Signature," "Look to the End," "Self-Portrait," "Loss," "Savour of Salt," and "After Grief," which focus not only on the general inheritance of "Livesayana" (a term Livesay uses in her 1977 *Canadian Bookman* article about JFBL), but also on the specific characteristics that Livesay claims to inherit from her father: professional determination, skills with words, logic, and rhetoric, and, most significantly and repeatedly, the closely examined facial features of her father as they appear in satisfactory or unsatisfactory measure in his daughter's physical appearance. This is the "half myself" that appears in the final line of "Unwritten Letter"; the mourner "lack[s] [the beloved's] face" in that she cannot see the face of the lost beloved before her, but this is also a genealogical "lack." She resembles the lost beloved father only partially, and she "lacks his face" both as a physical attribute and as a quality of his bold demeanour.

"Self-Portrait," a poem written in 1960 but not anthologized in Livesay's lifetime, appeared in Dean Irvine's edited collection of previously uncollected and unpublished Livesay poems, *Archive for Our Times*, in 1998. In this poem, Livesay's physical inheritance from both her mother and her father is painstakingly offered as a lifelong problem with self-image; by inheriting characteristics from both parents, her face pleases neither her father (whose contempt for her mother's appearance is startling, in this poem and others) nor herself. It is worth noting here that Livesay's mother, the poet and translator Florence Randal Livesay, died in 1953, but she is not included in the address of the poem. Livesay's first-person speaker refers to the mother figure in the distant third person while the father figure enjoys a position of prominence in the poem's first stanza as the "you" to whom Livesay addresses all questions about inheritance. Beginning the first line of the first stanza with "And," Livesay suggests in this first part of "Self-Portrait" an ongoing conversation between father and daughter about how to make meaning from familial resemblance:

> And from your mouth, my own misshapen teeth.
> My mother's eyes; in mine no cornflowers grew,

Leaves raced, the summer danced.
Your fine hair, father, scattered all too thin—
No silver wires curling in the wind
Like hers, I'll have. His pointed chin,
Her jaw, plain cussed, stubborn to the point
Of senselessness; at other times sheer pluck,
A gay insouciance sprang from the set of it. (126)

The switch in possessives from "your" to "his" is significant here as the first-person speaker moves from sharing the addressee-father's judgement at her own appearance, to assessing the awkwardness of her own body, supposedly "inherited" from the mother and openly despised by the father. The speaker of the poem makes it clear in the next stanza that the father's admonitions to "stand up straight" have the effect of shaming the daughter rather than merely correcting her. His criticisms that "destroy the pleasure of a walk" and "sow the self-distrust" in the daughter are followed by the daughter's responding judgment of the mother, a figure who remains absent and voiceless in the poem, more a point of comparison than a person. Rejecting what she calls the mother's "hatred of the body's good," the speaker describes how she "found . . . kin" by embracing "a trembling birch." The poem ends with the poet's body decaying in the woods, as "the earth / Pressed patterns on my skin and bone / No years erase; till fossil I become." This self-elegiac resolution to the humiliation of corporeal existence seems rooted in Livesay's ecopoetics as she returns to the tree as a symbol for the self: the eponymous self-completing tree that will serve as the title for Livesay's eventual autobiography of collected poems. The solution of self as a kin to trees who becomes "one with crushed leaf-mould" is rife with consolatory possibilities and, in addition, functions as an internal criticism of the inventory of legacy offered in the poem's first half. It is no coincidence that when the "wrinkles of the earth" impose their "patterns" on the speaker's "skin and bone," she is freed from the need to distinguish maternal inheritance from paternal inheritance. Instead Livesay attempts to slip the bonds of daughterhood while pointing out the impossible problems of responding to inherited attributes from two combative parents.

Livesay returns to this parameters of inheritance in 1957's "Signature," beginning with an epitaph from a tombstone that puns on her father's surname: "Livesay the name God them gave / And now lives aye indeed they have." The poem imagines the progress through history of a single, perpetually reincarnated Livesay soul who in the end chooses to give up its hold on the body to become the prairie wind: "The prairie gave breath; I grew and died: / Alive on this air these lives abide." Livesay is clearly not above a little punning, and her echo of the epitaph/epigraph's "Livesay/ lives aye" with her own "alive/lives abide" in the final couplet is another negotiation of legacy. Livesay's retention of her father's surname for publishing is significant from a feminist point of view, but it is also more evidence of Livesay's literal adherence to the Name of the Father, suggesting an authoritative paternal figure in the Lacanian mode. A later poem, 1971's "Look to the End," performs another reading of the Livesay legacy. The title is noted as a translation from the Latin of the Livesay family motto: *Respice ad finem*. The poem focuses on the speaker's aging, imperfect body, and while the paternal relationship is not the focus here, the patrimony of the motto watches over this poem, a warning and promise that the end deserves a look, complete with a question about the wisdom of doing so.

Finally, and most interestingly for regarding the feminist paternal elegy as a political challenge, by the 1970s Livesay was weaving the encomium of her early elegies with the inquiry of her "inheritance" poems into poems in which she proposes a female subjectivity that challenges the social limits of female mourning and inheritance. Livesay's father, for decades the addressee and/or audience for these father-haunted poems, is acknowledged in these later elegies as a difficult companion whose "inevitable nearness" is as problematic as it is desirable. In place of poetic equivocation about daughterly duty, Livesay takes up the voice of knowledge, and educates her dead father about gender, power, and grief. The most dramatic of the poems to illustrate this change in tone is the poem whose change in title, from "Daddy's Girl" to "Jove's Daughter," acts as the best example of Livesay's later paternal elegies. The shift in these poems is from lament to demand, with the mourning daughter persona pressing towards redefining subjectivity not as a function of mourning, but as a space into which she has been ushered by mourning. "Jove's Daughter," published in the feminist journal *Fireweed* in 1983 and later in *Archive for Our Times: Previously Uncollected and Unpublished Poems of Dorothy Livesay* (edited by Dean Irvine and published by Vancouver's Arsenal Pulp Press in 1998), switches out the Freudian expectations of "Daddy's girl" with a more mysteriously mythological title and intrigues with its stark contrast to Livesay's earlier elegies. Although "Jove's Daughter" positions the father once again as a god-like figure, this wry invocation challenges the last vestiges of worshipfulness left over from the encomiastic poems:

> The father seduced her; not by love
> but by the secret summons of the bone
> that builds brain targets, knocks them down
> and leaves the child immured, alone.

The father seduced her; his sin rings
round all her circular circuitings.
Not in the flesh did he
take her to bed
but in the embrace implied
the declaration never said
—Bind yourself round me—
(under the glove, the lead)
and she complied;
till her lover slit at the vine
slashed as she cried.

But every lover following, knew
she was not his, but Jove's shrew.

The poet writes herself away from the emptied daughteronomies of Electral obsession or Antigonal duty, and instead establishes herself as Minerva, daughter of Jove, one of the Roman Capitoline Triad of gods (with Juno and Jove), and herself the goddess of crafts, poetry, and wisdom. Both the archived typescript of *Her Father's House* and the published *A Winnipeg Childhood* take note of the "steel engravings" of "two Roman gods, Jove and Juno" mounted on the wall of the father's bedroom, where the figures repose with "only a sheet draped over them" (*Winnipeg* 8). But entering into this pantheon, even as a metaphor for power, has a price. Livesay's bold invocation and complication of seduction theory as an intellectual danger notes the intensity of a relationship that binds the daughter to the father even as it isolates her as his "shrew." Is this familial "shrewishness" the legacy that Livesay sought to define and claim for so many years? Metaphors of imprisonment persist throughout the poem, yet there is a wry wit at work in "Jove's Daughter" with its "brain targets" and "secret summons of the bone" that nonetheless point to an intellectual seduction that is familiar to homosocial master–student relationships from antiquity: an erotics of pedagogy. Livesay, through appropriating and even mocking the terms of incest horror, asks the kind of impertinent questions about daughterhood and inheritance that Gallop has suggested are not only feminist questions but are also the questions that the patriarchy most fears. Livesay does this not by suggesting that she is above the psychoanalytical reading, but, rather, that she occupies it and sees through its entrapment. The poem's ending—in which the daughter declares herself to be simultaneously subordinate and equal to the Law of the Father—is a feminist reversal similar to Gallop's use of the phrase "the daughter's seduction": who, we have to ask, has the power in this poem? The daughter in the poem is not a mere servant of Jove, but his shrew—feminine, sharp, vicious. The possessive is significant in this phrase, as we have to ask to what degree "Jove's shrew" is in service of Jove, driving lovers away, and to what degree in service against Jove: that is, the shrew that menaces him. What has this Father/God/Law wrought? In creating a daughter in his own image, the father has produced an heir and not a woman who is an exchange commodity. There may be encomium at work in "Jove's Shrew," but it is complicated by the claim on intellectual inheritance that Livesay proposes. It is also indicted by the impertinent question that hovers around the end of "Jove's Daughter" as the psychic autobiography's version of "reaping what has been sown": the implication that familial questions about gender and power cannot be evaded. In this poem, Livesay is more shrewd than shrew, pinpointing her ongoing affectionate relations with the dead and gesturing towards the legacy that can now be named. The shrew that carries the daughter's pack is not at a loss for words.

Undeniably, Livesay's later Minervan elegies are curious poems, equal parts feminist manifesto and paternal memorial, attempting to serve a legacy with emotional honesty and political inquisitiveness. They transform the imperative of mourning into a wider political discussion about gender and power. In other Minervan poems—"Heritage," "The Old Bawd" (in which Livesay notes, "The men I loved / never recognized / my devotion") and "The Sybil"—Livesay's attempt to define daughterly duty parallels career-long tensions in her political and poetic choices. "Unwritten Letter" represents a literary moment that presages Livesay's shift to elegiac inquiry rather than remaining satisfied with elegiac encomium, but "Jove's Daughter" suggests that this shift remains complicated by the ambiguity implied in her mythological allusion to her dogmatic father as Jove, and by "the inevitable nearness of [his] mind" to her own consciousness. Livesay scholars and readers of the daughterly elegy can regard the ubiquity of her father's mind as claustrophobic or as companionable. Either way, the stylistic and political movement of Livesay's paternal elegies move through a restrained performance of modernist daughterly duty to arrive at a feminist re-visioning of the daughter's mourning self as a political entity, troubled and sometimes enlivened by her debate with the dead father.

3

"So Much Militia Routed in the Man"

P. K. Page's Military Fathers

The darkness hid
a general toying with a broken water pistol.

Hid from his daughter, frail organza issue
of his now failing loin
the battle done:
so much militia routed in the man.
— P. K. Page, "War Lord in the Early Evening"

as soon as even the most daughterly woman writer might become a plausible writer, male artists as well as their female contemporaries perceived for the first time the father's potential fragility along with his compensatory ferocity.
— Sandra Gilbert and Susan Gubar, *The War of the Words*

In *The War of the Words*, the opening volume of Sandra Gilbert and Susan Gubar's three-volume study *No Man's Land: The Place of the Woman Writer in the Twentieth Century*, the authors suggest that the devastation of the two world wars on European and North American society placed male fragility and modernist literary daughterhood in a matrix that was as discomfiting as it was revealing. Aligning the productivity of emerging women writers alongside other women's war work during the First and

Second World War, Gilbert and Gubar suggest that one immediate result of the wars was a rise in women's confidence that was boosted by the shifting of social rules. Female writers began to awake to the "potential fragility" and "compensatory ferocity" of personal and cultural paternal figures as a result of militarized conflict and its aftermath. Evidence of such a shift, and of the discomfort such reassessment of paternal masculinity could manifest, shows up in a series of P. K. Page's poems written in the late 1940s and early 1950s, and this reassessment fuels the inquiry of her paternal elegies written in subsequent decades.

Page was a poet admired for her reserved sensibility, her spiritual sense, and her command of nuanced metaphor. Her literary debut was in 1944's *Unit of Five*, in which she was the only female poet of the "unit," sharing space with Louis Dudek, Ronald Hambleton, Raymond Souster, and James Wreford. Page's first book, *As Ten, As Twenty*, was published in 1946; her second book, *The Metal and the Flower*, won the Governor General's Award for Poetry in 1954. Like Livesay, Page had a long-term association with a man with a good deal of experience in publishing; in 1950, while working as a scriptwriter for the Canadian Film Board, Page met and married W. Arthur Irwin, former editor of *Maclean's* magazine and Commissioner of the Film Board. Also, like Livesay, Page had a lengthy career as a writer, publishing more than thirty books of poetry, fiction, and children's literature in her lifetime, the last, 2009's *Cullen*, just a year before her death.

Page was the daughter of Major-General Lionel Page, a command veteran of both World Wars who was awarded the Distinguished Service Order for meritorious service in combat. In an interview with Sandra Djwa in 1996, Page contrasts her interest in international politics with her tendency to "stay out of domestic politics," a strategy she learned during her childhood "as an army brat" ("Biographical" 42). Although her claim to remain silent on domestic politics is true in that she does not comment on government policy or the theatre of war, her phrase "domestic politics" is nonetheless apt for its suggestion of a tension felt by women in familial situations as a side-effect of the politics of war. A number of Page's poems written during and after World War II feature lyric explorations of social politics in which aging military men are observed by daughter figures who attempt to align the father's remembered ferocity or authority with his new (and sometimes frightening) fragility.

Proposing that Page's background as the daughter of a decorated military officer gives her an insider's perspective on how paternal fragility and aggression may yield the kind of liminality about which Eric Leed writes in *No Man's Land: Combat and Identity in World War I* is one proposition. Considering what such liminality means in terms of the female-written paternal elegy is slightly different, but both perspectives converge on questions of male power and female literary authority in the years following World War II. In one way, Page's literary daughterhood began very early; Lionel Page, like many other officer and enlisted men, wrote poetry, but instead of writing trench poetry that has been made familiar in the British tradition by Siegfried Sassoon and Wilfrid Owen, he composed entirely for the eyes and ears of his wife and daughter. While stationed in France during the First World War, Lionel Page, then a lieutenant-colonel with Lord Strathcona's Horse regiment, composed a series of children's poems. (As Paul Fussell discusses eloquently in *The Great War and Modern Memory*, World War I was a very literary war.) By 1918, Rose Page had illustrated her husband's verses and bound them together in a rag-paper book for the amusement of their daughter, Patricia Kathleen, who was two years old at the time. In 1991, Porcépic Press published Lionel Page's poems in a single volume titled *Wisdom from Nonsense Land*, including an Afterword by P. K. Page in which she muses about the poems' generation and about her father as a soldier-poet:

> I imagine my father, in the trenches, scribbling cautionary verses in a notebook for his new daughter, whom he barely knew; and to amuse his young wife whose three married years had been years of acute anxiety. He would have written them quickly, as he wrote verses all his life, when the fancy took him. And he would have known as well as I do that some of the rhymes were less than perfect and that he was reaching for the meter now and again.

While Lionel Page may have "reached for" some of the meter in *Wisdom from Nonsense Land*, his poetic talent is of less concern than is his daughter's early association of her father with both war and poetry. That being said, it is undeniable that Page was sensitive to assumptions of autobiography in her own work, and unlike Livesay, Page did not take up an ongoing conversation with her father in her poetry, nor did she seek the kind of intense union of opposites that defined father–daughter kinship for Livesay and her father. Page's approach is more nuanced, and as she asserted on several occasions when asked, her elegies have more in common with the high modernist use of an objective correlative than with an autobiographical "de-facement" as Paul de Man uses the term to represent a negotiated speaking self in poetry. While Livesay's paternal elegies engage directly with the autobiographical in their use of family of origin material, Page's early poems are determinedly distanced from autobiography in order to suggest that the father–daughter relationships depicted in the poems are as symbolic as they are realist, and as much to do with a shift in the cultural understanding of father–daughter relationships—as Gilbert and Gubar suggest—as they are about a subjective personal vision. Livesay's paternal elegies begin in a mode that is very close to confessional and branch out into the mythical, but Page does just the opposite by swathing the father figures of her early poems in layers of metaphor. The elegiac convention of these early poems is muted, though the melancholic tone is unmistakable. A sense of paternal dissolution dominates in these poems; death is implied as the inevitable next step rather than an event that has already occurred. These early poems are in many ways proto-elegiac: poems that presage death by regarding the failing power of the body, and do so by engaging with some elegiac conventions.

But this is not to say that Page never uses autobiographical material, despite her early resistance to doing so. She admits to a turn towards more autobiographically based material at times in the later stages of her career, and is wry about her approach to personal subject matter in a 1987 interview with Eleanor Wachtel: "I've never claimed to write autobiography. Yet there is a fair amount of autobiographical material in my work—more so in the later than in the early. Usually people start writing about themselves and then grow up and extend their range of interests. I seem to have done the opposite. I started writing about other people and other things—all that early stuff about typists and stenographers and children. Now I find myself writing more about myself" ("That's Me" 62).

"Writing more about myself" does not mean giving up her finely developed sense of metaphor, as an examination of Page's later poems will reveal. Nor does it mean the sudden adoption of a confessional tone, nor even a rewriting of family narrative, as Livesay chooses to do. Page, throughout her career, remains steadfast in her dedication to the writer as a kind of multiple self whose vocation demands a relinquishment of any personal frame of reference. For example, Page's refusal of what she calls "the tyranny of subjectivity" in her 1969 essay "Questions and Answers" (*Glass* 191) seems ironic in a feminist context, but if subjectivity is understood as invariably linked to confessionality and the assumption of autobiography, then Page's refusal to be read solely from this perspective is a point well taken, and a point that could be construed as a political stance, despite Page's impatience with such a designation. Page's respect for multiple perspectives in poetic argument is best represented in her poem "The Selves." Douglas Freake contextualizes Page's multiple selves as a device to gain the ironic distance that eventually, and progressively, emphasizes "the discovery of a self that is related to the universe on levels that the heightened and intensified consciousness that poetry itself makes possible" (98). Considering the kinds of results that Page achieves with these multiple selves, Suniti Namjoshi points to the clash of internal and external worlds as Page's fundamental poetic material, noting that much of Page's work concerns "the individual's attempt to bring the microcosm into alignment with the macrocosm," and that "the outcome might be either frustration or despair" ("Double" 25–26). The delicate balance of personae and perspectives while negotiating between the social and the autobiographical are hallmarks of Page's poetry.

In poems written in the postwar period of the 1940s and 1950s, Page represents the male body as debilitated by war and rendered vulnerable by modernism's changing views of heroism and masculinity. However, during the 1960s and 1970s, her poems begin to question the ways that military authority serves, and sometimes fails, as a metaphor for paternal authority. Finally, in her poems of the 1980s and 1990s, she offers a more autobiographically based father figure and raises the question of a daughter's legacy. Page's father poems begin with paternal figures who seem equal parts myth and man. The later poems argue for a more expansive subject position for the daughter, one not based on a tyranny of subjectivity that insists on a single autobiographical perspective for the poet, but rather explores father–daughter kinship as a fit subject for modernist poetry.

When she appeared on the Canadian literary scene in the 1940s, Page's early work included an intense interest in the minute negotiations of power and class during and immediately following the Second World War. In his response to Page's first full collection, *As Ten, As Twenty* (1954), Desmond Pacey makes special note of the book as a "sensitive woman's response to the world of want, war and fascism" (167). Such assessments of Page's work are not unusual, and while Page never believed herself to be a commentator on gender politics, readers often thought otherwise, particularly as concerned the appearance of cold, distant men in her work. In 1971, A. J. M. Smith noted the frequent appearance of "selfish, isolated, lonely men" (19) in Page's poetry. In 1996, Nancy Paul cites Page's concern with the "mineral-hard resistance of men who shut themselves up in their egoism" (122), referring to these figures as "fisted male[s]" to which Page responds as an "Apollonian shaping artist" (130). But it is poet and critic Travis Lane who provides the most astute observation of personalities in Page's verse when she writes that Page's "descriptions of people are stylized, mythologized, almost impersonal," creating characters like "figures on an arras" (104–5). As a mythologized figure, the military father becomes a symbol of protection from and integration with the bellicose modern world, a man caught between authority and doubt, and between cultural iconicity and corporeal fragility. The father's struggles between his public service and his private life, between command and kinship, are paralleled by the daughter's struggle between the desire for familial love and the desire to fulfill societal ideas of duty. Page examines the paternal archetype to suggest that the waning command and eventual dissolution of the officer-father warns the daughter about the price of subjectivity and the humility of corporeal existence.

Father Once Removed: Dissolution and Duty

Page's context for addressing such gender negotiations may be considered as historical as it was personal. The cultural figure of the twentieth-century soldier has been an ambiguous figure for decades: part myth, part hero, part madman. In *No Man's Land*, Eric Leed discusses how veterans of the First World War were perceived in their home communities as "liminal" figures, men who existed "between the boundaries of settled societies, the figures that practice transformations upon themselves, roles, morals, values, spiritual and physical states" (195). Identifying veterans as men who were "defined and refined by war, stripped of every social superfluity," Leed emphasizes how the returning soldier can represent civilians' fears of "disorder" and "petrifaction" (195). Though the veteran "embodies the anxieties, acts out the guilts [*sic*], and attenuates the boredom native to domesticity," the returning soldier must also live forever with "an experienced knowledge of the fragility of his own substance and humanity" (194–95). Leed's alternately fragile and aggressive soldier traverses the inner domestic and outer political world, belonging to both and, wrenchingly, to neither.

Noting the disturbance of modernism on the vestiges of normative Edwardian masculinity, Page's poems read father–daughter kinship through the trope of the returning soldier even as they discover the apprehension of the female gaze upon the dissolution of a once-powerful body. These struggles to balance kinship and command make Page's father poems a volatile mix, especially considering the potential invasiveness of the daughter's gaze. In Livesay's "Lament," it is clear that the daughter capitulates the power of her gaze to the father's mastery of worldly abilities under the force of elegiac tradition, but Page's gazing daughters are more ambivalent. The gaze in these poems is always curious, sometimes compassionate, and occasionally critical, and the military context lends the daughter's gaze a certain frisson of taboo; she is looking where she should not. In *The World Wars Through the Female Gaze*, Jean Gallagher contends that "acts of seeing and attempting to understand war—particularly in relation to the gendered subject—necessarily usher in a species of unease that can never be exorcised from sight in a belligerent culture" (160). Linking military trauma with modernist aesthetics may be nothing new, but identifying that "species of unease that can never be exorcised from sight" remains a vital project in a feminist context. By exploring the "unease" between officer and civilian, father and daughter, age and youth in a belligerent culture, Page's poems interrogate not only familial memory, but also the Western cultural expectation of daughterly duty. How much does the military rectitude of these father figures make them visible or invisible to the daughter?

Certainly the poems acknowledge how much the female gaze remains an uneasy social and literary privilege, even (or especially) within a familial structure. Such a brand of unease accompanies the gaze of the female poet upon the militarized male body, and Gallagher suggests, intriguingly, that unease is entirely to be expected when a gaze does not always discover a complete or unified image. Gallagher examines the ways that "an emerging alternative model of fragmented or indirect visual apprehension" makes the body available to the gaze only through "failures, gaps or blocks in vision" (6). In an analysis of the limits and the possible revelations of this visual apprehension, the female non-combatant's gaze most often reveals "two figures that resist representation in wartime propaganda: the wounded or destroyed body of the soldier and the body of the female observer who looks in directions other than those authorized by the closed circuit of soldiers' vision" (158). The female tradition of resistance to belligerent action that blossomed throughout the years of the First World War questions the rhetoric of the military machine and its accompanying cultural constructions, particularly as they dictate codes of gendered behaviour. In keeping with this tradition, Page examines and questions cultural heroism as modelled by the military ethos, but she focuses upon the aging military commander as the locus of the daughter's visual apprehension.

This is a good time to consider the curiously cautious position that Page's poetry occupies in the canon of Canadian modernism. In 1996, two critics discussed Page's negotiated position in gendered modernism, addressing Page's career-long reluctance to be read as a poet whose femininity was important to her work. Even her use of the initials "P. K." was a nod to modernist writers (Eliot, Auden, Yeats, Lewis, Lawrence, H. D.) who chose this symbolic reduction of personality in the names under which they published. Laura Killian, in her article "Poetry and the Modern Woman: P. K. Page and the Gender of Impersonality" and Nancy Paul, in "Redressing the Balance: Female and Male in the Early Poetry of P. K. Page" each address gender negotiation in Page's poetry in the context of Canadian literary modernism. But it is Paul who analyzes most thoroughly the ways that the "moral agency" of male figures victimizes the female characters in Page's work (122), and she concludes that Page is "self-consciously following in a male tradition, while simultaneously purporting a feminine modesty in her public statements" about her poetics (130). Paul's identification of this gender split in Page's work illuminates the poet's reluctance to limit her work to mid-century standards of "female" writing, and, in addition, Paul suggests that Page subtly criticizes the social rigidity—disguised as moral agency—that appears in Page's male characters. If she is indeed accessing male modernist moral agency in order to cast light on its limitations, Page eventually uses this stance to investigate exactly how a daughter's elegiac duty to a father figure may be shaped by socio-cultural readings of military-paternal authority. Page moves towards a discovery of melancholia as a part of the daughter gaze, and then begins to demand her father's attention in later elegiac work.

Gallagher's concept of fragmented vision suggests the struggle for kinship between Page's men who have invested in a culture of virility and restraint, and daughters who observe the dissolution of that investment. The unauthorized direction in which the female observer looks may be towards her estranged father; these poems emphasize the father's psychic wounds as corporeal affect. While Nancy Paul asserts that Page's "sympathies tend to come back to the lonely men" (130), this assumption of sympathy supports rather than challenges that "closed circuit" of militarized vision against which Gallagher warns. If we accept, with Gallagher, that a daughter's gaze at her military father is "continually subject to the various forces that constitute wartime visuality and subjectivity," including attempts to redirect or constrain the daughter's gaze (7–8), then we cannot ignore the idea that duty, as it satisfies or frustrates daughterly devotion, is as important as sympathy within these poems. Duty, in fact, may be close enough to defiance to act as a shaping force.

To read the daughter's gaze on the debilitated father's body as sympathetic or defiant is a daring project from the outset, and this perspective has been largely ignored by major movements in psychoanalytic theory. In *Aging and Its Discontents*, Kathleen Woodward submits that old age is less like a tragedy and more "like a postmodern drama of interminable postponement," noting that both Freud and Lacan ignore the aging process in their haste to theorize the death drive (43). In order to maintain his authority, the father must remain unavailable to his daughter's gaze or, at the very least, remain subject to Gallagher's "failures, gaps or blocks in vision." As Page's officer figures struggle with the loss of authority, their corporeal frustrations suggest Woodward's assertion that "the body at the limit of its life is the bedrock of the real" (19). To inscribe this limit as "bedrock" seems to assert the subjectivity of the aging body at the same time as it places the aging person's subjectivity "at the limit," a fundamental elegiac paradox.

This paradox appears most noticeably in "War Lord in the Early Evening," Page's poem in which the sight of the father's demobilized but resolutely militarized body becomes compromised by the gaze of his young daughter, which is also the gaze of the adult narrator, and eventually becomes the gaze of the reader. Readers of Page's poetry will be familiar with a setting to which she returns again and again: twilight in a formal garden. This trope offers a pastoral atmosphere while maintaining the tone of a nocturne, and others critics have remarked upon Page's use of the formal garden as a site of spiritual revelation (Namjoshi, "Double" 25; Sullivan, "Size" 36). The garden at night, for Page, is also a site of strange growth and unusual transformation. In "War Lord in the Early Evening," the father figure is a retired general who attempts to control the generative space of the garden as the silent girl watches his every move. The general's daughter witnesses the dissolution of her father's authority, even though her gaze is impaired—for the reasons that Gallagher has suggested—by the darkness that hides the general's "broken water pistol," the phallic metaphor for his "now failing loin." Showcasing the relationship between paternal vulnerability and the daughterly gaze, the general as "war lord" becomes a hyperconscious representative of regulated and socialized patriarchy, and the daughter a disturbing observer of her father's performance of commanding masculinity as a metaphor for paternal law. When Page writes "the battle done / so much militia routed in the man," she puns on "rout" and "route" to suggest that the military ethos has deserted him, and that the military ethos travels the route through the father to the daughter (and to the reader). And there is still room for one final paradox: this "routed" father, hidden by the shadows of evening, endures because of his liminality, not in spite of it.

These poems show aging military men estranged from civilian domesticity and thwarted by their own investment in military exigency. Stripped of command by age and debilitation, Page's officer figures are bereft of the status granted by their uniforms but are still reliant upon the authority granted by such status. In many ways, Page resists using overtly autobiographical elements of the paternal elegy, shying away from confessionality and its attendant sexual politics. But Page is interesting as a daughterly elegist precisely because of her impulse to critique paternal militarism—especially considering her frequent return to the material over a span of six decades—and her early resistance to autobiographical motifs. These poems lean towards the elegiac while refusing to articulate a complete admission of sorrow, a committed lament for the dead, or a passionate search for consolation. Page does not appear to debate or even consider Freud's work of mourning as a model; instead she takes up the "disturbance in self-regard" (143) that Freud designates as melancholic, and complicates the scenario with daughterly self-reproach that masks the sublimated guilt of the officer-father. Such self-reproaches are most evident in the daughter's migraine headaches in "Portrait of Marina," in the daughter as the "frail organza issue" of the general's "failing loin" in "War Lord in the Early Evening," and in the daughter as "a blank space in the air" in "Voyager." In contrast, the daughter's first-person narrative in "Father" objects to being "crunched in a tiny space" with only his "dread of [her] grey gaze" as a weapon. Page's iterations of the failing paternal body, complicated by military rigor, are insistent and compelling as the observing daughter struggles with the pressures of veridiction. What is truth-telling in these finely wrought lyric poems? Shaw's notation that "lyric anxiety" is a necessary "mark of truth" in the elegy is definitely at work in Page's poetry (147). In struggling against a strictly autobiographical depiction of the father, Page synthesizes the elegiac mode with the melancholic; through her refusal of autobiography in her early poems, she reinforces the power of veracity in her later elegies.

To engage with autobiographical material within the confines of elegiac convention demands attention to the balance of Paul de Man's "contractual agreement" (76) with autobiography and the power of mythic parallel. Livesay's work with "Jove's Daughter" suggests that recourse to mythology can be a useful tool for the paternal elegist to "tell the truth but tell it slant," as Emily Dickinson famously suggested. There is a degree to which elegiac convention usurps the autobiographical impulse in order to remake the mourner's sorrow and the loss of the beloved as mythological in both size and scope. For Page, as for Livesay and other female elegists discussed in this volume, myth becomes the method by which daughters can write fathers: a way to mix veridiction with vindication.

As the subjectivity of the daughter figure gains strength in Page's poems, she declares herself to be the subject of her own inquiry. Trapped between the impossibility of earning the father's attention and a surprised discovery of her individual perspective, each of these daughters arrives at a realization that complete closure is functionally and poetically impossible. Undoubtedly, questions of authenticity haunt these poems outside of the strict terms of the unspoken contractual agreement of autobiography, and consciously so, for such work with Eliotean objective correlatives contribute to the antiphonal modernist style of Page's poetry. All attempts to consider autobiographical material in Page's poetry require an engagement with contradiction, especially when considering that Page emphasizes that autobiographical material can be aesthetically limiting to any given poem ("Entranced" 115). However, Page also clearly identifies the autobiographical basis for several of her later poems, "Father," "Alphabetical," and "Voyager" in particular ("Biographical" 36; "Entranced" 126; "That's Me" 63).

At the beginning of her career, Page kept this liminal father figure at a considerable ironic distance. Her early poems, such as "Spring" (from 1946's *As Ten, As Twenty*) and "Portrait of Marina" (from 1953's *The Metal and the Flower*), offer quasi-military father characters that function as "figures on an arras" to use Page's own metaphor and Travis Lane's critical apparatus. Both poems show their male protagonists caught in painful or problematic resistance to transformation. "Spring" seems to have captured a particularly problematic but enduring figure; the original 1946 poem was re-titled "Now This Cold Man..." to emphasize the frozen male figure in *The Glass Air: Poems Selected and New* in 1991, and modified once again to appear as "This Cold Man" in the first volume of *The Hidden Room: Collected Poems* (1997). In addition, Page has said that the "fearful salty man" who commanded a "four-master" in "Portrait of Marina" was sparked by her memories of Maritime fishermen who "looked so splendid in their oilskins—like gods," but "got drunk on lemon extract" at the local bar, and Page laments the fishermen's economic reality along with her own bewilderment at the contradiction of the men's god-like stature and very human flaws: "[i]t had been a disillusioning period in my life. And it was World War II, remember" ("Biographical" 43). The aged skipper of "Portrait of Marina" is one such "disillusioning" and perhaps disillusioned figure; the poem traps the reader between the father's demand for respect and the daughter's pain. The skipper is a pitiable tyrant; his command is still intact, though his sphere of power is private rather than public. Without a crew, he can give orders only to his daughter. He who was once splendid in his oilskins, like the Prospero figure to which Page compares him, now "sews the ocean of his memory" with a "furious needle" that he cannot thread himself, and "his stitches, interspersed with oaths / had made his one pale spinster daughter grow / transparent with migraines." Those oaths and his frequent calling of her name "fretted her more than the waves." The "dimity young inland housewife" who is three generations removed from the skipper will romanticize the embroidered picture and her "great-great-grandpappa" grown "docile as a child again," but his daughter Marina, "the sole survivor of his last shipwreck," grows "warped / without a smack of salt." Constance Rooke notes Page's tendency to create poetic characters who struggle against "a frightening dissolution, which means that the individual is unable to place himself in the surrounding world" (180–81), and this poem offers two characters threatened by such dissolution: the aging father and his spinster daughter. The mythologized father figure, though only quasi-militarized as the retired captain of a fishing vessel, struggles between his need for kinship and his need to command and between his private vulnerabilities and his public persona.

The old man in the garden of the poem eventually known as "This Cold Man" is also caught in painful dissolution, though in this poem Page renders the dissolution more problematic. The mystery of "This Cold Man" lies in Page's rich use of double meaning, so that the poem may be read simply as an extended metaphor for the renewal of the earth, or, more darkly, as an objective correlative for the liminal figure of the solider. If we read the poem's image of the man sinking into the ground as metaphoric, then the old man personifies winter dissolving with the return of spring. However, a more literal reading—one that recalls that many soldiers met their deaths by sinking beneath the mud in the trenches of World War I—cannot help but align the image with the anxiety that Rosemary Sullivan identifies in Page's tendency to layer "incipient terror under the smooth, urbane surface of her early poems" (Sullivan, "A Size" 35–36). Such terror may be read in Page's double-edged diction in "This Cold Man," which implies dissolution even as it suggests transformation. The old man's "stiff eyes slip," indicating doubt that seems out of place on Old Man Winter. Though he "kneel[s] in welters of narcissus," his body is a "fossil frame" that is "held tightly locked"; does this connote a fearful paralysis? The choice of flower, too, is significant for its allusion to the beautiful youth who wastes away while admiring his own beauty. When "sharp green shoots ... whistle for him," they evoke both the new growth of spring and conversely, the diction of weaponry—sharp bayonets, guns that shoot, bombs that whistle before exploding. A. J. M. Smith points out that this poem is driven by Page's "concentrated angry wit" (25), and this wit paints a nightmare that parodies the elegy's convention of the pastoral dream of redemption and renewal. The "cold man" is not "mounted high" as Lycidas is, and there are neither "fresh woods" nor "pastures new" for the elegist, if there can be said to be an elegist narrating this poem. These disturbing associations undermine the fantasy of regeneration, though they do not annihilate it. In "This Cold Man," as in "Portrait of Marina," the mythologized father figure, a spirited but debilitated old man, struggles to maintain his ego and his vision, but is compromised by the inevitability of death.

From these metaphoric and reasonably distanced renderings of father figures, Page moves into more identifiably paternal, and elegiac, territory in "War Lord in the Early Evening." In this poem, the general's wish to impress his daughter with his "gentle and disarming" manner is destroyed by his expectation that he can control nature. As in the two earlier poems, the father figure's lingering belief in the Romantic sublime as something controllable by human action is annihilated, and this poem's inquiry is piqued by Page's use of a narrative "I" in the final stanza of the poem, as well as by her curious use of comic action—a moderate rarity in Page's poetry—to show the dissolution of the father's authority. The general orders a hose with which he may water his roses, but the result resembles a phallic farce more than a sublime reverie. The garden hose arrives in six sections of "assorted sizes" with no connecting fixtures. The general's attempts to assemble a working garden hose are in vain, and his frustration and social embarrassment recall Kaja Silverman's warning about the vulnerability of constructed sexuality in the aftermath of military conflict: "Even under the most auspicious circumstances...the fiction of a phallic masculinity generally remains intact only for the duration of the war" (63). The sectioned hose functions as a metaphor for dismantled masculinity, a construct that struggles to survive outside the symbolism of conflict. Determined to demonstrate his sensitivity and adamantly refusing to recognize the limits of physical reality, the war lord commands his servants to hold the section of the hose together. This father's call is as ridiculously ineffective as the ancient skipper's call is painfully powerful. The five fountains of water that spurt into the servants' faces as they bind the hose parts together with their fists are both farcical and grim references to an uncontrollable aging body. Though Kathleen Woodward claims that aging is a form of castration, her theory seems only half right in this poem, where abundance and lack issue from the same unreliable source. The recalcitrant hose and the general's "broken water pistol" yield only a "trickle" from his "failing loin," all echoing Silverman's comment that military trauma manifests as a "psychic disintegration...of a bound and armored ego, predicated upon the illusion of coherence and control" (62). Though the hose is a phallic symbol, it also operates as a metaphor for command and obedience. The failure to water the roses is couched in bellicose terms; it is a "battle done" with "so much militia routed." Proposing the general's impotent command as a case of "*sic transit gloria mundi*," Page glosses the ignominy of his defeat with the irony of the mock epic, suggesting that "War Lord in the Early Evening" is a melancholic satire on phallic tropes.

But Page is not yet finished with this disassembled officer. Sullivan warns us that the "recurring image of stasis in a metaphoric garden...is Page's private image of hell" (36). The war lord's struggle to define himself through his own command moves beyond satire when the narrator intervenes with a statement of wistful melancholia in the final lines:

> *Sic transit gloria mundi.* I would rather
> a different finish.
> It was devilish
> that the devil denied him that one innocent wish.

These lines contain the poem's only reference to the narrative "I." The assumption that Page is projecting an omniscient narrative voice cannot entirely escape the implication that this first-person speaker adopts the voice of the daughter who has remained silent throughout the poem. Does the narrative "I" represent the nostalgic wishes of the daughter grown to adulthood? Does her exposure of this difficult moment indict her as forever melancholic? If the "different finish" is the daughter's wish for the preservation of her father's dignity, does the father's wish to maintain his authority constitute an innocent wish? "His now failing loin" certainly indicates a "different finish" from the ideology of phallic mastery. Has the devil granted his every other wish, innocent or not? How "innocent" is such a construction of innocence? Page's introduction of a devil's discourse suggests that the war lord is caught in a Faustian bargain. Whether or not we choose to interpret this poem as a melancholic satire of masculine authority, the penultimate stanza emphasizes that the general is "hid[den]" from his daughter by "darkness." He cannot provide succour; he is not the regenerative vegetation god that he strives to be at the poem's beginning, tending the roses with his "beneficent care." The light and roses fade in the "early evening" of his life. His call is obeyed, but to no effect; innocent or not, his glory is about to pass from the earth.

"His Safe Return": The Officer-Father as Lost Beloved

In her poem "The First Part" from 1985's *The Glass Air*, Page admits to a "[g]reat desire to write it all. / Is it age, death's heavy breath / making absolute autobiography / urgent?" The urgency of this autobiography, "absolute" or heavily mythologized, recalls Gilbert and Gubar's discussions of the freedoms and concomitant pressures of modernist literary daughterhood, pressures that both Laura Killian and Nancy Paul have suggested Page refuses, or at least forestalls. In conjunction with locating paternal fragility as a subject of modernist literary daughterhood, Gilbert and Gubar claim that female modernist writers struggle with an "affiliation complex...a desirous (even if agonistic) interaction" with a paternalized literary tradition, a tradition that is inevitably bound up with questions of inheritance (169). Warning that these affiliations are often deeply ambivalent, Gilbert and Gubar note that the father–daughter paradigm "is so haunted by history" that it cannot provide an "entirely satisfactory motive for female creativity" (171–72). Whether or not a modernist affiliation complex is part of Page's "great desire to write it all," this very lack of satisfaction describes the tensions of female filial piety.

Such a debate about the scope of female filial piety is fully on display in "Voyager," an eloquent example of Page's father–daughter poems, originally published in 1981's *Evening Dance of the Grey Flies*. The poem describes a classic mourner's dream in which the lost beloved returns but does not recognize the mourner. The long-dead father haunts his family with his refusal to look at them, until "reluctant to return / bored to be home," he sets off again into his alternate dimension, as though death were the ultimate military tour of duty. With the painful irony that often accompanies haunting by the lost beloved, the brusque commanding officer leaves in order to seek his family, those whom he cannot see right in front of him: "he / sought us in other places / studied maps, set out in search." Page writes with wry anxiety about age and the persistence of memory, an anxiety that is only heightened by the daughter's inability to sustain the father's attention in her own dream. The father's refusal to see his daughter even within the bounds of her own subconscious is dispiriting. Interestingly, this poem contains no overt reference to the father as a military man, though the father's return does echo a soldier's return. The father's disregard of the family displays the anxious attenuated boredom of Eric Leed's portrait of a returning soldier, and the family reacts as though he has in fact come home from war: "And we were always so eager, / welcoming each time, pleased / at his safe return / glad at the sight of / his face." Leed reminds us that the veteran's idealization of home was "an inevitable process in the trenches," and that this image of the ideal home environment was so powerful that many veterans found their return to the everyday realities and stresses of home profoundly disillusioning (188–89). The father's difficulty in recognizing his family parallels the awful irony of the returning soldier; he served in order to protect his family, but they seem like strangers to him when he returns to them at the end of the war. In "Voyager," the father's selective blindness is set against the ability of his military retinue (either fellow officers or men under his command) to observe the family, and the family's ability to see and recognize the father.

Even as "Voyager" reflects frustration with father–daughter kinship, the poem refuses to blame the father, but rather acknowledges his estrangement from his family in a world where he has the power of command but is denied the quotidian pleasures of a private citizen. "Voyager" reconfirms that the return of the elegiac figure of the lost beloved is forever desired because it is forever deferred. Though her melancholia keeps the daughter-elegist inconsolable, she resists the temptation to render the father as solid and knowable. In fact, her melancholic rhetoric assists her identification of the father's blind spot. She dwells in "a blank space in the air," and deprived of even his "glance of recognition," she cannot make herself visible to him. As he "set out in search" of the family that he remembers but cannot see, the daughter acknowledges, with chagrin, that this is intimacy as dictated by war and death: "the closest we have come / to meeting / during thirty years of dreams." Consolation, if it was ever a possibility, is indefinitely postponed in "Voyager."

The process of maintaining ongoing relationships with the dead, affectionate or otherwise, has its attendant frustrations, especially in attempts to renegotiate the father–daughter paradigm. Female affiliation haunts the elegy with its desire to delineate, and perhaps dismantle, the fidelity demanded by the father's death, and to investigate the unsolved question of the daughter's legacy. Whether this means that consolation is flatly refused or simply unavailable is another matter. Is the rhetoric of consolation offered by tradition satisfying or useful for the female elegist? Many of the changes in Page's work emerge from a confrontation with the modernist aesthetic to forge a more open dialogue with the father. Featuring confrontation of the dead as a twist of the elegiac tradition, Page comes close to a negotiated consolation in "Father" from her sequence, "Melanie's Nite-Book." In a 1996 interview, Page declares that while many of the poems in the sequence were fictional, and aligned with the fictional persona of "Melanie," the poem "Father" is very autobiographical: "The emotional feeling towards my father [in the poem] was true... I loved my father very much, and I always felt we belonged to each other. But we were never fully reconciled before he died" ("Biographical" 35–36). The expectations and tensions surrounding a reconciliation of fathers and daughters are enduring tensions in women's paternal elegy. In "Father," the officer-father appears impeccably aloof in his uniform, and the daughter (who assumes first-person speaker perspective) must once again—as she does in "Voyager"—beseech his attention.

The echo of "father" in "farther" underscores the distance between the two figures, and it is hard to ignore the allusion to the daughter of Jephthah's utterance, "My father, if thou hast opened thy mouth" (Judges 11:36), in Page's adoption of seventeenth-century Biblical syntax: "Father, o farther / in what heaven circlest thou? / Daily and dearly / ask I for thy succour." The daughter is "awaiting... benediction" from the father, even as the father begins to "crave [the daughter's] grace." He "tremble[s]... with dread of [her] grey gaze / the twin of [his] grey gaze." He craves forgiveness as she craves praise until she at last suggests a truce, predicated on a bargain that underlies the elegiac contract: "Let me your spokesman / and your axeman be." In order to strike this bargain, the daughter calls up the power of "that one word which severs as it heals." Given the syntax of the poem, that word may be "truce," but Page leaves the possibilities open. The "one word," unspoken and unwritten, is conspicuous by its absence. Page's conflation of the powerful unspoken word as a device that both severs and heals is intriguing from a psychoanalytic point of view. While castration is invoked by the cutting tool, the fact that the "one word" severs and heals simultaneously suggests something reminiscent of the cutting of an umbilical cord. Alternatively, the healing/severing dichotomy echoes Occam's razor, cutting away the unnecessary plurality of discourse around father–daughter kinship. The unspoken word becomes the tool that severs the tension between father and daughter, and points to forgiveness as a healing force.

That same unspoken word dissolves a good deal of the melancholia as well, as in this poem like no other of Page's, the daughter commands her father's attention, not coincidentally by imitating his own officer's stance. The speaker of the poem changes from the daughter as a good soldier who is "obedient, house-trained / heel-trained, at [her father's] call" into a fellow officer figure, an opponent formidable enough to require a truce. The daughter reinscribes herself as the father's "spokesman" and "axeman" in the poem's final lines. The returning father in "Voyager" is completely cut off from familial care, despite the welcome he receives. The general of "War Lord in the Early Evening" calls for "beneficent care" but receives only humiliation, and his daughter's silence and beauty cannot succour him. But in "Father," the daughter forges a truce, reconciling Gallagher's unease of the female gaze in a belligerent culture with a militarized father–daughter homosocial pact. At last, the daughter becomes her father's comrade-in-arms. She is "spokesman" and "axeman." She is, in other words, even momentarily, a good son: someone who positions herself between her father and the abyss, and gives the father the opportunity to recognize himself in her words. Whether he recognizes his daughter in her "male" guise is a complication that Page does not reveal.

Page's most recent father–daughter exploration may be found in her poem sequence "Alphabetical," first published in 1998 as a chapbook by Reference West, and republished in her 2002 collection, *Planet Earth: Poems Selected and New.* "Alphabetical" references each letter of the alphabet as a tile in a personal literary mosaic, and the military father resurfaces in the sections that explore the letters "q" and "r," represented by the words "question" and "reference." The father appears in this sequence as an instructor figure, a man with an educated mind who admonishes his daughter that her "questions are often laziness" and teaches his daughter intellectual "independence" by encouraging her use of reference books. John Orange's 1988 interview with Page records her characterization of Lionel Page as "a free thinker" who was "great on mind over matter" ("Conversation" 76). In "Alphabetical," the father inspires the daughter to "push towards objectivity" (and significantly, not towards subjectivity), and the "R" section recommends that such objectivity ought to be sought in "reference books in general, those / faceless authority figures in disguise." Is it too much to read the military references in these lines, the "general" as a "faceless authority figure... disguise[d]" in words? Is this a reiteration of the "war lord" and his "broken water pistol," hidden in the murk of masculine authority while offering his daughter an inheritance of knowledge and the ability to assert her "mind over matter"? Faced with the comic lack of "that trickle, that distil," the narrator of "War Lord in the Early Evening" wonders how to read the father's reduced offering: "Was this philosophy? It wasn't plumbing." Behind the blunt humour of the statement, the question lingers: what is left for the daughter in that "trickle, that distil" of the officer-father's knowledge? The officer-general of "Alphabetical" attempts to be "a faceless authority figure" but stands revealed by the daughter's gaze, trapped in his own "routed" body.

Page's officer-father poems testify not only to the tensions of father–daughter kinship, but also to the presence of the debilitated male body within the trope of the paternal hero. The abjection of this body is not necessarily a failure of masculinity, but a failure of the heroic concept of masculinity and a contribution to feminist discussions about constitution and dissolution of masculinity in modernist verse. Dismantling the authority of power and the privilege of rank, Page renders fragments of the father visible, no longer "hid from his daughter" in the darkened garden, through her investment in a creative melancholia that challenges the limits of daughterly devotion. The negotiation of a truce means that the daughter need no longer choose between the soldier-father's ferocity and fragility, but may see that which has been routed from and through the man. The father's body, "trembling with dread" in the daughter's gaze, offers itself up to transformation, and submits to that truce that severs even as it heals.

4

"Absence, Havoc"
Jay Macpherson's Rebellious Daughters

While we loved those who never read our poems,
Answered our letters, said the simple things we
Waited so long for, and were too polite to
    See we were crying,

Irony fed us:
—Jay Macpherson, "Some Ghosts & Some Ghouls"

Harold Bloom notes in *The Anxiety of Influence* that a younger male poet—an ephebe—establishes himself as the rightful inheritor of a senior poet's legacy by composing an elegy that underscores his stance as the writer most appropriate and most able to enact (and eventually, to best) the artistic ideals of his literary father (15–16). The daughterly elegiac mode is not so easily defined, nor is it so publicly acknowledged. A female ephebe must demand the right to elegize her father figure, and in addition she must argue for the right to inherit an artistic legacy within the elegiac tradition. The daughter's argument for inheritance must be especially strong when the literary father's legacy is composed of attributes or privileges that are considered to be masculine. If we regard this argument for inheritance as part of the discovery in the daughterly elegiac mode, then we cannot be surprised at the ways and means female poets have undertaken to write and rewrite the conditions of inheritance, nor at the rebellious positions they have taken up in order to pursue the privileges of inheritance. In many cases, the daughter must actively assert her daughterly position and even rebel against her father in order to prove herself the rightful inheritor of a tradition, either literary or familial.

In the poetry of Jay Macpherson, the lost father becomes a wandering beloved that the daughter pursues by way of allegory and allusion, and the work eventually becomes a codified inquiry into women's place as readers and writers of great works of Western literature. As Macpherson's literary daughters mourn for their magus-fathers, they discover the fathers to be sinister and the paternal transformative magic to be unavailable to the daughter. The daughter's anagnorisis, in Macpherson's poetry, is the discovery of her subjectivity beyond the father's influence, and beyond the influence of his alchemical logos. She charts a journey from good modernist daughter to defiant mourner of the paternal world in two books that regard the havoc that absence wreaks along with an oxymoronic "welcome disaster." In *The Boatman and Other Poems* and *Welcoming Disaster*, Macpherson works with a mythology that may seem to intimate autobiography, but ultimately gestures toward the failure of elegiac convention to serve a discourse of female mourning. Lorraine Weir notes that the "[p]ublic parallax" of Macpherson's poems operates as "a technique of revelation" that contrasts with her technique of masking her writing persona, and that this play of public and private desires is part of Macpherson's subversion of literary colonization by the culture of patriarchy ("Toward" 62). Weir's caveat that it is vital to read Macpherson as a wily rhetorician rather than as a servant to her own allusions bodes well for reading Macpherson's work as guided by elegiac rebellion. Macpherson reappropriates the conventions of elegy to question the role of mourning daughters in Western literature and, in doing so, criticizes the father figure in his learned guise as alchemist, magus, or anagogic man.

As the epigraph that opens this chapter suggests, irony feeds Macpherson's work, not only—as the poem implies—because the daughters labour after those who do not notice their efforts, but also because she shows mournful daughters who learn rebellion through their grief. In *The Boatman and Other Poems*, Macpherson revives doomed Biblical and Shakespearean daughters who mock the old sinful order even as they mourn its loss. In *Welcoming Disaster*, she writes the mourning daughter as a living ghoul who haunts the absent father, and, ultimately, as a character who notes that the mythology that she has appropriated cannot serve her as she wishes. Macpherson's use of this kind of irony begins in the late modernist mode in 1968's *The Boatman and Other Poems*, and edges out into proto-feminist territory in 1974's *Welcoming Disaster*. Raymond Williams points out that one of the ironies of modernism is that it "quickly lost its anti-bourgeois stance, and achieved comfortable integration into the new international capitalism" (35). Female modernist poets like Macpherson must have felt acutely the irony of writing in what purported to be a new tradition, but was instead one in which women continued to define their subjectivity through the approval of literary men, "those who never read our poems" ("Some Ghosts & Some Ghouls").

Macpherson's poetry has received little critical attention in the past two decades, beyond a handful of articles and Weir's thoughtful 1989 monograph. Weir notes that critical discussion of Macpherson's work is "sparse, occasionally generous, but always incomplete" ("Jay" 180). However, critics who have written about Macpherson agree upon the elegiac tone of her work. James Reaney writes that Macpherson is "a poet who makes both elegiac and comic equally rich" (29), while Suniti Namjoshi notes the importance of the Orphic journey to both *The Boatman* and *Welcoming Disaster* ("In the Whale's Belly" 55). Northrop Frye's review of *The Boatman* notes that Macpherson's "elegiac poems are the most resonant, and they make the strongest impression" ("Letters" 436), while David Bromwich asserts that "Macpherson's more ambitious poems have been elegiac," in particular those that "lament... an alienated and/or repressed element of the self" (336). He suggests that Macpherson's use of allusion in *The Boatman* has a distinct elegiac purpose, in that "it helps us to cross the distance between ourselves and our losses" (337).

But even such apparently easy agreement does not mean that Macpherson's work is widely regarded as elegiac. Critical discussion of her first book, first issued in 1957 as *The Boatman*, tends to focus on Macpherson's manipulation of classical and Biblical mythology into a narrative that retells the story of the Biblical flood, complete with the hope for human redemption in a post-apocalyptic world. Macpherson populates her text with sleeping shepherds and fallen women, the saved and the unsaved, demonstrating her scholarly familiarity with the literary Christian philosophies of Blake and Milton. (In an article published in *University of Toronto Quarterly* in 1992, Macpherson names Milton's "Lycidas" as an early literary fascination that eventually became the subject of her master's thesis.) Northrop Frye was Macpherson's dissertation advisor from 1955 to 1959 when she concentrated on the literature of the late Romantic period for her doctoral degree. Not surprisingly, many reviews and early articles about *The Boatman* emphasize Frye's influence on Macpherson's style and subject matter, and, certainly, Frye's expertise in Blake and his explorations of Christian consciousness had some influence on Macpherson's poetics and her hermeneutic work. But while it is easy to detect Frygian influence in

Macpherson's apocalyptic vision, strong evidence of her independence may be found in her concern with female subjectivity within her work, beginning with the 1968 edition of *The Boatman and Other Poems* and extending to *Welcoming Disaster*. For the purposes of clarity, I will refer to the 1957 version as *The Boatman*, and the 1968 edition as *The Boatman and Other Poems*.

The Boatman elegizes the fallen world while exploring a Blakean philosophy of sin and redemption, positioning the poet as an artist figure who, like Philomel, sings in "unmeasured grief," but who also, like Procne, "[p]erforms as she is able" and, together, the sacrificial virgin and the vengeful wife tell a story that "[r]aises both Cain and Babel" ("While Philomel's Unmeasured Grief"). Macpherson's poetic voice in *The Boatman* combines wit with an elegant Christian philosophy; it offers a vision of a fallen world redeemed by Noah as the figure of anagogic man, he who holds the future and, indeed, the whole universe in his head: "what sways when Noah nods? / The sun, the stars, the figures of the gods" ("The Anagogic Man"). However, in 1968, Macpherson's addition of sixteen new poems to *The Boatman and Other Poems* intentionally disrupts the unity of the original text's ending. The added poems introduce several daughter figures who, unlike the "fallen women" of the 1957 *The Boatman*, distinguish themselves with their vitality: they refuse to die. Their presence in the post-apocalyptic world implies the possibility of an anagogic woman who could match the powerful figure of Macpherson's glass-headed anagogic man. The mercurial, multi-voiced narrator of 1968's *The Boatman and Other Poems* includes the voices of several defiant daughters, including a revived and aggrieved Ophelia, the silent daughters of Job, and a fictional, fourth daughter for King Lear, the cruel but constant Jenny Lear. These daughters occupy Macpherson's added seventh section of the 1968 version as living indictments of their fathers' behaviour, as well as of the traditions in Western literature that killed off these women in their original plots.

Macpherson resurrects these lost daughters and arms them with defiant wit. They are rebellious survivors who mourn their lost fathers even as they insist upon a place in the post-apocalyptic world, and their presence reveals Macpherson's concern about the place of women in the anagogic revelation of *The Boatman*. Placing these lost daughter figures among those who survive the Flood suggests Macpherson's dissatisfaction with the original ending of 1957's *The Boatman*. The grief and violence of the daughters in the seventh section, particularly the self-destructiveness of Jenny Lear, ushers in the gothic, mourning daughter of *Welcoming Disaster*: a woman failed by psychoanalysis and by mythology. By amalgamating her rebellious daughters into *Welcoming Disaster*'s single melancholic narrator, Macpherson creates a daughterly persona who haunts the dead in an attempt to understand her loss, and, in doing so, writes an elegy for the literary father and for her self.

The "disaster" that is welcomed in Macpherson's second book is nothing less than the crisis in legitimation funnelled through a bid for female subjectivity that does not rely upon paternalized permission. Within the struggle to differentiate love from reason, Macpherson contemplates the possibilities of writing beyond the influence of the father, articulating what seemed to be, in Canada in 1974 for a woman of Macpherson's generation, an unrealizable dream of *écriture feminine*. Like many modernist writers, Macpherson alludes to the great books of Western literature in order to debate the value of knowledge. However, in both of her books of poetry, and, significantly, in her rewrite of her award-winning first book, she casts doubt upon the efficacy of male-centred knowledge systems, suggesting instead the need for a fully realized female literary subjectivity. Her elegiac tone mourns the obedient daughter as much as it mourns the mythological father, and her melancholic turn from the rhetoric of consolation ironizes both the consolation and the subjectivity available to her daughter persona.

In *Welcoming Disaster*, the paternal figure appears in a variety of literary and theoretical guises. Macpherson fashions a literary father from the figure of the alchemist which she identifies in *The Spirit of Solitude* as a "hypnotist" or "abominable showman (Frye's term)," who bamboozles people with "the glittering world of illusion" while pursuing the dark arts in the "surrounding darkness" of secrecy (194). Rosemary Sullivan notes that *Welcoming Disaster* begins "with the poet metaphorically orphaned" ("Macpherson" 498), struggling in vain to define herself with the magic formula of her father's symbology. The alchemist figure of *Welcoming Disaster* appears as an anagogic man who has become demonic through his possession of absolute power—some combination of the Old Testament God, Noah, William Blake's Nobodaddy, and Northrop Frye—and Macpherson indicts the rhetoric of modernism as the alchemist father's "world of illusion," the paternal logos. In desiring the key to his secret art, the daughter desires the father's knowledge, and as Macpherson herself points out, the pursuit of "[k]nowledge as treasure is usually ironic, and apt to bring destruction instead of fulfillment" (*Spirit* 184).

Whose Father? Whose Effect?

The paternal figure featured in Macpherson's poems appears to be closely related to Julia Kristeva's "imaginary father" as a rereading of Freud's "father in individual prehistory," a father who represents love rather than law (Oliver 69). Kristeva proposes this "loving, giving and gratifying" father figure (*Black Sun* 92) in direct opposition to the commanding Lacanian Father figure. While Macpherson's explorations of the father figure leave no doubt about the father's power in a symbolic system, the abandoned daughter is greedy for his attention: so much so that *she* haunts *him* after his death. Significantly, she does not fear his authority, but rather covets his sense of certainty and creation. Kristeva describes the imaginary father as the male figure who establishes "the link between pleasure and symbolic dignity... as he leads his child from primary to secondary identification" (*Black Sun* 92–93). So necessary is he as a figure of psychic gratification in *Welcoming Disaster* that Macpherson configures his "absence" as first "havoc" and then "winter," invoking chaos and then hibernation as manifestations of the daughter's grief.

The father–daughter kinship explored in these texts cannot be separated from Macpherson's practice of "parody, pastiche and allusion" (Bromwich 334). The paternal in Macpherson's texts does not refer to the autobiographical, biological father, but rather to the symbolic father, who, for all his ephemerality, strikes a formidable figure, that of a "tranced master" ("Masters & Servants") in *Welcoming Disaster.* The limits of autobiographical criticism show themselves here. While Macpherson dedicated *The Spirit of Solitude* to her father, James Macpherson, her circumspect nature, rarely giving interviews and remaining reluctant to speak personally about her poetic work, prohibits me from making any argument that these elegiac poems refer specifically to James Macpherson. However, since the division of cultural/symbolic Father from individuated father is never easy, Macpherson's creation of a mythic, alchemist father suggests strongly that F/fathers may be found both within the boundaries of the family and, significantly, beyond them. Without a doubt, the father figure is a major force in both of Macpherson's poetry collections; as the Father, he is the anagogic man who knows the secret of alchemy, just as he is the maker of rules and an unquestionable authority. Macpherson's shift in narrative persona from the distanced, multiple-personaed narrator of *The Boatman* to the "greedy devourer" of "Some Ghosts & Some Ghouls" in *Welcoming Disaster* anticipates the failure of psychoanalytic language as a discourse that cannot capture the deep ambivalence of female mourning.

Applying Freud's or Lacan's theories to Macpherson's work only points out the difficulties both psychoanalysts had in construing female experience, particularly the limitations of theories of hysteria (for Freud) and female signification (for Lacan). Macpherson's revived Ophelia may be read initially as a Freudian hysteric, but Macpherson grants her a resilience that belies such easy pathology. Jenny Lear may be read as a monster of femininity whose cruelty springs from a suppressed desire for her father, but what can Freudian theory make of the wit in her wickedness? A Lacanian reading would suggest that the rebellious daughters and the greedy devourer desire the symbolic father's language and signifiers but are thwarted by the limits of the father as "register," or image of the world. Such a reading seems ungenerous given Macpherson's poetic skill and the subtle layers of her examinations of power and love in father–daughter kinship.

Kelly Oliver suggests that by claiming a loving father, the female theorist (and, I would add, perhaps the female poet) can lay claim to being the "imaginary son, the rightful heir" (67). But in *Welcoming Disaster*, the mourning daughter discovers that she cannot lay claim to the knowledge dispensed by the father-alchemist figure, and her lack of access to his mythological systems shapes her mourning practice. Macpherson's characterization of the father figure as an "enchanter" and "magister" who is the source of all magical knowledge aligns with the Kristevan imaginary father as "a metaphorical function that gives way to the metonymic paternal function" (Oliver 66). The figure of male magic and mastery holds the power of the word and of love, and, at first, the narrator's intense anguish at his absence invites comparisons to Kristeva's interpretation of a "loving father who helps the child overcome abjection" (*Tales* 26). But there is something too similar about Kristeva's concept of the imaginary father and the Lacanian lawgiver—Father as arbitrator of law and the symbolic order—even though Kristeva insists that her idea of the father is both "stern" and "playful" (*Tales* 46) while Lacan's father is completely authoritative. Something of this tension plays itself out in *Welcoming Disaster*; in "Some Ghosts & Some Ghouls," the fathers are with "coldness adorned," while the daughters are "guilty most of suffering." But Macpherson goes on to suggest that these fathers will reap the reward of making daughters in their own image:

> They were our teachers: what we are, they made us.
> Cautious our converse, prudent our behaviour,
> Guarded our faces: we behind them lurking,
>   Greedy, devourers.

Despite Kristevan objections that a "crisis in paternity" is characterized by "the lack of love" rather than "the lack of law" (Oliver 69), the imaginary father remains a shadowy figure, one that has been—so far—at the mercy of the limits of paternal representation. Thinking about Macpherson's grieving and eventually rebellious daughter figure as Alice Jardine's "woman-in-effect" (48) seems to be a more productive way to re-think daughterly negotiations of inheritance. In *The Boatman and Other Poems*, the daughter figures are so decidedly "outside" of the text that they could be construed as "abject-in-effect." Separated from their original plots yet surviving, these rebellious daughter figures embody the Kristevan "narcissistic crisis" of abjection *par excellence* (*Powers of Horror* 14). The mourner of *Welcoming Disaster* goes a step further, assuming the persona of the melancholic daughter who is abandoned by an intellectual father, so that she "nurtures horror... a work of disappointment, of frustration, and hollowing—probably the only counterweight to abjection" as Kristeva notes in *The Powers of Horror* (210). When Lorraine Weir suggests that the text of *Welcoming Disaster* teases out the parallels between eschatology and epistemology ("Jay" 195), these parallels connote the relationship between nurturing horror and welcoming disaster.

Welcoming Disaster displays a marked tendency for the elegy to swing between expressed grief for the lost beloved and the elegist's grief for the self. The speaker of *Welcoming Disaster* begins by longing after the lost and abandoning father figure, but soon her loss grows to encompass her systems of thought and ways of expression until she is mourning the loss of a world. The play between the elegiac object and the elegiac subject, or between the elegized and elegist, is part of the disaster that the daughter welcomes as a part of establishing subjectivity. Such a project is fraught with potential pitfalls. Jardine cautions, "The 'woman-in-effect' can only be thought beginning with how the monological structures we have inherited are constantly reimposed and rearranged, and (particularly) with how women both mime and reject those structures and even become their most adamant support systems" (48).

Macpherson acts out this kind of mime and rejection with her use of eschatology to welcome a new epistemology and to mourn for the daughter figure while miming an elegy for the father. In aligning language use so closely with feminist thought, Jardine emphasizes the need to identify moments at which women writers realize that the systems of thought in which they have been working serve neither their subjectivity nor their desires. Jardine uses the term "gynesis" to describe the feminist tenets of language inquiry, "the putting into discourse of 'woman' as that *process* diagnosed in France as intrinsic to the condition of modernity" (25; emphasis in original). Concerned about the essentialism of reducing women to sexual difference or to biological function, Jardine proposes a mercurial subjectivity for the female subject rather than a stable unified identity.

An overarching goal of modernity, as Jardine defines it, is the examination of and eventual participation in "processes that disrupt symbolic structures in the West" (42), and from this position, Macpherson's project reveals the structures of elegiac convention. She begins as a wry commentator on myth through the visionary wit of *The Boatman*, but undercuts the redemptive conclusion of that text with her addition of the resurrected daughters in the 1968 reissue of the text. Macpherson's exploration of apocalyptic revelation in *The Boatman* yields to her revisionary inquiry into women's place in the redemptive world. On the heels of the resurrected daughter poems, the narrator of *Welcoming Disaster* acts out the daughter's abjection and her loss of faith in that paternal world and its promise of redemption. The elegiac mode serves as Macpherson's literary compass; her play upon elegiac convention and its accompanying myths is vital to contemplating the difficulties of daughterhood in modernity and in literary modernism.

Resurrection and the Daughter: After the Anagogic Man

James Reaney sums up the end of 1957's *The Boatman* by referring to "The Book of Riddles," the final section of the original text: "The last section in effect says to the reader that Creation, Fall and Redemption are part of a dance whose final figure is the scene in which the Fisherman, in the very last poem, having corrected the Fall is corrected himself for all time" (34). Reaney's analysis is inarguable as far as "The Book of Riddles" is concerned. However, it is the defiantly uncorrected voice of Jenny Lear that ends 1968's edition of *The Boatman and Other Poems*, as Jenny commands that the curtain be brought down on what Lynda E. Boose calls the "unstructured" state of daughterhood (21). What that curtain represents, as vicious and strangely vulnerable as Jenny Lear appears, is the coming literary and critical "disaster": the dismantling of the rhetoric of daughterly sacrifice. By adding this seventh section of "Other Poems" in the 1968 *The Boatman and Other Poems*, Macpherson destabilizes readings of the 1957 text.

The resurrected daughters of Macpherson's seventh section are figures of defiant abjection, manifesting in affective modes: assertive grief (Ophelia), plangent silence (Job's daughters), and vicious glee (Jenny Lear). The distance between Ophelia's grief and Jenny's glee is a mere handful of pages, and the enigma of Job's daughters serves as a bridge between them. The wordlessness of Job's daughters seems balanced between acquiescence and accusation. Certainly these resurrected daughters presage the "eerie" and "ruthless" tone that results in what Atwood has called Macpherson's "rigorous and sometimes bloody-minded self-analysis" in a review of *Poems Twice Told* ("Jay" 411). To the degree that we can read bloody-mindedness as a common attribute in Macpherson's daughter characters from the 1968 *The Boatman and Other Poems* onwards, we can identify with it a protofeminist glee that emerges from Macpherson's criticism of the fractured mythos of modernism. There is a certain amount of irony in considering that these resurrected daughters of the added other poems are as potentially sacrificial as the young women of 1957's *The Boatman*; the poor child who is "ruined from the womb" ("Poor Child") seems strongly akin to the "daughters mild and fair" in "A Garden Shut" who are "spit rudely on" the unicorn's "sexual thorn." It would be true enough to say that Macpherson practises feminist "re-vision" in the way that Adrienne Rich defines it, as "entering an old text from a new critical direction... not to pass on a tradition but to break its hold over us" ("When We Dead Awaken" 35). However, the literary daughters Macpherson resurrects are ambiguously feminist, "all in their various ways betrayed by impulses that reach out for the conditions of an unfallen world" (Macpherson, *Spirit* 146). As Macpherson titles an early poem in *Welcoming Disaster* that alludes to a line from Matthew Arnold's "The Scholar Gipsy" (1853), even these rebellious daughters are "still waiting for the spark from heaven."

Nevertheless, these "bloody-minded" daughters perform a feat of liminality; they assert their femininity in the timely addition of the seventh section of *The Boatman and Other Poems*, and their presence questions the position of women in the earlier version of the text. The rebellious daughters are refugees from that fallen world, and they cannot quite find purchase in the new redemptive world. Though the glass head of Macpherson's "anagogic man" holds "[t]he sun, the stars, the figures of the gods," that head cannot seem to fathom the idea of women. His head encompasses "[a]ll us and our worlds," and Macpherson warns that "to startle him" is to allow "some / Poor soul to its destruction come," and that seems to be the case with women in the original text of *The Boatman*. In the 1957 version, the "fallen women" do not survive the apocalyptic Flood, and any "woman-in-effect" seems to be the "soul" who cannot be encompassed in the mind of the anagogic man; the female soul "[s]lipped out of mind and past recall / As if it never was at all."

The lack of critical attention to these added poems speaks of another kind of liminality in Canadian literary history, for only Margaret Atwood has commented on the poems of *The Boatman and Other Poems*' seventh section in her 1982 review of *Poems Twice Told*. Even Weir's extensive discussion of Macpherson's texts does not venture near these poems. In "Jay Macpherson and Her Works," Weir concludes that by the end of 1957's *The Boatman* "[c]ommunity triumphs over the temptations of solitude the avenger, and the word triumphs over silence" (209). But the addition of the seventh section changes that; the resurrected daughters of the "Other Poems" are without community, ghettoized within the text. In affecting a literary resurrection of daughters who were originally sacrificed in line with the father's death or debilitation, Macpherson creates a new world out of an elegy for the fallen world.

But it would be a mistake to imply that the daughters of the "Other Poems" appear out of nowhere. On the contrary, Macpherson lays the groundwork for their 1968 appearance early in the original 1957 edition of *The Boatman*, in the section titled "O Earth Return: A Speculum for Fallen Women." In a series of ironic lyrics, with skill so deft that her tone is notoriously easy to misread as misogynous, Macpherson reflects upon the tendency for Biblical and classical mythology to condemn to annihilation whores and virgins alike: sexually savvy woman die in sin and shame, while virgins are martyrs to their innocence. Reading these poems in the first decade of twenty-first century, it is difficult *not* to read this "speculum," that instrument of observation and diagnosis, as an instrument of Macpherson's irony. The early version of *The Boatman* contains no human women at all once the Flood has begun. In the final "Book Of Riddles," the only females are supernatural ones who could not drown: angels, mermaids, and phoenixes. The addition of the "Other Poems" to the 1968 edition suggests a wry take on the Old Testament valuation of daughters as generative beings who exist in order to carry the Lord's Blessing. Deliberately uncooperative daughters change the ending of *The Boatman*, while their presence in the revised text reminds readers that the Fisherman "hoick[ed] . . . in" by God's "patient grin" should be read with considerable irony. Macpherson's determination to worry the myths she appeared to support in the first six sections offers a chance to read *The Boatman and Other Poems* as a text that enacts more than a dutiful daughter's obedience to her cultural, literary, and Christian fathers. With one foot in and one foot out of Macpherson's apocalyptic world of revelation, these elegiac daughters position themselves over the abyss of modernist daughterhood in order to question the place of women in the post-Flood world, and in the symbology of Western literature.

The resurrected daughters' demand to be taken seriously is of primary importance in the post-Flood world. When Ophelia warns in "The Woods No More" that "None shall make a game of me," she cautions readers that Macpherson's argumentative daughter figures are deeply ambivalent to the tensions of patriarchy. To be "made a game of" implies participation in and capitulation to mockery of the daughters, the kind of passive victimhood that Macpherson coolly writes into the first three sections of *The Boatman*. With this seventh section, Macpherson changes the rules of the game. These daughters dare to question the concept of redemption, but their most rebellious act appears to be survival itself, and by surviving, they call into question the place of women in Western literary culture, trapped as they are between Biblical typology as the Frygian "Great Code" of cultural formation and as a force that is systematically fatal to women. If the anagogic man represents the hermeneutical force of *The Boatman*, then the surviving daughter as anagogic woman counters with a female figure that refuses sacrifice and idealization.

Atwood asserts that "[t]he central voice of *The Boatman* is one of a complex and powerful grief, and its central symbols revolve around separation and loss" ("Jay" 409). Part of this complex and powerful grief is the separation of women from God as a father figure who views his daughter as either a virginal object of sacrifice or another sinful woman. Critics who suggest that Macpherson is too indebted to Frye are missing the irony of her creation of a God who "hoicks" men into His grace and forgiveness, but abandons women to oblivion, textual absence, or interpretive obscurity. Weir's suggestions that Macpherson asserts a high modernist sense of the death of God, and that the text must account for itself in a Godless world, are particularly useful in regarding the fate of the resurrected daughters ("Jay" 176–78). Macpherson begins the "Other Poems" of the seventh section by introducing doubt into the narrative of the "master text" as a defence against a surfeit of "feminine" emotion:

> Ophelia on the threshold of the season
> Stands doubting, fears, lets fall
> Green love, green sorrow, shaken without reason:
> Poor maiden, not the girl for fall. ("A Winter")

The idea of an Ophelia who stands on the threshold instead of plunging in, who dares to doubt, who "lets fall / Green love, green sorrow" rather than herself being befallen with love and sorrow is a revelation. This Ophelia is ruled by thought rather than affect. Neither sexual nor dead, Macpherson's Ophelia is not a fallen woman in any sense; she has already achieved more than the sexually doomed women of "O Earth Return" and "The Plowman in Darkness." Indeed, Macpherson's Ophelia is "not the girl for fall" so much as she is not the girl who *will* fall. We have left the fallen Shakespearean world in which Ophelia must be sacrificed on the altar of male desire and paternal death. Macpherson's Ophelia is more cautious at her threshold, "shaken" by the promise of winter. She is no paragon of reason, but she "lets fall" the two emotive concepts that dog her in *Hamlet*: love and sorrow. In "The Woods No More," Ophelia rediscovers her grief but, although her "tears run down" and her "heart is sore," she warns that "none shall make a game of me." She is no longer a pawn in a game of political romance; she has removed herself from the tragic equation, and no longer offers her drowned body to precipitate or resolve male desire. By the end of the poem, she warns her lover to "make no bones"—a warning against sexual congress and death, and, perhaps, against accusations of frivolity or being "without reason." Make no bones and no games of her; do not die, do not make fun, do not make love. This Ophelia is a young woman as dedicated to mourning both her father and herself as she previously was dedicated to madness. In "A World of Glass," she is "a small damp female" who pushes her weeping body against the glass as she cries. The display of such an image connotes this grief as very public and determined, as well as an active refusal of a diversion into madness by way of grief. In refusing sacrifice and asserting her grief as a spectacle, Macpherson's Ophelia suggests that the acknowledgement of grief can be, in Gillian Rose's sense, a quest for justice.

In "The Beauty of Job's Daughters," a poem that Atwood praises for its "outwardly formal, flexibly-handled lyricism" (409), Macpherson debates the value of beauty in relation to justice. The first line, "The old, the mad, the blind have fairest daughters," seems to pun on "fair," meaning both beautiful and just in this context. The daughters spend the first three stanzas of the poem supplying Job and his visitors with a welcoming environment: "[w]ide shining rooms more warmly lit at evening, / Gardens beyond whose secrets scent the air." The question of whether Job is old or blind or mad, or possibly all three, is rendered moot by Macpherson's description of how he has "[a]ttained in age to inwardness of daughters." The implicit intimacy and unwavering faith of this "inwardness" seems deeply suspect, even as the word implies that Job's silent daughters serve his inner life and his sons may serve him in the larger social world. To receive such daughterly devotion is a heady prospect, even more so when Macpherson suggests that Job is so entranced by the attentions of his daughters that nothing else seems as interesting or delightful:

> Not wiles of men nor envy of the neighbours,
> Riches of earth, nor what heaven holds more rare,
> Can take from Job the beauty of his daughters,
> The gardens in the rock, music at evening,
> And cup so full that all who come must share.

This full cup, the bounty that must be shared (or flaunted) in its abundance that surpasses all other pleasures, warns the reader of the impossibility of this paradisal dream. Neither earthy evils nor heaven's temptations can move Job from the devotion of his daughters, who prove to be figments of his fevered imagination, mere "desert stumps." These devoted daughters have already served as sacrifices to God. Macpherson places this poem third in the "Other Poems" section, so that the hint of steel in her Ophelia is followed by this dismantled dream of the daughter as devoted servant. The woman as redemptive beauty, the woman who serves and demands nothing, the all-giving maternal figure in the body of a young girl, is a romantic construction. It is no wonder that the old, the mad, and the blind have the fairest daughters; these examples of womanhood are constructed from the hallucinations of social delirium made manifest. The poet's choice of "desert stumps" as corollaries for the daughters is not a complete parallel with the pillar of salt into which Lot's wife turns, though the stumps are nevertheless reminiscent of the lonely annihilation of that cautionary tale. The difference is, of course, that Lot's wife is turned into a pillar of salt when she looks back on the city where her daughters met their death, and we cannot know the final fate of Job's daughters; are they indeed the stumps in question, or have they vanished into lives of their own long ago?

If Ophelia lives to complain of injustices done to her, then Jenny Lear emerges in her two poems ("The Love-Song of Jenny Lear" and "Love-Song II of Jenny Lear") as a daughterly law unto herself. Combining the characteristics of Goneril, Regan, and Cordelia, Jenny is Lear's fictional fourth daughter, the one who stays with him, but refuses to sing with him in prison "like birds i' th' cage" (*King Lear* 5.3.9). She is not above exploiting Lear's infirmity under the guise of daughterly care; her attentions to him are sassy, crudely flirtatious, and sometimes cruel. Her irascible nature mirrors her father's temperament, and allows her to survive by virtue of a rough poetic justice; she is, in many ways, the daughter that Lear deserves. As much as Macpherson has fun with the bawdiness of the limerick form, she offers a Shakespearean daughter who is a walking contradiction of devotion and disobedience. On one hand, Jenny Lear proves to be a successful device for stirring up the reader's sympathy for Lear; with her verbs straight out of broad sex farce and sadism, one shudders to think of Jenny's harsh ministrations to Lear's frail body. But in positing the "fairness" of daughters as a traditional literary virtue, Macpherson also implies that Jenny's actions are "just desserts" meted out to Lear. Despite her cruelty, she acts as a textual tonic after the multiple passive deaths of lolling shepherdesses, sacrificed virgins, and the pale and righteous weepiness of Macpherson's Ophelia. Jenny is no model of filial piety, but she is righteously vital, and, as her two poems complete the 1968 version of *The Boatman*, she demands a serious reading for her audacity alone.

In her first "Love-Song," Jenny sneers at Matthew Arnold's Margaret of his popular 1849 poem, "The Forsaken Merman," who leaves her merman husband and amphibious children in order to return to Christian devotion on land. Macpherson echoes Arnold's rhyme of "whirl" and "pearl," in a parody that displays Jenny's contempt for Margaret's piety and sets up her assertion that she herself is "more of a hell of a girl." Though Lear is glossed as a Neptune figure, Jenny does not appear to show any signs of leaving Lear to a watery repose like the "king of the sea." Instead, she implements a program of rigorous torture, thinly disguised as care. She recommends a walk by the sea and a "horrid long talk," and pushes the limits further to imply sexual and physical violence:

> Poor old fish, you're no walker at all,
> Can't you spank up that elderly crawl?
> I'll teach you to hurdle,
> Led on by my girdle,
> With whalebone, elastic and all. ("The Love-Song of Jenny Lear")

By the poem's end, when Lear is at last allowed to shut his eyes and seek the blindness that plagues him spiritually throughout Shakespeare's play (but an affliction that he may devoutly wish for as relief from Jenny's ministrations), she becomes a kind of cannibal "crunch[ing] down [his] bones / Guts marrow and stones." Jenny's consumption of the father in order to "raise [him] up dancing again" is a method of resurrection that satirizes Cordelia's tender care of Lear in the play's final act, and Jenny herself is a parody of the returning daughters who redeem their sinning fathers in Shakespeare's late Romances: Perdita in *A Winter's Tale*, Marina in *Pericles*, and Imogene in *Cymbeline*. Cordelia attempts to do the same for her father but dies before Lear secures redemption. Jenny's "Love-Song II" repudiates daughterly piety and suggests a deeply ambivalent perspective on this daughterly role. It is brief enough to quote in its entirety here:

> Were I a Shakespearean daughter,
> Safe restored through fire and water,
> You the party in the crown
> — Someone get the curtain down.

Is the call for the curtain a call for the play to end, or her wish for the father's death? Is she indicating that Lear is not worth saving, or that she herself is ill suited to the role of the redeeming daughter? Suffice to say that Jenny considers herself a different species of daughter—"more of a hell of a girl"—and is not shy about saying so, though we are left wondering at the suddenness of that falling curtain. Is her voice aggrieved or mocking, or even ashamed? It is worth noting that, instead of the "hoicked" fisherman that ends the original *Boatman*, Macpherson's 1968 edition ends with Jenny Lear's decisive rejection of a daughterly restorative function.

Jenny Lear is not the Anagogic Woman, but in bringing the curtain down on sacrificial daughterhood, her voice ushers in the daughter-mourner of *Welcoming Disaster.*

"Absence, Havoc": Gothic Mourning in *Welcoming Disaster*

Macpherson's 1974 *Welcoming Disaster* was originally published as a 63-page chapbook of short lyric monologues. The text is divided into five sections that describe the narrator's reactions to the loss of her creative powers, preceded by the disappearance of a paternal magus figure. But *Welcoming Disaster* remains something of a textual enigma; it has received little critical attention since its publication, even though *The Boatman* won Macpherson the Governor General's Award for Poetry in 1957. About *Welcoming Disaster,* W. J. Keith assures readers that the text "reveals hints (like *The Waste Land*, we might add) of a palpable if subtly personal trauma" (32), while Suniti Namjoshi calls it an exploration of "the world of nightmare" ("In the Whale's Belly" 55). Michael Hornyansky points out the text's "ominous simplicities" and calls Macpherson's prosody "a very curious blend of the cryptic, the elliptic, and the conversational" (337).

Suffice to say that *Welcoming Disaster* has received only a fraction of the critical attention that it deserves as a poetic sequence, as a feminist text, and as part of the gothic tradition in Canada. Margaret Atwood, who, as Macpherson's former student at the University of Toronto, acquired at least some of her sense of the gothic tradition from Macpherson, writes that *Welcoming Disaster* resonates with "echoes of all those nineteenth-century ghosts, from Catherine Earnshaw on down," with "vampiristic or sinister-double relationships" and with "Faustian pacts with darkness," emphasizing Macpherson's use of the "lore of magicians, ghouls, mazes and crossroads" ("Jay" 410). Certainly the illustrations in *Welcoming Disaster* invite a gothic reading. The poem "Conjuring the Dead" is accompanied by a reproduction of the woodcut from the 1620 quarto of Christopher Marlowe's *Doctor Faustus*, showing the scientist in his learned robes raising the devil, though significantly, the *Welcoming Disaster* emblem shows only Faustus brandishing his book within his charmed circle (14). Later in the text, section III, "The Dark Side," is adorned with a *memento mori* of a grinning death's head, decorated with cherubs, bats, and an ourobouros, taken from a 1776 Puritan headstone in Massachusetts (Weir, "Towards" 205). When Atwood writes that the poems in *Welcoming Disaster* "make the hair stand up on the back of your neck" ("Jay" 411), she does not specify whether this effect is a result of fear or admiration, although I suspect both reactions are appropriate.

One of the hair-raising qualities of these poems is the omnipresence (or lurking "omniabsence") of the dead. In *Welcoming Disaster,* the dead seem to proliferate at an alarming, nearly geometric rate, perhaps because the protagonist insists upon the "closed communion, pact profound" between the dead and the living ("Conjuring the Dead"). Later in the same poem, Macpherson writes this relationship as morbidly satisfying on one level, but also acknowledges that it remains frustrating enough to leave the speaker "stupid—cumbering the ground." Although she has conjured them, the dead react in good elegiac fashion; they do not stay in contact with her, but neither do they have the decency to vanish. Corpses languish in cellars, in graves, in ruined castles, in lost books, in cinema seats, in coffins, and behind locked doors; they linger because they are haunted by the poems' protagonist. She craves union with the dead in general and with one "wandered love" in particular ("Absence, Havoc").

If we are to consider *Welcoming Disaster* a wittily melancholic blend of gothic and elegiac traditions that work towards feminist concerns, then thinking about the timing of publication is important. Macpherson wrote this text in the late 1960s and early 1970s, as feminist theory was emerging in Europe and while younger Canadian poets, such as Atwood, Gwendolyn MacEwen, and Susan Musgrave, were beginning to modernize the gothic with feminist concerns. In the introduction to their 2007 collection *Postfeminist Gothic*, Benjamin A. Brabon and Stéphanie Genz assert that "the Gothic has always resisted a monological definition and exceeded the laws of genre and categorical thinking" (1), adding that scholars of both gothic and feminist literature must "now demand a self-criticism with respect to their own totalizing gestures and assumptions" (7). Justin D. Edwards's recent study, *Gothic Canada*, casts a wary eye on those same totalizing gestures when he proposes that Canadian gothic literature struggles with "the grip of an ambivalent impulse that arises equally from a wish to a counter wish, from attraction to repulsion," between the colonizing impulse and the wish to escape the force of colonization, creating "an obsessive mindset, in which Canadian writers continually return to ghostly figures who haunt" (xxi).

The struggle for subjectivity in *Welcoming Disaster* develops into elegiac concern that is also obsessively existential; can an elegiac subject exist outside the master discourse, even if (or especially if) she loves and serves the master discourse? How can a female poet, as Macpherson characterizes her narrator, grieve after the fatherly myth and discourse that abandons her? The daughter-narrator of *Welcoming Disaster* argues for subjectivity at the same time as she mourns the lost world of myth from which she enacts her exile, even as she probes the myths for answers to how to grieve and how to find consolation. The narrator's displacement from the psychic space of her poetic tradition results in a Kristevan abjection of the narrative voice: the "abject is the violence of mourning for an 'object' that has always already been lost" (*Powers* 15). Given Judith Butler's suggestion in *Antigone's Claim* that a daughter who mourns her father represents "kinship's fatal aberration" (15), it should come as no surprise that the crisis of abjected love surfaces in the poems of *Welcoming Disaster.* That the abject daughter provides a poetic and psychic parallel to the lost object of the father is only underscored by Kristeva's warning that "the abject has only one quality of the object—that of being opposed to *I*" (*Powers* 1). Macpherson's melancholic daughter of *Welcoming Disaster* is the abjected self, estranged from the myths and symbolic systems that have served as the father's talismans. As the narrator claims in "Masters & Servants," she is "born unfree" and serves a "tranced master." Kristeva is explicit in her definition of abjection as a force of preservation, a "narcissistic crisis" that draws a great deal of energy from desperation: "The abject shatters the wall of repression and its judgments.... Abjection is a resurrection that has gone through the death (of the ego). It is an alchemy that transforms the death drive into a start of life, of new significance" (*Powers* 15). The "alchemy" of *Welcoming Disaster* acts out an abjection that is also a resurrection of the mourning daughter, and the grieving narrator remains trapped in the paradox of welcoming disaster.

Using not only gothic motifs but also a gothic structure, *Welcoming Disaster* inquires into the gender dynamics of elegiac convention and explores the possibilities for renewed, and renewable, female subjectivity. Though the text of *Welcoming Disaster* is rendered entirely, and remarkably, in sapphics, ballads, and other formal verse, the poetic narrative describes that of a traditional gothic novel, parsed here with its attendant "misleading clues, postponements of discovery, [and] excessive digressions" by Claire Kahane:

> Within an imprisoning structure, a protagonist, typically a young woman whose mother has died, is compelled to seek out the centre of a mystery, while vague and usually sexual threats to her person from some powerful male figure hover on the periphery of her consciousness.... she penetrates the obscure recesses of a vast labyrinthean space and discovers a secret room sealed off by its association with death. In this dark, secret centre of the Gothic structure, the boundaries of life and death themselves seem confused. Who died? Has there been a murder? Or merely a disappearance? (334)

This description, so accurate and yet so tongue-in-cheek, points to the standard features of a gothic plot while suggesting that the enigmas of the tradition invite subversion, and further, that the questions that fuel the gothic novel are potentially strong enough to crack the structure itself.

While a poetic sequence is not and never will be a novel—nor should it attempt to be—Macpherson's sequence shows a surprising amount of correlation with and witty subversion of Kahane's description, suggesting, as Brabon and Genz do, that gothic literature's best definition relies on its adaptive modality rather than its insistence upon the novel form. Applied to *Welcoming Disaster*, Kahane's delineation of gothic plot reveals enough commonalities to be useful, and enough divergence to be intriguing. While an individual short lyric should not need to function as a plot summary, Macpherson's poem "Absence, Havoc," offers a condensed version of the narrative arc of *Welcoming Disaster*, and identifies some of its major thematic and philosophical concerns: the speaker's acknowledgement of loss, the havoc wreaked by abandonment, the longings and frustrations fulminating from that loss, and the confusion about the boundaries between absence and presence. These concerns are as elegiac as they are gothic; they are as much about grief and mourning as they are concerned with fear and confusion.

> Absence, havoc—well, I missed you –
> Near and dear turned far and strange,
> Dayshine came disguised as midnight:
> One thing altered made all change.
>
> Fallen? stolen? trapped? entangled?
> To a lower world betrayed?
> Endless error held your footsteps,
> On your brow a deepening shade.
>
> Long I sought you, late I found you,
> Straying on the farther shore:
> You indeed? A swaying phantom
> Fades, that flickered on before.
> Lost, no rescue: only dreams our
> Wandered, wandered loves restore.

The poem's form and its appraising tone also deserve some attention: the thoughtful "well" before "I missed you," the arch coolness of "You indeed?" This careful poetic diction contrasts with Macpherson's language of gothic excess, culminating in the speaker's desperation to "restore" her "wandered, wandered love." Formally, "Absence, Havoc" appropriates a sonnet's rhyme scheme and subject matter, but its trochaic tetrameter pushes against the conversational tone of iambic pentameter, and pits melancholic desperation against controlled prosody. This precision of form consistently frames the heat of obsession in *Welcoming Disaster*, as Macpherson produces a text that puzzles out the ways in which the contemplation of elegiac absence can quickly spin out into gothic havoc. The illustration that accompanies "Absence, Havoc" is a reproduction of a large figure caught in the centre of a Cretan maze, reinforcing Kahane's theory of the gothic heroine's search through labyrinthean paternal space for the maternal uncanny at its centre, the female (corporeal) secret hidden deep within the male (intellectual) structure (67). At her most audacious, Macpherson implies that absence and havoc are contiguous entities, inseparable from rituals of mourning and from a poetics of melancholia that seeks to articulate female subjectivity forged from significant loss.

Macpherson suggests the dominating influence of a male muse with her wandering magus figure, not the least because his "absence" is equated with nothing less than "havoc," the wanton destruction of worlds. The destruction of a world, and of a female mind situated in such a world, is the gothic subject matter of *Welcoming Disaster*. Kahane contests that the terrifying gap at the heart of gothic enclosure, the "secret room," as the space of the maternal, specifically the body of the absent and uncanny mother (336); Susan Greenfield similarly asserts that the traditional gothic plot as written by women explores "missing mothers and their suffering daughters" (13). Atwood claims that the descent into the underworld—known as a *nekusis*—in *Welcoming Disaster* is an attempt to search for "lost mothers" ("Jay" 411). However, evidence of mothers, lost or otherwise, are scarce in *Welcoming Disaster*, particularly as the beloved father, a recalcitrant, mercurial figure, dominates the narrator's attention with his refusal to respond to her grief. But the text's gothic frame supports a "secret room" at the centre of the text's "imprisoning structure" that plays the maternal uncanny role and reveals the father's evil abstractions to the mourning daughter.

Welcoming Disaster operates within a double frame, pursuing the paternal elegiac tradition while drawing on the maternal gothic, yielding what Valdine Clemens calls an "antidote" for the "excessively cerebral consciousness" that is "the ache of modernism" (2), while also debating the possibilities of defining female subjectivity in mid-century Canadian poetry. The mother of *Welcoming Disaster* is so absent as to be nearly unimaginable; in a text in which the dead are easily imagined and even desired, the unimaginable is not that which has vanished from corporeal being but that which has not yet been conceived intellectually or physically. Just as the beloved father stands in for patriarchy in *Welcoming Disaster*, so the absent mother stands in for proto-feminist subjectivity that remains desirable but indefinable, unpronounceable, and/or unspeakable at that time in Canadian literary history. Kahane emphasizes that the gothic plot does not only emphasize the search for the mother, but also outlines the beleaguered daughter's attempts to delineate herself from the mother: "a dual unity preceding the sense of separate self" (336). Such a project is not easy, in the psyche or in the text, and may result in plot convolutions and possible gender confusion as "female characters continually attempt to escape by repudiating their womanhood" (347). The good daughter can attempt to harrow hell in the tradition of a *nekusis*; she can read the right books; she can even try on the magus's robes, but she can never be the good son. Nor should she be.

Macpherson's strategy in *Welcoming Disaster* is twofold. First, she adopts gothic conventions in order to use them as textual apotropaics, ritual "deceptions intended to trick the spirit world," like piercing the heart of a vampire with a wooden stake (Barber 46). Then, she adapts the elegiac tradition in order to articulate a gap at the heart of female subjectivity. Macpherson draws on an even older tradition in order to adapt her poetic daughter persona to the role of the inquisitive gothic heroine; she writes her within the tradition of male melancholics, but gives melancholia a female twist. Macpherson shows her daughterly narrator as deeply inquisitive about the magus's disappearance, his alchemical abilities, his "book of laws" ("Lost Books & Dead Letters"), and about her own melancholic powers to haunt even as she is haunted. In pursuit of the "near and dear turned far and strange" ("Absence, Havoc"), Macpherson's narrator proposes an intricate poetic and philosophical puzzle, beginning with a question that dominates the gothic tradition: "Is love haunted?" ("Substitutions"). There is an implied question here, or perhaps two: Who haunts love? And how?

The attempt to establish a daughter's hauntology, both as a mourning practice for the lost father and as a gothic strategy of self-definition, can be read in Macpherson's section titles and in the narrative arc described by the poems. In Section I, "Invocations," the daughter-narrator appeals to the muse of memory, as well as the apostrophe of the magus's lost book (like Prospero's drowned volumes) to restore her creative powers, but to no avail. This failure to invoke inspiration is at least partially ironic, but the failure here is a failure of affect; love and creativity are intertwined here, and the lack of love drives the poetic narrator to the desperate state in which she resorts to "conjuring the dead." Section II, "The Way Down," describes her frustrated wish to embark on a *nekusis*, a journey to the Underworld. In her article, "Toward a Feminist Hermeneutics: Jay Macpherson's *Welcoming Disaster*," Lorraine Weir proposes that Macpherson models this *nekusis* on the Sumerian myth of Inanna. But for much of *Welcoming Disaster*, access to the Underworld is denied to the narrator, so that she is forced instead to haunt ghosts for news of her lost beloved. Section III, "The Dark Side," shows the narrator exploring the possibility of tricking evil by trying on the facade of death. The final two sections, "Recognitions" and "Shadows Flee," document her elegiac revelation, the recognition of a maternal secret, and the narrator's emergence into a world that has been altered by the force of her own desire.

Donna Heiland contests that patriarchy itself is a gothic structure built upon the "suppression—and sometimes the outright sacrifice—of women" (11). Charting the distance between absence and havoc, as well as between love and haunting, Macpherson inquires into some of the larger questions facing Canadian female modernists in the mid- to late twentieth century. If modernism itself constitutes a gothic structure of masculine literary privilege, the feminist project of writing back allusively to master narratives of Western literature, and sometimes to its "masterly" practitioners, may have resulted in a reconstruction of gothic secrecy in these subversive texts. Certainly one of the best kept secrets about Macpherson's work is that it is subversive rather than worshipful. In this text, the magus figure is less a flesh-and-blood father than the phantom of literary tradition: an alchemist unwilling or unable to apprentice his daughter to his transformative art.

The magus figure in *Welcoming Disaster* is the anagogic man with the key to the mysteries of religion and the secret of transcendence. But as Linda Bayer-Berenbaum points out, transcendence in the gothic tradition is almost universally related to evil; not only a defiance of Christian law, it also defies the laws of nature, and flouts humankind's "inescapable connection to the world around us," the "immanence" that makes us human and allows for the possibility of the sublime (21). Such immanence is not exclusively paternal by definition, but in *Welcoming Disaster*, the alchemist does not transmute himself so much as he entrances himself to a self-serving evil that grows rich on "treasures coined from pain, from anger, / Spoiled love" ("Masters & Servants"). Reading the magus-father as entranced by evil suggests another way to read the rebellious daughter in Macpherson's work. Atwood has commented on the "ruthless" tone of *Welcoming Disaster*, and her recommendation of Macpherson's "rigorous and sometimes bloody-minded self-analysis" connotes Macpherson's hijacking of the gothic tradition to reconfigure it as a feminist apotropaic, a way to ward off the "evils" wrought by a rigid male tradition and its modernist succession. In "Poets & Muses," Macpherson writes of the need to "reverse the story," to be "Muse-redeemed, return and live," and immediately invokes a Biblical patriarch, Solomon, only to judge his wisdom to be impotent compared with the power of the Muse. In "Lost Books & Dead Letters," the narrator laments the loss of ancient books of knowledge, but notes with chagrin that the "book of laws" is very much in evidence and in use. Chillingly, she claims that the book of laws is older than God Himself, and that the book foretells both her birth and her incipient sorrow. Her only hope is to write her way out of the book of laws and into "the book of life" held by the Muse: "Let me not be put to silence, / From thy page blot me not out."

The book of laws, with its double echo of the Lacanian Law of Language and Law of the Father is Macpherson's sign for desire and violence, a Romance symbol rendered gothic by its power and its prescience. Donna Heiland notes that "transgressive acts at the heart of gothic fiction generally focus on corruption in, or resistance to, patriarchal structures" (5), and Fred Botting identifies father–daughter kinship as a dynamic of gothic excess that evokes incestuous overtones even as it refutes them: "Familial and sexual relations, power and suppression, turn on the roles and figures of father and daughter" (20). In *Welcoming Disaster*, the daughter-narrator's haunting of the paternal figure asserts a female melancholia that holds the key to an emerging female subjectivity in mid-century Canadian modernism. In the nineteenth century, female writers combined the gothic tradition with the elegiac with spectacular results, hinging their narratives on the desperate resolve of the mourner to regain the lost beloved at any cost: think of Christina Rossetti's "Goblin Market," as well as Emily Bronte's *Wuthering Heights* and Mary Shelley's *Frankenstein*. Elegiac convention predicates the desire of the living mourner to risk her humanity for a last sight of the beloved, the mourner's assertion of unending grief, the obdurate refusal of consolation; these conventions find fertile ground in the gothic tradition of portraying cultural anxiety as corporeal and eschatological excess.

Without a doubt, love is haunted in *Welcoming Disaster*, principally by the alchemist-father's "book of laws" ("Lost Books & Dead Letters"). The narrator worships these laws as immutable, and she cannot anticipate how profoundly the father's law will betray her. When the father departs to his unknown destination, the power of his law deflates. The daughter's invocations fail; the "old spells" of his mythology are unworkable, "hollow." She tries to manipulate the myths into performing for her, but in frustration, she determines that it is better to haunt than be haunted. In "Lady Haunts Ghosts," she takes on mourning as a job of work. Because her "phantoms" are "too weak" to haunt her, she must "take the whip and urge them" into her world. Once in their presence, the lady of the poem ravishes the ghosts for sustenance: "Back in the light I rummage them, ransack them, / Breathe them and suck them, wolfish, famished, rake for / News of my lost ones, gone where gods of darkness / Keep, unforgiving." This is bloody-minded work indeed. The narrator calls herself, variously, a "ghoul," a "goblin" and a "familiar," and a "lost soul" who is run by "greed, pride and envy." She labours at "conjuring the dead," but finds even the living are trapped in "magic circles" and "dead-engrossed, they make no sign." The lost magus figure for whom she mourns is at once an "enchanter" and a "man of stone, of ivory, of glass" who will not (or cannot) yield to the narrator's "conjuring," but instead remains "tranced" by his lost power. The interplay of these two figures produces what the poet calls "complicities." The narrator indicts her words as inadequate to the task: "painful, cautious offerings," and accuses herself of being a "cherished bosom-serpent," recalling the gleeful viciousness of Jenny Lear from *The Boatman* along with Lear's injunction that "sharper than a serpent's tooth it is / to have a thankless child" (*King Lear* 1.4.295–96).

Macpherson carries this tone of vicious neediness into section III, "The Dark Side," in which the daughter enters a "castle with the mystic name" and descends a "stairway to the underground / Where the lost ones shall be found." There she sits a lonely mourner's vigil resolving to "nevermore behold the day," the better to "keep a lasting watch above / My undying monster love." Even as Macpherson invokes horror-movie phantoms throughout this "Karloff Poem," "monster love" seems to describe the tenor of the daughter's affections as much as it describes the body she seeks. Judith Butler warns that such insistent and ambivalent mourning functions as "a transgression that gives kinship its prohibitive and normative dimension but that also exposes its vulnerability" (*Antigone's* 10). *Welcoming Disaster* proposes a mourner who attempts to haunt the dead through a descent into the Underworld, and finds that the journey and consolation of that myth fails her. She cannot find an entry to the underworld, and, finally, she abandons her project of haunting the dead, only to find the father at last in a place she never thought to look.

In "The Well"—a poem Atwood includes as an epigraph to her final chapter of *Negotiating with the Dead*—Macpherson shows the daughter drawing near the empty space at the heart of the gothic structure: the maternal absence, a hole in the ground, an *omphalos*. She searches for the father in "the well of truth, of images, of words," and at first she sees only her own "pupil head" backed by a sky of stars. But the maternal space of the well gives her, at last, an answer about the whereabouts of her haunting, haunted father. The water reflects the sky, and when the daughter turns to look up at the image in the sky that has been reflected in the water, she sees the image of Orion, "the winter-king." The mythic reversal is perfect, and a solution to her anxiety. In searching for the lost father on "the way down," she finds him above in the firmament. Frye designated winter as the mythos of irony and satire, and far from representing a Christian apotheosis, this discovery of the "winter-king" reveals the magus father as a "fiend" who lives according to a reversed law of physics and morality: "his up is down: his height is set / In Hell, and yet he shines." The irony of this reversal shocks the daughter. The father is not languishing in the Underworld but is instead a demon pinned to the sky for the purposes of cosmic shaming. This image of the magus is not a romantic intellectual rebel or a sardonic hero, but rather, a revelatory image of evil.

However, being bloody-minded means possessing inordinate powers of perseverance, the kind of perseverance Frye notes is needed to pass through "a dead center," like the hole in the ice where Dante and Virgil climb down Satan's body in order to climb up Mount Purgatory (Frye, *Anatomy* 239), and passing through the ironic reversal of her perspective wakes the protagonist to understanding. As the daughter turns to see the image of the father in the sky, she embarks on what Butler calls a "melancholic turn" (*Psychic* 195) towards subjectivity. By abandoning her dependence on traditional tropes of consolation, the mourner turns back to contemplate the enormity of her loss and so faces the "loss of autonomy that is mandated by linguistic and social life" (*Psychic* 195–96). The "melancholic turn" allows mourning by asserting subjectivity, an "ego [that] is other than itself; what melancholia shows is that only by absorbing the other as oneself does one become something at all" (*Psychic* 196). The mourning daughter's demand is answered at last; she turns to identify her lost beloved, and in doing so, recognizes the fruitlessness of her search and is granted the means to recognize her own subjectivity.

She is ready now for the irony that is played out in "They Return." As the elegist has "long desired," the dead return, but all is not well: "they are changed." The dead are not the loving beings of her memory, but rather appear "Armoured each in private shade, / Sullen, helmed against the light." "Absence, winter," instead of being "shed like scales" as the narrator anticipates in the first verse, invokes the very name of the dead, and they lay the blame for their uncomfortable return on the living: "Their resentment fills our arms, / Sifting from their ribs like night." Because this scenario recalls the excesses of Poe, the ending of the poem offers a sobering shock or horror. Understanding, at last, that these returned dead have had their "human places" not only devoured by death and entropy, but also "sold to darkness by our fear," the narrator has room to admit her complicity in the final two lines of the poem: "They, returning, bring us back / Absence, winter, what we gave." The absence that began the elegiac sequence has now been returned to the narrator, in a matched pair with winter's irony. The dead cannot return not only because of a spiritual injunction placed upon them to remain in the world of the dead, but also because they can never be equal to the elaborate encomia which the living heap upon them.

Comfort and hope for the future, such as Macpherson allows them, come not from a mother figure, but from the unlikely figure of a stuffed bear, specifically named as a substitute for the absent magus: "Filling in for / Him not there" ("Substitutions"). Macpherson mocks the tendency for psychoanalytic theory to infantilize female desire and female protest, and her creation of a daughter-narrator—complete with teddy bear as an ambiguous "substitute"—is a parody of elegiac substitution and its attendant psychoanalytic readings. In designating the bear as both "doll" and "god," the narrator refuses to be reduced to an embodiment of the Electra complex or a recalcitrant child. Michael Hornyansky notes that the bear's inclusion in the text is "a big risk," but as a symbol, it is "psychologically right and has been poetically anchored in myth" (337). Macpherson pulls off this audacious conceit—a combination Atwood claims, quite rightly, that "only Macpherson could get away with" ("Jay" 410)—principally because she uses the stuffed bear to mock the common psychoanalytical perception of women as id-dominated children. The narrator may be written as a child, but she is not a child in the psychoanalytical sense; she is, rather, Macpherson's wry comment on the socio-cultural infantilization of women's desire and its manifestations in grief.

The fourth section, "Recognitions," shows the daughter turning to the teddy bear as a substitute for the discredited father-hero. In the poem "Discovery," the daughter credits the bear with destroying the father in a heroic subplot: "was it you then... Laid a powder plot, and blew the / Man of glass to smithereens?" The gothic heroine has now reached the centre of her labyrinth, and we discover the other death that has remained a secret until this point in the text. Though the bear seems poised to become the gothic hero, Macpherson addresses the rest of the poem to "a feeble-minded child" who is desperate for revenge. The child in question is at once the girl-child who owns the bear, and another separate child, a miscarried or aborted baby whom the speaker calls "poor changeling, never born... the first of me to die." The accompanying emblem, showing a serene adult figure in a coffin with a child's body in the crook of her arm, reinforces the image of the lost child, as do the final six lines of "Discovery":

> Lie there, fertilize my garden:
> See what earth will make of you.
>
> Though, I never meant to lose you,
> Little thorn of poison tree:
> Nights I lay me down beside you,
> When I wake, am still with thee.

The "secret room" of the text shows both a vengeful child and a loving mother; the girl-child has both connected with her mother and separated enough to become a mother herself, although the pain of the loss of the baby is acute in these poems. "What Falada Said" proposes the mother and the lost child as "a constellation / Turning: maimed child, barbed mother—torn, rent open / Womb, bladed baby." In a gesture of protection, the hero-bear makes the journey that the daughter cannot; as her "surrogate" in the land of the dead, he becomes a symbol of pastoral renewal, buried beneath "the world-tree" where the daughter discovers herself "reposing in his shade" and can see the way "punished giants, monsters dim— / All the heaven turns on him." Is Tadwit the bear himself a "punished giant" or a "monster dim"? The narrator's willing sacrifice of the bear, after all her pains to assert his substitutive value, is surprising, but by becoming the still point in the earth around which the stars turn (in contrast to the Orion-father who is impotently pinned to the sky), the bear fulfills his symbolic destiny as the daughter's substitutive "messenger" to the dark side.

Macpherson's daughter figure draws energy from an inquiry into her own state of abandonment. The inquiry itself is ghoulish in its intensity; the persona is determined to endure the rigours of mourning by haunting the lost beloved. The ghoul-mourner fears the loss of words; she begs to be included in the orthodoxy of knowledge as the Father has defined it; and ultimately, she learns to live with both absence and havoc. She may continue to crave the unveiling of a revelatory consciousness of a mid-century proto-feminism, for she reaches an uncomfortable comprehension that the myths she loves do not, and cannot, represent her effectively. Whether or not this makes Macpherson the kind of poet Frye calls "a poltergeist in the city of God" (*Anatomy* 128), an artist who haunts religion for answers rather than for inspiration, remains to be discussed.

In the end, the daughter's quest brings her to the "conjecture" she imagines at the end of the text's fifth section, "Shadows Flee." In "Playing," Macpherson poses an intriguing series of questions. She wonders about life for the daughter beyond the tenets of the father's rule, querying about the lack of success at what she calls "Square One" and speculating about the operation and rules of "Square Two," which she believes "never got marked on this / Board." The narrator is clear that "life on Square One" was an exercise in paradox and frustration: its "surface not solid, though / Hard as a stone." In spite of her industry, she gets nowhere: "I venture runs, but I'm / Always bounced back." She considers what might be involved in the move to the next "square" in the game:

Hardly a player,
Nothing to win,
Clocking how long I might
Take to clue in.
Now we've exhausted the
Charms of Square One,
Maybe you know a
Game that's some fun?

Despite her progress, the daughter's despair goes unabated, and she must fall back upon the struggle for her own subjectivity as a consoling performance, a "game" that might be "some fun." Her mourning ushers in the meta-performance of the text, the poet's turn from the rhetoric of daughterhood to the approach of subjectivity, "Square Two."

In the text's final poem, "Notes and Acknowledgements," Macpherson thanks her mentor, in perfect rhyme: "Best of readers, Northrop Frye, / Cast a sure arranging eye." The temptation to cast an ironic eye over this couplet is considerable, but it helps to situate *Welcoming Disaster* as a revelatory or apocalyptic text in the Frygian sense. Although Weir notes that the text operates as "an elaborate strategy of camouflage which strives paradoxically for both concealment and revelation" ("Toward" 61), *Welcoming Disaster* strives toward the possibility of a feminist future in very careful terms. Macpherson operates within Jardine's "profound paradox" of a woman writer who searches for a reconfigured subjectivity: "she proceeds from a *belief* in a world from which—even the philosophers admit—*Truth* has disappeared" (31; emphasis in original). Jardine warns that the tension of such paradox may result in "at least three possible scenarios: a renewed silence, a form of religion (from mysticism to political orthodoxy), or a continued attention—historical, ideological, and affective—to the place from which we speak" (31–32). *Welcoming Disaster* charts the narrating persona's struggle with all three of these circumstances: the ghoul-mourner fears the loss of words; she begs to be included in the orthodoxy of knowledge; and ultimately, she learns to live with the absence of a "father" to guide her to firm epistemological ground.

Sylvia Söderlind, in "Ghost-National Arguments," suggests that within Canada, mourning is less of a national impulse than a regional one, of special concern to "lost nations-within-the-nation: Quebec, Acadia, Newfoundland, and the First Nations, all of whom rattle their chains on occasion" (676). Can we hear women writers as a nation-within-the-nation in *Welcoming Disaster*? The narrator's displacement from the psychic space of poetic tradition makes her an outsider in her own text: "blot me not out" indeed. The difference between nurturing horror and welcoming disaster is a fine distinction, but such a distinction is vital to the carvinalesque project of defining female subjectivity. Each desire contains the seeds of disaster: the beloved paternal is monstrous; the barely imagined maternal is painful; and the knowledge gained by the thwarted journey is not transcendent, but rather, resoundingly corporeal. The daughterly subject of *Welcoming Disaster* has been set in motion by her recognition that it is not the stuffed bear, but rather the spirit of havoc that becomes her most reliable "guide to dark places—finder of lost direction— / Tearspring-diviner, and where the wordhoard lay" ("The End"). The elegiac wordhoard is the treasure to which the daughter at last lays claim, even as the text ends.

Part Three

Differently Conceived Nations

The Mourner's Journey

5

"Do What You Are Good At"

Margaret Atwood's Authorizing Elegies

> This year we are making
> nothing but elegies.
> Do what you are good at,
> our parents always told us,
> make what you know.
> — Margaret Atwood, "Four Small Elegies"

> to ignore the nation is to fall into the trap of trying to escape from the past by silently reinscribing its forms. Beyond the nation lies more nations, differently conceived.
> — Jonathan Kertzer, *Worrying the Nation*

Margaret Atwood's contributions to paternal elegiacs cannot be viewed as discrete from her contributions to Canadian literature and criticism, although it would be an error of equal magnitude to consider her paternal elegies from 1995's *Morning in the Burned House* as nothing more than continuations of elegiac narratives and tropes that she has been exploring as early as her first book, *The Circle Game* (1964). This position, between the need to consider Atwood's work as part of an emerging tradition of female-written paternal elegies in Canada and the need to acknowledge that it is impossible to treat Atwood as though she is not an industry unto herself, is not completely contradictory, but neither is it comfortable. Atwood is unique in this study, as she is in Canadian literature and criticism, for the weight that her astonishing output and considerable career history brings to the attempt to situate any single book of hers into a tradition that emphasizes anything other than the Canadian nationalism or her own oeuvre. This is not to say that Atwood's work has not ventured far and wide in its examination of genre, subgenre, tradition, and innovation. The problem is that from the vantage point of the first decade of the twenty-first century, any examination of Atwood's work comes with its own set of problems and possibilities. The quotation from Jonathan Kertzer that opens this chapter pinpoints some of the anxieties inherent in reading Atwood's *Morning in the Burned House*. If we "ignore the nation" (i.e., efface Atwood's position in the Canadian canon), we are merely reinscribing "the nation" in another form: in this case, a literary nationhood of the elegiac mode. No matter what the difficulties are in thinking of elegy as a national genre—and the pitfalls are many—it is important to remember that situating the elegy as somehow beyond the nation would only invite the temptations to create "other nations, differently conceived." Put another way, like Virginia Woolf's "undiscovered countries" of illness in her 1926 essay "On Being Ill" or W. B. Yeats's "terrible beauty" of Irish martyrdom in "Easter 1916," an affective "nationality" born of mourning is certainly possible, but how does such a citizenship position itself in relationship to what we usually understand as national literature? How do conceptions of nation and region influence our readings of Canadian elegiac work? It is here that I would like to begin by considering Atwood as an exemplar of our national literature and as a catalyst for introducing the problems of reading cultural nationalism alongside with the paternal elegy.

To begin to consider Atwood as a national elegist would mean being confronted with a blizzard of examples of elegiac tone or narrative in her corpus, of which *Morning in the Burned House* is only one of many examples. Janice Fiamengo points out in one of the first articles published on *Morning in the Burned House* that the text takes up "Atwood's complex negotiations with elegiac convention, most particularly in her tentative and ambivalent affirmation of memory" (151), and suggests that Atwood's seemingly "anti-elegiac voice" is actually "anti-sentimental" (149–50). Fiamengo's contrast of the rigours of elegy against sentiment is a point that deserves discussion, and I offer as a test case Atwood's "Four Small Elegies" from 1978's *Two-Headed Poems*. The poem crystallizes a dynamic that Atwood has often addressed in her elegiac work: the need to address and mourn a nation's historical violence—often the violence that attends colonization—that exists alongside of and complicates the need to create a literature that "makes what we know." Making difficult national and personal histories recognizable and public is aligned with a kind of elegiac counter-public, though Atwood's role in "making what we know"—in the Foucaultian sense—suggests that her canonicity overrides what may have been a subversive intent to challenge neat historical categories of victor and rebel. Along with this urgency, the spoken assertion of the elegiac impulse—"This year we are making / nothing but elegies"—and the parental injunction to "do what you are good at" and "make what you know" are packed with unspoken implications about the rhetoric of mourning, particularly how such rhetoric is used in the project of nation-building.

"Four Small Elegies" begins as an elegy for the women and children killed by British soldiers and Scottish volunteers who raided villages in Quebec in 1838 with the intent of quelling a citizen's rebellion. However, the presence of Scottish volunteers in the raid quickly complicates the poem with the history of Scottish immigrants to Ontario. Atwood's post-poem note identifies the Scots as those who came to Canada as a result of the Highland Clearances, when they were accused of being Jacobite rebels against the crown after the British victory at the Battle of Culloden in 1745, and "cleared" from the Highlands of Scotland by British troops. "Those whose houses were burned / burned houses. What else ever happens / once you start?" asks Atwood in "Four Small Elegies," and the need to "do what you are good at," as a reference to the raid and the act of elegizing, is deeply ironized by this question. What else could ever happen in a cycle of violence and memorialization? Raids and elegies can be nation-builders, Atwood implies; both teach us to "make what we know." These "burned houses," as artifacts of affect and of history, refuse the nation even as they build the nation from the ashes.

Refusing to depoliticize mourning or to create a simple system of oppressors and victims, Atwood points out that the adoption of vengeful violence is a toxic legacy that has—in many cases—"made the nation." If we "make what we know," are we making a nation from elegy? Are we making heroes of violent melancholics? Are we making history as we know it, or as we would like to construe it? In a later stanza, Atwood writes, "The elegies are new and yellow, / they are not made, they grow," and for the remainder of the poem, elegies spring forth at a geometric rate in swamps and in parking lots, as profuse and uncontrollable as wildflowers. Atwood's metaphor for the elegy as something that is at once a made object (or artifact) and a grown object aligns with her assertion that "elegy is a natural Canadian form" ("Dire Things" 29). What might make a subgenre like the elegy natural to a particular nation remains to be seen, but perhaps more importantly to elegiac studies in Canada, we must acknowledge the elegy as a national framing device that a writer like Atwood makes because she "knows it" and grows because she is "good at it."

The Arc of Mourning: Genre and Authorization

The position I take up in regarding Atwood as an elegist, and especially as a paternal elegist, has been influenced by her image as a national cultural icon: someone who is as famous for her critical commentary on Canada's position in the world as she is for her fiction and poetry. Atwood has been working with the elegiac mode for perhaps all of her writing career; Sara Jamieson notes elegies in *The Journals of Susanna Moodie* (n63) and Coral Ann Howells suggests that an elegiac impulse informs the narrative structure of both *Surfacing* and *Cat's Eye* (70). One might add Atwood's Booker Prize–winning *The Blind Assassin*, and even her dystopic fictions *Oryx and Crake* and *The Year of the Flood* to the list of novels that draw inspiration from an elegiac plot structure, for these novels, too, are informed by a narrative of profound loss. In *Negotiating with the Dead*, Atwood states clearly her belief that "*all* writing of the narrative kind, and perhaps all writing, is motivated, deep down by a fear of and a fascination with mortality—by a desire to make the risky trip to the Underworld, and to bring something or someone back from the dead" (156; emphasis in original). However, while these literary desires do reflect an elegiac tone, they do not necessarily account for the work that the elegy performs in its poetic form, particularly the convention of lamentation leading to inquiry, and inquiry to discovery. For Atwood, as for many female elegists, some negotiations are with the dead, and some are with the elegiac tradition itself. Still other negotiations, for Atwood and for readers of her work, are with the force of Atwood's career and reception, for it is impossible to read Atwood's exploration of paternal elegy without considering the role that Atwood's canonical status and international reputation plays in the reception of and scholarship about *Morning in the Burned House*. Atwood has proven, and continues to be, a polarizing figure in Canadian literature and criticism: the writer whom everyone knows and about whom everyone has an opinion. While *Morning in the Burned House* is not by any means Atwood's most widely read work, it is to date the most widely read and widely reviewed work of the female paternal elegy in Canadian literature, and its inclusion in this book is necessary not only because of its subject matter and approach, but also for the cultural position the book occupies as a text that authorizes the practice of the female elegy in Canada.

When *Morning in the Burned House* was published in 1995, it drew attention because of its genre; it was Atwood's first book of poetry since 1984's *Interlunar*. These eleven years between poetry books seems particularly notable given that Atwood produced a dizzying five poetry collections, as well as two novels (*The Edible Woman* and *Surfacing*) and a book of criticism (*Survival*), in the ten years between 1964 and 1974. Of course, this is not to accuse Atwood of laziness. During this eleven-year hiatus from poetry, Atwood wrote and published *The Handmaid's Tale*, *Cat's Eye*, and *The Robber Bride*, three books that enhanced Atwood's reputation as a Canadian novelist with enormous international appeal and the sales to match. Though Atwood has often said that she wrote more poetry early in her career because the shorter genre fit more easily with her day job of university instruction, this practical reason does not efface the fact that Atwood's poetry collections—and her elegiac poems in particular—perform different cultural work than that performed by her novels. The eleven years between *Interlunar* and *Morning in the Burned House*, and the subsequent twelve years between *Morning in the Burned House* and 2007's *The Door* (another collection that includes a number of elegies) was time taken by Atwood to reconsider the ways that elegy writes, and refuses to write, the nation. For who is the subject of the sentence "this year we are making / nothing but elegies"? In *Morning in the Burned House*—a book that seems to be made up of "nothing but elegies," nearly twenty years after "Four Small Elegies" appeared in *Two-Headed Poems*—the national "we" gives way to a more reciprocal "I/you." While certainly the "we" is overtly political and the "I/you" is provisionally personal, the feminist politics of Atwood's work align with the possibilities of a feminist rhetoric of mourning to suggest not only that the personal is the political, but also that the "I" as contentious and as various a subject position as a violently collective "we."

In her 2007 book *Literary Celebrity in Canada*, Lorraine York maintains that the ongoing negotiation in which Atwood is most thoroughly engaged is between her public and private selves. The "uneasy eminence" (116) that York chooses as the defining quality of Atwood's celebrity status is an important factor in considering the position that *Morning in the Burned House* occupies in both Canadian literature and in women's developing elegiac tradition. And who better than Atwood—with her intelligence, wit, courage, decades-long career, and considerable powers of literary authority that "Canadianize" almost any project she produces—to raise the attendant issues of affect, inquiry, and duty in women's elegies for fathers? Atwood's eminence may be "uneasy" partially because of the ways that readers and commentators of all kinds impose expectations of affect and assumptions of autobiography onto her work, and, if so, *Morning in the Burned House* is especially laden with such expectations.

For example, Kathryn van Spanckeren asserts that the poems in *Morning in the Burned House* strip away Atwood's ubiquitous irony, and that she employs "newly sensitive language" to arrive at the conclusion that "nature can console if we will become emotionally open" (117–18). Citing a heretofore unexpressed, or inexpressible, "vulnerability" (111) on

Atwood's part, van Spanckeren claims that *Morning in the Burned House* "breaks new ground in its use of autobiographical material" and "makes a claim to emotional authenticity, containing as it does a sequence of elegiac poems on the death of Atwood's father" (106). However, if we consider *Morning in the Burned House* with Shaw's paradox of veridiction, we will recall that the truth-telling necessary to the elegy's genesis is not necessary to its larger literary life; the poet must balance the often varying emotional truth against the demands of elegiac convention to produce the culturally loaded subgenre of the elegy. Adding national and/or feminist politics, the power differential of gender and genre, and debates about language and rhetoric to the mix in a feminist paternal elegy, and an elegist (and a reader) can be forgiven for not being able (or willing) to pinpoint where the "truth" begins and ends in an elegy.

Yet an unalloyed belief in the cathartic truth-telling power of elegy has proven to be a popular strategy with this book, and one of the results has been that *Morning in the Burned House* has been received as Atwood's poetic griefwork, unmediated by her characteristic irony, shorn of her feminist, national, and environmental politics: in other words, in these pages, we will find Atwood vulnerable at last. But, as I have argued throughout this volume, such a belief effaces the complexity of the poems. Critical reluctance to delve further into Atwood's ironic elegiacs has been as curious as it is significant. Reducing the elegies to intimate familial confessions without considering their social and political implications means missing the work that *Morning in the Burned House* sets out to do as an elegiac sequence, and the popularity and relative power of such assumptions are an important reminder that even writers of Atwood's renown and stature are frequently misconstrued.

Just as it is impossible to read *Morning in the Burned House* without considering Atwood's national literary reputation, it is also impossible to read any work of Atwood's without thinking about her links—both chosen and imposed—to cultural nationalism and the construction (and continuous reconstruction) of the Canadian literary canon. In his chapter "Margaret Atwood, Inc.," in 1991's *The Postcolonial Exotic*, Graham Huggan (by way of Pierre Bourdieu) discusses the process by which texts and authors become "consecrated" symbolic capital through scholarly and general reading: "Such attempts to make canonical works constitutive, however ironically, of national cultural identities is always likely to lead to oversimplified interpretations that mythologise the history on which they presume to draw and comment" (220). He goes on to warn that however obvious such literary canonization may seem, the results are frequently ideologically potent. Atwood, for Huggan, has become the exemplar of a national literary representative whose public image has been wrought through valuing and revaluing her symbolic capital: "Atwood's national image as a no-holds-barred cultural commentator has been augmented by her international image as a translator and interpreter of Canadian culture. These images, when taken together, have fuelled the common (mis) perception of Atwood as a 'representative,' or even 'quintessential,' Canadian and Canadian writer" (214).

But as potent as that public image of Atwood as "representative Canadian writer" may be, Atwood's status as cultural icon is neither unitary nor unambiguous. Lorraine York suggests that Atwood's fame is very much a double-edged sword: a force that Atwood is savvy enough to manipulate, but which also has a decided effect on her public behaviour and statements about her work. York notes that Atwood's formidable education and work with literary tradition, as well as her considerable intelligence, makes her "well able to diagnose her own condition as a public commodity" (78). York's medical metaphor is an apt choice to describe the cultural pathology of celebrity. Atwood may be considered both doctor who diagnoses the national consciousness and patient who manifests the symptoms of the national consciousness as an entity that digests literary sustenance. This "Canadian literary power," to use Frank Davey's phrase from the book of the same name, is practised by Atwood even as it is practised upon her, and this makes Atwood, in many ways, unlike the other poets included in this study. Even the most indisputably canonical poet in this book—Dorothy Livesay—has, despite her awards, her work in multiple genres, and her sixty-year career, neither Atwood's international reputation nor her cultural cachet.

This cultural cachet, or Atwood's symbolic capital, is powerful enough that any reader might have an impulse to read *Morning in the Burned House* primarily as an Atwoodian text and only secondarily as a series of paternal elegies. Certainly Atwood is skilled in the management of literary genre; her foray into elegy could be compared to her accomplished successes with other genres such as historiographic metafiction (*Alias Grace*), dystopic speculative fiction (*The Handmaid's Tale*), or adapted fairy tale (*The Robber Bride*). However, the compulsion to situate *Morning in the Burned House* in a niche in Atwood's oeuvre can be reductive even when the analysis is academically rigorous. Critical scholarship about *Mourning in the Burned House* has reflected this with the emergence of two branches: the Atwoodian and the elegiac. Of the Atwoodian readings, Coral Ann Howells discusses Atwood's use of doubling and reversals, Kathryn van Spanckeren discusses poetic tricksterism and the environment, and Charlotte Beyer examines Atwood's dramatic monologues of feminist re-vision as they apply to spiritual concerns. Janice Fiamengo, Sara Jamieson, and Priscila Uppal make reading the text as a series of elegies their explicit aims, and, in doing so, all of these critics suggest that the elegiac tone of the collection is neither simple nor merely affective. Fiamengo, the most experienced Canadian literature scholar and Atwood specialist, concentrates on mourning as "an unfinished process repeated across texts" in Atwood's work, and focuses especially upon consolation as ambivalent in *Morning in the Burned House* (145, 160). Uppal situates her study of the text in a tradition of family elegies in Canadian literature, even choosing the name "The Burned House" as a chapter title in *What Are What We Mourn*. Jamieson reads the text through consideration of a gendered elegiac tradition and notes Atwood's frustration with "a fairy-tale model of filial devotion impossible to emulate in real life" (42). In spirit, Fiamengo, Uppal, and Jamieson offer readings that are closest to the heart of this study, and rather than reproducing their good work, I will concentrate on further possibilities for reading *Morning in the Burned House* as a text that marks a particular paternal elegiac watermark in feminist Canadian poetry, and as a text that offers an intriguing exchange of authorial prominence and autobiographical assumption.

Mourning and Uneasiness: Atwood's Oeuvre

The first section of *The Daughter's Way* deals with the various ways in which Dorothy Livesay, P. K. Page, and Jay Macpherson worked within and against the tenets of modernism in their paternal elegies. While the 1970s and 1980s saw resurgence in maternal-inflected texts, by the 1990s, women writers in Canada began to address paternal influence on feminism, taking up the inquiries of the modernist writers and applying it to late-twentieth-century feminist ideas and critical theory. The cultural moment delineated by so many female poets writing their fathers' deaths in the late nineties may not have consciously arisen from modernist work, but the sense of permission to broach the topic is owed to these precursor poets nonetheless. The watershed year for women's paternal elegies in Canadian literature was 1995, a year that saw the publication of Anne Carson's *Plainwater*, which included the long prose poem "The Anthropology of Water," Lola Lemire Tostevin's *Cartouches* (both discussed in later chapters of this book), and Atwood's *Morning in the Burned House*. Add to this the fact that Lorna Crozier's *Inventing the Hawk* appeared a little earlier in 1992 and Kristjana Gunnars's *Zero Hour* appeared in 1991, and the idea that the early 1990s saw something of an elegiac critical mass among female poets in Canada does not seem far-fetched. Atwood's presence in that critical mass is significant not because she is doing what others are not, but, rather, because her work gets the attention that other texts do not, and that critical attention goes a long way to authorizing the paternal elegiac as a literary question for Canadian female poets.

Along with considering *Morning in the Burned House* as a hinge text in the history and criticism of Canadian feminist elegies, Atwood's position as the literary daughter of Jay Macpherson, as a former student of Northrop Frye, and as an ardent reader of Margaret Avison and P. K. Page places Atwood in a position to speak from both sides of the interregnum periods of the 1980s. Atwood's interview with Mark Abley in 1995 concerning *Morning in the Burned House* reveals the poet discussing her position relative to the modernist tradition, outside of the confessional mode, and firmly established in an inquiry into elegy's negotiations with veridiction. In response to Abley's questions about the difference between "writing about a painting or a movie star" and "writing about one's family," Atwood stresses that although elegies begin with autobiographical detail, they quickly lose that version of the "truth" to emphasize concerns with genre, myth, and reader response: "when you write a poem, and the reader reads it, the reader is not reading about you. The reader is reading about himself" ("Dire Things" 3).

She goes on to discuss the expectation of fidelity to biography as "a kind of voyeurism" that exists outside of the poem as an entity: "For the poem as poem, or for the novel as novel, it's immaterial. The thing either convinces on its own merits or it doesn't" (3). Abley responds that while he understands what Atwood has said, he still believes that Atwood is being "somewhat evasive" about the basis for the poems (3). Atwood's reply is acerbic, cutting through the layers of polite debate and switching gears to remind Abley of his role as an interviewer: "So it's really a biographical question. Do you want to wring some feeling from me? Do you want to get me to express some emotion? Is that what you have in mind?" (3). If Abley is indeed, as Atwood intuits, digging for a show of emotion from Atwood, he is hardly alone in doing so. The project of getting Atwood to admit to feelings, to show vulnerability, and to discuss affect for affect's sake in her writing has been ongoing since the start of her career and could be said to amount to a national obsession. Early interviewers who came to interview the new young female poet, perhaps expecting hippie-like fuzzy thinking and a desire to "express emotion" got more than they bargained for not only because these attributes are not prominent in Atwood's personality, but also because she could often tell from their attitude that they had not read her work. In fact, Abley's prefatory comments to the interview remind readers that Atwood has "a justified reputation for eating unwary interviewers for breakfast" (1).

In the interview with Abley, Atwood repeats the same formalist outlook that she has always touted: questions and terms of discussion are to be found in the text, not in the author's life. While the poems in section IV of *Morning in the Burned House* spring from the occasion of Carl Atwood's death, their appearance is not solely the result of affect. In Atwood's words, she is "writing about dire things because they exist" (29), and not pursuing a personal project of morbid fascination or pure affect. "Elegy is a celebration," she reminds Abley (29). This interview offers an exchange that recurs many times in media interviews with Atwood and, to a lesser degree, in her own public talks and critical essays: a moment of clarification when Atwood, pushed either by the interviewer or by the frame of the occasion, resists the ways that reductive readings diminish complex ideas, and challenges the categorization, the misapplied term, and/or the tendency of the reading public, including scholars, to recast her work as simple.

Atwood's statement that "elegy is a natural Canadian form" was made in the interview to redirect the discussion and to remind the reading public that Canada exists in a world of literary traditions from which it can never be fully separated and to which it will never be fully committed. Canada's most famous writer offers up a typical soundbite in her own defence: a tendency both York and Huggan note in their studies of Atwood's celebrity. In refusing to allow *Morning in the Burned House* to be reduced to therapeutic autobiography, Atwood's defence forecloses upon the genre as endemic to nation as nature even as she purports that elegy is both "a natural Canadian form" and a "celebration." Though she utters the phrase while arguing against the assumptions of autobiography, Atwood's claim that the elegy is "naturally Canadian" functions as a warning against reducing a national literature to a haunting consciousness. In the previous chapter of this volume, Jay Macpherson's reclamation of gothic tradition in order to rout it for proto-feminist purposes showed that appropriating the conventions of a genre does not necessarily mean that the conventions are desirable, only that they are powerful vehicles that can take the writer (and the text) somewhere else—beyond "Square One."

The Elegiac Revelation: Making Atwood New?

Reviews of *Morning in the Burned House* are nearly unanimous in hailing the book as a marker of a "new" Atwood. In line with Kathryn van Spanckeren's contention that "the challenge, for Atwood's poems ... is to address real issues and dare vulnerability" (111), Nicholas von Maltzahn claims that "the final poems ... bespeak a new dimension in Atwood's poetry" (10), and Dale Jacobs in *Prairie Schooner* says that the collection "is, in the true sense of the word, a revelation" (183). Charlene Diehl-Jones, in

Books in Canada, sees "a new turn of mind" in the elegies (30). Not only is this Atwood new, critics rejoice, she is also more emotionally available. In *Border Crossings*, Robert Enright is even more effusive, comparing Atwood to Yeats and praising the poems' "unprecedented emotional resonance and grandeur...characterized by an almost impossible sense of focus. The lines strike you as inescapable, like death and passion" (58). Later in the review, Enright compares Atwood favourably to both Tennyson and Browning, and notes that "there's so much being said that you can hardly read for meaning.... It's the best book of poetry Atwood has written so far" (60). George Woodcock in *Quill & Quire* asserts that the paternal elegies in section IV are the poems that distinguish this book from Atwood's earlier work, and that "the deep compassion of these poems and their curiously level tone of grieving objectivity make their remarkable among recent Canadian verse," and concludes with the crowning achievement: "We not only have Atwood here at her prime; we may also have her as a whole" (25).

These responses—and there are considerably more in this vein that I have not included—and their claims to newness and intimacy are curiously insistent and just as curiously assumptive, as though the combination of Atwood's controlled self-image, an autobiographical tinge, and the elegiac contradiction ignited a critical group hallucination about *Morning in the Burned House*. To be sure, the collection is about mourning, and the elegies are undeniably moving, but there is a triumphant tone to the observations above. They herald with glee (or perhaps with relief) that Atwood has at last shown her true, weeping, vulnerable face to her loyal readers/subjects and has done so while delivering the finely crafted poetry to which her followers have become accustomed. Perhaps this is a consummation devoutly to be wished, but is it true?

The reception of *Morning in the Burned House* as the book in which Atwood "gets personal" and finally admits her humanity seems largely a self-fulfilling prophecy. Mark Abley calls the book "a startling volume, both somber and intimate in spirit, and written with Atwood's customary stylishness. We expect nothing less from her; and she delivers" (Atwood, "Dire" 1). This final sentence, acting as an introduction to Abley's obstreperous interview with Atwood, is intriguing; does Atwood deliver what we expect only because we expect it? "This year we are making / nothing but elegies," she states in "Four Small Elegies"; in 1995, were critics making nothing but autobiographical assumptions?

What is at issue in this book of elegies—some for history's lost women, some for the environment, some for Carl Atwood, and some for Atwood's double-pronouned "I/you" figure—is neither grief nor vulnerability but a stark view of the fateful order of mourning, a view of entropic decay that owes its perspective to biology as much as it does to personal affect. The poems in *Morning in the Burned House* consider the rhetoric of mourning as profoundly problematic and full of rituals that no longer signify. Death, the collection implies, has its own order, but survival places the mourning subject in an unspeakable world. I am resistant to reading the text as a breakthrough in Atwood's work largely because the language of therapy is never very far from discussions of mourning, and while Julia Kristeva's point in *Black Sun* that literary depictions of melancholia have a therapeutic effect is perfectly valid, there is a difference between Kristeva's psychoanalytical analysis of melancholia through literature and the choice to read literature primarily as a therapeutic device. The discovery at the heart of elegy—the anagnorisis—is as resolutely political as it is personal, and I am often suspicious of therapeutic theories of literature because they are infinitely useful for concealing the political power of writing by women.

It is the political exigency of Atwood's paternal elegies that intrigues. She allows the Canadian national pastoral to offer deliverance and even apotheosis to the paternal figure, while consolation remains impossible for the mourner. Part of the difficulty of reading *Morning in the Burned House*, and one of the reasons why critics have had such problems pinpointing what happens in this collection—Sara Jamieson is right to call the poems "deceptively simple" (38)—is that Atwood discusses affect by exploring the limits that lack of affect imposes upon the mourner. She explores not grief but emptiness, not melancholia but an abandonment of language, and not mourning but the linguistic void that surrounds mourning. She does this through a device that is familiar to Atwood readers: the doppelgänger or "mute twin" figure who serves as guide through the underworld of mourning and an accrual of affect arrested by its own intensity. But the twin figure, the mourner's "mute sister, / left-handed shadow cast by an absence / that moves you nevertheless to love" ("The Signer") is more than just a Jungian psychopomp; she is also the embodiment of affect, and she speaks a different language than the mourner.

Responding to Fiamengo's contention that "the characteristic Atwood voice... would seem to be aggressively anti-elegiac" (150) and that section IV's paternal elegies are "shorn of the poet's hallmark wit, irony and mythic allusions" (145), Priscila Uppal notes that Atwood is rather "anti-nostalgic" and that within the collection, "irony and elegy complement each other" (50). Uppal further notes that "with only the platitudes and ineffectual conventions at the speaker's disposal, without the opportunity to actively participate in meaningful ritual, the work of mourning is left unperformed" (50). Uppal is correct. The poems of inquiry in section V are a direct result of that non-performance; in each poem, Atwood's protagonist rakes over the rhetoric of mourning and finds it inadequate to the task of addressing the reconfiguration of time and self demanded by the death of the father. The final section of *Morning in the Burned House* is haunted, but not by the ghost of the father figure, who has received the pastoral apotheosis of a canoe trip down a dream version of the Ottawa River. Atwood's twin figure, familiar from her various uses in *The Journals of Susanna Moodie* (especially as a double voice) and as the Other in *Two-Headed Poems*, appears here as the ghost of female melancholia, a spirit that answers the question "what are you supposed to do / with all this loss?" ("Down"). Perhaps more intriguingly given the leanings toward autobiographical assumption already noted in Atwood's readers, the recurrent nature of the twin figure makes it possible to read the twin as the ghost of Atwood's public personae. Conscious that I am proposing a "doubled double," or two ways of reading a figure who already performs as a mirror of the speaking subject, I do not wish to complicate things needlessly, but rather wish to make it clear that it is impossible to read any single work by Atwood without reading "Atwood" as signature, as national culture critic, and as literary phenomenon.

Incandescent Alterity: *Morning in the Burned House*

Though Atwood is often read as a student of Northrop Frye, her wry iterations of myth, her resistance to the Orphic journey, and her ironic take on the Jungian psychopomp all suggest that it may be more useful—at least for this study—to think of Atwood as a good student of Jay Macpherson. But just as Macpherson has said little about possible autobiographical readings of *Welcoming Disaster*, Atwood has been resistant to readings that reduce the elegy to a personal expression of grief made available for public consumption. In *Morning in the Burned House*, the mourning daughter is temporally dislocated into "nothingness in motion" ("Shapechangers in Winter") until she recognizes her "dark twin" who reflects her gestures of mourning back to the daughter-narrator. Coral Ann Howells posits that the text examines a "dynamic process of mourning and a mobile relocation of the subject at the end" (70) through the negotiation of a "radically altered frame of reference for the surviving subject" (74). While Howells is clear that any focus on stable subjectivity is a tempting but false consolation, she also problematically states "the structure of elegy also resembles epic in its pattern of odyssey and homecoming for the subject" (74). The *nekusis* or descent pattern does suggest a hopeful return, but the descent always requires sacrifice in exchange for revelation, and the return of the journeyer is shadowed by the difficult knowledge attained in the Underworld.

Atwood, contra her own gloss on the Orphic *nekusis* in *Negotiating with the Dead*, throws a spanner in the works to suggest that the descent is not only painful, frightening, and risky, but notes, as Macpherson does, that it may well be denied to the daughterly mourner. In that case, what *are* you supposed to do with all that loss? Atwood has employed the descent pattern so frequently in her texts that Rosemary Sullivan, in her biography *The Red Shoes: Margaret Atwood Starting Out*, named a chapter "a descent through the carpet," referencing Atwood's early poem of the same name. Despite evidence of the descent pattern in poems like "Down" and "Shapechangers in Winter," a more consistent and compelling pattern in *Morning in the Burned House* can be found in Atwood's dislocation of time and fragmentation of consciousness. This dislocation begins as uneasiness about aging in "You Come Back" and "Waiting" in section I, appears as the monologic hindsight of history's powerful women in section II, and takes on global proportions in the environmental and scientific mortality of section III. "A Pink Hotel in California," one of the first poems in the collection to presage the father's death, sets up a temporal and geographical dislocation for the narrating daughter between a hotel room in 1994 California and a cabin in the northern Canadian forest in 1943, a setting familiar from Atwood's earlier work, particularly in *Surfacing* (1972) and *Cat's Eye* (1988).

The difference between the elegiac subject (the narrating daughter) and the elegiac object (the dying and eventually dead father) is important. The father's confusion, full of the awful tensions of the contemporary elegy, dominates the poems of section IV in "Wave," "King Lear in Respite Care," "A Visit," and "Flowers," but it is the daughter's sense of displacement in "A Pink Hotel in California" that ushers in the struggle against an entropic nothingness in section V. Instead of engaging the work of mourning in all its patriarchal values (or alternatively, embracing melancholia in either self-denying or philosophical models), Atwood rejects both models when she rejects the descent pattern as insufficient for an exploration of mourning a parental death. Where Macpherson employs the language of the gothic to render her text proto-feminist, Atwood addresses her own status as a cultural signifier in her rejection of the Orphic descent. The thematic juxtaposition of "Down" with "A Pink Hotel in California" suggests that the daughter-narrator resists the mourner's *nekusis* and, further, that it is only by extricating herself from the descent pattern that the daughter-narrator can discover her own potential for an incandescence that cuts through both the patriarchal constructs of mourning and the bleak philosophies of melancholia.

What could be more appropriate for an Atwoodian text than to read its tropes against the critical conventions that have accrued around Atwood's work? In *Negotiating with the Dead*, Atwood notes that that the figure of the poet "can bring the knowledge held by the Underworld back to the land of the living" (174), and while this is indisputable concerning the literary-historical tour that Atwood conducts in *Negotiating with the Dead*, whether or not it describes the central action of *Morning in the Burned House* depends upon how we read the ending of that text. If the twin figure is the ghost of female melancholia, then the knowledge that Atwood's daughter-narrator brings back from an undefined Underworld would be a rhetoric of mourning that includes daughter figures free from sacrifice. Such a rhetoric would need real ties to the quotidian world; if Atwood's mourning daughter figure cannot escape to the Underworld to pursue romantic knowledge, then she must meet mourning in the commonplace but revealing light of the physical world.

Returning to my proposition that the twin figure is the ghost of Atwood's persona, we might consider Lorraine York's characterization of literary fame as an enervating spirit pertinent to an elegiac reading. Citing Atwood's identification in *Negotiating with the Dead* of writerly "duplicity"—that is, one persona who lives as an everyday citizen of the world and another "more shadowy and altogether more equivocal personage who shares the same body, and who, when no one is looking, takes it over and uses it to commit the actual writing" (*Negotiating* 35)—York notes that "fame, which exacerbates that split between public and private writer, is, in this dramatization, a scene of death": a metaphorically gothic murder complete with "body snatcher" motif (York 121). So York concludes, with considerable aplomb, that "Negotiating with the dead is more than an archetypal descent into the realms of mortality and knowledge, though for Atwood it is certainly and profoundly that. It also means negotiating with the living death that is fame" (121). This "living death" is full of its own kinds of everyday selves, which is one reason why the twin figure of Atwood's section V is best read as both the doppelgänger of fame and the ghost of female melancholia. They are figures with whom Atwood has "done what she is good at"; she had made what she knows and what we—her readers—think we know.

One aspect of the cruel everyday world that the mourning daughter must confront in section V of *Morning in the Burned House* is the stark contrast between the everyday world, with its "ruins...that do not look like ruins" ("Girl without Hands"), and the dream world of melancholia, which is both "nowhere familiar" and "somewhere I've been before," a place where the daughter wakes "to the sound of nothing" ("The Ottawa River by Night"). The bitter contrast between an elegiac idyll and the ruined world is conventional, but Atwood's differentiation between the elegiac ocean and the real one with "sick whales / and oil slicks" ("The Ottawa River by Night") and the violent romance of a river that bursts its banks only to leave "trash caught overhead in the trees" ("Vermilion Flycatcher, San Pedro River, Arizona") suggests more than just a melancholic refusal of a dirty world: rather, it connotes a dislocation of the mourning daughter in a nightmare world. When the daughter's mute twin appears she acts as both mirror and warning that melancholia holds as much danger as relief. To move beyond mourning, the daughter must see that the "myopia" of being "bored out of my mind" is the key to memory and to mourning ("Bored"). Considering Nancy Holland's contention that the "father's ghost" haunts the daughter in the shape of his concept of the "eternal idealized woman" that the daughter can never achieve (67), Atwood's female ghost in section V operates as an idealized mourner, a woman whose otherness exposes the dislocated daughter to her own doppelgänger.

Throughout section IV, Atwood gives the reader fair warning of the daughter's growing sense of self-estrangement and experience of time as "doubled," manifested as present and past through the medium of her father's illness. "Man in a Glacier" uses an image from a "box of slides in the cellar" to situate the father as "alive or else preserved, younger than all / of us now, dark-haired and skinny," reminding the daughter that "this freeze-framed / simulacrum or slight imprint" cannot approach the "everlastingness" for which she longs. In "Bored," Atwood emphasizes the father's scientific patience, his legacy of "looking hard and up close at the small / details," a habit that his illness erodes. Ironically, Atwood's short book *The Labrador Fiasco* shows close observation to contain a metaphorical fallacy of its own when the dying father looks at a gleaming hardwood floor and deduces that the shine indicates he is on a river (37). The myopic view in "Bored" is itself partial sight, depriving the narrating daughter of the larger focus of time spent with her father, a larger view that is only ever available in hindsight. From her position in the future, the daughter claims that her younger self "could hardly wait to get / the hell out of there to / anywhere else," but now her father's illness has recast those boring moments as sublime in their particularity: "sunnier" with "more birdsong." Her wish to return to the past and abandon all knowledge of mortality makes her final claim one of frustration and desire:

> Perhaps though
> boredom is happier. It is for dogs or
> groundhogs. Now I wouldn't be bored.
> Now I would know too much.
> Now I would know.

This "knowing" presents part of the daughter's inheritance from her father, but between "boredom" and the weight of her future "knowledge," the daughter is trapped in a reverse Cassandra position that frustrates temporal existence. However banal it may be to recognize disaster too late, such recognition can be agonizing. The discovery that human beings cannot "stop, or live backwards" ("Man in a Glacier") is central to these poems. Atwood nominates "Chemistry and Physics" as "our bad godmothers" whose curse upon humanity is entropy accompanied by consciousness: "*You will not sleep forever.*"

Though her father's death initially hastens the daughter's dislocation, that dislocation is the means by which she becomes aware of her potential for alterity. For instance, in "The Ottawa River by Night," the father's disappearance down the river recalls apotheosis: a divine vanishing that blesses the mourner with his absence. In this poem, the father navigates the rapids "so skillfully / although dead," towards a "safe arrival" that may not be in a Christian heaven but is definitely Christianized in its view of the afterlife as a haven. As the father canoes not towards the "real sea" but the "other sea," he transforms into his vigorous youthful self; his pain is over, and his passage to another better world is complete. However, one of the strengths of this text is that Atwood seems not the least tempted to translate paternal apotheosis into consolation for the daughter. In fact, as the father becomes more like his younger, competent self, the daughter becomes increasingly estranged from herself. The gap between the expectation of consolation and its determined lack creates a tension for the daughter to discover, in Melissa Zeiger's terms, what lies "beyond consolation" for her. "The Ottawa River by Night" may be Atwood's most distinctly Canadian elegy, from the echo of Tom Thomson in the father's canoeing disappearance to the suggestion that the Ottawa River—passing by the Parliament Buildings and the Peace Tower, dividing Ontario from Quebec—functions as the waters of Lethe, bringing nothingness rather than peace to the mourner. On second thought, she determines that it is "not nothing" but something she can no longer identify, a sense of temporal displacement that echoes the father's fateful "wave [that] washed over him" until his family "remained to him in fragments" ("Wave"). Similarly, at the end of "The Ottawa River by Night," the daughter—now a mourner without a body to mourn—is left to decode her effective *and* affective location: "It always takes a long time / to decipher where you are."

In trying to "decipher" her location, the daughter takes up her father's sense of displacement, but the legacy of alterity left by the father operates as a model for her. However, the father finds his alterity through his journey toward death; how then will the daughter perform this work of mourning that seems to, in the Antigonal mode, require self-sacrifice? Part of Atwood's answer can be found in the longest poem in the text, situated just before the section on the father's illness. "Half-Hanged Mary," the poem inspired by Atwood's ancestor Mary Webster who was hanged as a witch in the 1680s, presents an image of a woman who accrues power through her fragmentation; she may be "half-hanged" but her survival of the hanging makes her fully conscious. She is "all fullness, all vacancy" by the end of the poem, a conflation of opposites that emphasizes her new-found power of alterity. Through her engagement with death, Mary achieves a kind of worldly apotheosis, cut down like Christ from her rope but feared rather than revered. Nevertheless, "[h]oliness gleams on [her] dirty fingers" and she "speak[s] in tongues," knowing that her only "audience is God, / because who the hell else could understand me? / Who else has been dead twice?" Mary fuses together her naïve victim self who was "hanged for living alone" and for "having blue eyes" with the cynical other she discovers during her all-night vigil: "Before, I was not a witch. / But now I am one." In a similar manner, the dislocated daughter figure of *Morning in the Burned House* must be transfigured by an encounter with an other in order to perform her task of inheritance. Mary's alterity makes her over into a powerful seer; the mourning daughter eventually recreates herself as the "incandescent" being of the title poem, "Morning in the Burned House."

The father's departure leaves the daughter "filled with dread," despite the presence of "birdsong," unable to eat or rise from her bed, figuratively "lying on [her] deathbed" ("Up"). She is surrounded by nothingness, rather than being filled with emptiness. This is not an interiorized image of Derridean mourning but an external image of being encompassed by nothingness, as in these lines from "Up":

> Where is it coming from, this echo,
> this huge No that surrounds you,
> silent as the folds of the yellow
> curtains, mute as the cheerful
>
> Mexican bowl with its cargo
> of mummified flowers?

The narrator is in stasis. It is not only the present that oppresses with its emptiness; "the future" has become "immense as outer space" and the "density" of the past, with its elegiac "drowned events," fills her lungs "like gelatin." The temporal collapse that characterized the father's confusion and illness remains with the daughter; the symptoms do not vanish with the lost beloved but remain with the mourner, a transferred "inheritance" that seems very Freudian indeed. But the nothingness that precedes the appearance of the twin figure is an exteriorization of grief, an inheritance of shifting space that plagues the daughter with visitations of violent murder, ambush, and drowning ("Vermilion Flycatcher, San Pedro River, Arizona"), as well as with a fear of space as annihilating ("The Moment"). The nothingness erodes the daughter's perception of her self and her own agency, and melts the landscape before her:

> you can't hold any of it. Distance surrounds you,
> marked out by the ends of your arms
> when they are stretched to their fullest.
> You can go no farther than this,
> you think, walking forward,
> pushing the distance in front of you ("Girl Without Hands")

The poem identifies distance as the space of mourning, but its limitations and emptiness imply that it is more like a refusal to mourn, and the concomitant refusal to see "each leaf / and stone quickened and specific" that holds the daughter in stasis. Nothingness, like Gillian Rose's aberrant mourning, refuses the alterity of the other. As much as the mourner wishes to remain inside "that clean circle / of dead space you have made / and stay inside, / mourning because it is clean," she recognizes the "girl without hands" as the Other when she appears. The girl is a ghostly apparition who is, ironically, more solid than the shimmering pyramids and offices surrounding the protagonist. The girl without hands is also "surrounded" by a soundless scream; like the mourner, "[e]verything has bled out of her." The girl without hands begins the process of transfiguration for the mourning daughter with her touch that feels like "nothing" but changes everything. The ghost of female melancholia touches the daughterly elegist; the effect is not one of breakdown and breakthrough, but, rather, of transformation from an unbearable grief to an incandescent reality.

The twin figure reappears in the next poem, "The Signer," still mute but now with hands as eloquent as her "absent" touch has been. She is acknowledged as the daughter's "unknown twin," "mute sister," and her "left-handed shadow" who can "translate [the daughter] into bone." This figure guides the soul of the narrator back to life by taking on the grief duties of the ultimate mourning daughter; as the girl becomes affect personified, the daughter-narrator is drained of her own melancholia when she discovers that she cannot exist in nothingness. In a twist on

Judith Butler's melancholic turn, Atwood's narrator leaves stasis for the potential of alterity.

After the appearance of the twin as Other in "Girl Without Hands" and "The Signer," Atwood introduces the metaphor of shape-shifting, a trope that has signified slyness from its earliest appearance in 1964's *The Circle Game* ("Eventual Proteus"). But in *Morning in the Burned House*, "A Fire Place" and "Statuary" emphasize inevitable temporal change rather than a willful mythic force, and Atwood's choice of eventual "shapechangers" over the more science-fiction style "shape-shifters" seems apt. In each poem, the effects of entropy mirror the force of mourning, distinguishing grief from nothingness, and alterity from depression. The burned place in the forest (another featured trope in Atwood's work) is a body with "a gash," "a scar," something that humans tried to save "with hand-pumps and axes to a damp and acrid standstill" ("A Fire Place"). Such a standstill is intentionally deceiving, for the burn turns to new growth, bringing people and animals to feed off its berries and eventually sprouting "scrubland, a light-green / sticky new forest." "A Fire Place," as a burned spot in a forest, and a "fireplace" as a hearth that warms and sustains human life, recalls the daughter's advice to the confused father that it is "better to watch the fireplace / which is now a beach" ("A Visit"). The father makes a final allusive appearance in "A Fire Place," in the guise of the "youngish (now dead) men" with "high-laced lumberjacks' (obsolete) boots," an echo of the paternal image from the old slides in "Man in a Glacier." Atwood's nod to pastoral renewal as a convention of consolation should not go unnoticed here, but her persistent image of the earth as a human body that "rips openings in itself" only to "skin over" the "wound" ("A Fire Place") points to a deep ambivalence about what it means to have a body and to lose it.

"Statuary" picks up on this idea, beginning with a comic grotesque on lopping off of body parts, but soon settling into an aesthetic of erosion that emphasizes the entropy of the human body. Language decays as the body does, Atwood warns: "Our mouths erode in the rain / you send, and all our bright definite / nouns and quick verbs with them." The poem is addressed to a "you," in this case the "nothingness / that by its moving / edges defines time." The statues speak as beings shaped by the weight of absence, the force that creates "those knotholes the world turns itself inside out through" and that ultimately grants the statues an ambiguous form of life that "lets us fly / and embody, like you. Until we are like you." The tension between absence and presence remains a paradox at the end of "Statuary." The statues are simultaneously embodied in flight and "ground down" to a profound absence. They are "like you" despite (or because of) the fact that they are "pebbles / on the shore of a vast lake that doesn't... exist yet." The force and motion of nothingness, glossed earlier in "Girl Without Hands" as profound grief, presages a more existential concern: somatophobia, a fear of dissolution or fragmentation of the body.

"Shapechangers in Winter" returns to three tropes that are nearly iconic in Atwood's corpus, neatly divided into three parts within the longer poem: part one reiterates Atwood's "descent through the carpet" motif; part two revisits the primitive human/animal perspective that appears in *Procedures for Underground* ("Midwinter, Presolstice," "Habitation," "Procedures for Underground") and *Power Politics* ("At first I was given centuries," "They are hostile nations"); and part three echoes the final poems of *You Are Happy* with their winter claustrophobia and sense of danger. By the end of "Shapechangers in Winter," the Other reappears as "you," the speaker's partner. The poem begins by reminding readers of the "nothingness in motion," a concept introduced in "Statuary," "the power of what is not there" that Atwood's narrator sees as either "indifference / on the part of the universe, or else a relentless / forgiveness." Atwood uses the nothingness to precipitate the descent pattern in part one of "Shapechangers," in which the "pressure" of "nothingness in motion" pushes the perspective down through layers of the earth and then "sideways, out into the city," and further out to encounter "the air, and then the scintillating ions, / and then the stars. That's where / we are." When in part two, Atwood's narrator refers to her shape-changing tendencies, she does so with nostalgia, as though the desire to escape in a different form has become foolish: "Once we were lithe as pythons, quick / and silvery as herrings, and we still are momentarily, / except our knees hurt." Atwood questions recognition and kinship, citing "eye problems: too close, too far, you're a blur. / I used to say I'd know you anywhere, / but it's getting harder." These "eye problems," reminiscent of the "myopia" of "Bored," are, on the one hand, a reference to aging, but they are certainly more than that; recognition, in mythological terms, augurs either great joy or great pain. Which will this be? If the mute twin here has shifted to become a beloved figure—living or dead—it is also hard not to think of the ghosts of Atwood's personae becoming less and less recognizable. We used to think we would know her anywhere, but it's getting harder.

The irony of the shapechangers, who lose their power to change and are harder to recognize in their stasis, becomes the turning point for the final part of the poem. Part three shows us an acute sense of dislocation, with the narrator and the "you" figure "lost in a six-dimensional forest" at the solstice, "[t]he year's threshold / and unlocking." The solstice's temporal shift prompts nothingness to perform its trick with space: "The walls of the house fold themselves down, / and the house turns / itself inside out."

The house shifts shape but the humans do not, and in the destruction of the house, the narrator is left to recognize the Other as a partner with whom she will endure the nothingness. As the dark and cold converge on the narrator as another form of nothingness, the Other remains constant even when "the visibility is zero: *Yes. / It's still you. It's still you.*" These final lines are an affirmation of subjectivity, a recognition of identity against the force of nothingness that prepares the narrator for her transfiguration in the text's final and title poem, "Morning in the Burned House."

The burned house, a conflation of the collapsed house from "Shapechangers" and the burned space of "A Fire Place," is another Atwoodian trope, the "small cabin" that appears so often throughout *Procedures for Underground.* That the time can be identified as morning suggests that time has stabilized. Past and present are conflated now, and the narrator is double-bodied at last in the realm of the Other. At once a child and an adult, she is "eating breakfast" in a house that has already burned and she herself is still burning in a fire of transformation. This is the final step in becoming Other; the protagonist is at once present and "non-existent" in her "cindery... radiant flesh." The poem's final word, "incandescent," from the Latin *candeo*, "to be white," describes the narrator's flesh and the hot light of the fire, as well as the whiteness or blankness of nothingness, now finally assimilated into the daughter-narrator. This incandescent daughter is reminiscent of Jay Macpherson's "Phoenix," part of Macpherson's "Book of Riddles" in *The Boatman*:

> That fire is my element, consumes and lights me,
> Heals and accuses and again requites me.
> I feed on the dew of heaven and live without desire:
> Reader, consider a life in the fire.

While Macpherson's Phoenix is no figure of mourning, there is a suggestion of the kind of paradoxical destruction and creation in the fire's ability to "heal," "consume," and ultimately "requite" the narrative "I," as it does with the mourning daughter of "Morning in the Burned House." The Phoenix's invitation for the reader to "consider a life in the fire" is typical of Macpherson's monologic address to the reader, and when Atwood's mourning daughter chooses the transfiguration of "a life in the fire," it is with a wry joy that is not new to Atwood but may be shockingly new to those who expect the elegy to be separated from philosophy. Gillian Rose's use of the same homonymic pun on morning as the end and beginning of mourning suggests that a productive melancholia is not only possible but necessary to the postmodern present: "mourning (or absence) must become our norm (or presence) for there to be morning (dawn or future), and not interminable dying" (103). In embracing alterity as part of the father's legacy, Atwood's mourning daughter completes her task of inheritance through transfiguration. Her incandescent subjectivity moves into the future, leaving "death worked and unworked" behind her (Rose 101). This transformation leaves Atwood negotiating not with the dead but with her own poetic persona to discover a median position that chooses "incandescent" rather than "transcendent" transfiguration.

6

The Pilgrim and the Riddle

Anne Carson's "The Anthropology of Water"

> When is a pilgrim like a photograph? When the blend of acids and sentiment is just right.
> — Anne Carson, "The Anthropology of Water"

Choose Your Duty: The Paradox of Pilgrimage

Almost every elegy could be described as a literary journey through the genre's conventions, or as an affective charting of the path through mourning to arrive at consolation. However, using a discovery-oriented journey as a metaphor for mourning practice presents a number of problems. Let it be accepted as true that undertaking a long journey of devotion—a pilgrimage, be it literary or spiritual—demands the daily exertion that is demanded of any devotional practice, including the work of mourning or melancholia. But although consolation is an attractive concept as a destination at which the mourner will arrive, the work of mourning is not so easily folded into a cartographic movement. Chapter Four examined the ways that the narrator of Jay Macpherson's *Welcoming Disaster* is ultimately remade by her inability to access the *nekusis* trope, and in this chapter, I return to the tradition of the mourner's journey as a promising and problematic trope for the female elegist.

In Anne Carson's "The Anthropology of Water," the long, elegiac prose poem from her 1995 text *Plainwater: Essays and Poetry*, a mourning daughter undertakes a traditional pilgrimage only to find that defining herself as a pilgrim-philosopher thwarts mourning rather than facilitates it. Carson's text reveals the ways that mourning resembles a journey for which we cannot plan. Her narrator's pilgrimage to the medieval Christian shrine of St. James functions as a quest for viable mourning practices, framed by the narrator's attempts to read the father's final attempts at speech, impeded by Alzheimer's-related dementia, as elegiac testament. "The Anthropology of Water" considers the difficulties of male–female relationships (filial, sexual, and fraternal) as these relationships are molded by the father–daughter relationship. Along the way, the daughter's relationship to the father is explored as a parallel to the pilgrim's relationship to the saint as the inspiration for pilgrimage and contemplation. For Carson's pilgrim, "Love is the mystery inside this walking" ("Anthropology" 145).

A reader could hardly fault the narrator's instinct in attempting pilgrimage as a way to complete mourning. After all, for centuries millions of people have used the practical and spiritual aspects of a pilgrimage to enact penitence, enter into contemplation, pay spiritual debts, and relieve unrelenting psychic pain. From this standpoint, pilgrimage seems not only to align with the mourner's journey but to enact an affective journey. The pilgrim, as a devotional practitioner, blends physical exertion and deprivation with spiritual contemplation, excoriating the body in order to exhilarate the soul. Victor Turner suggests that pilgrimages are "liminal phenomena" (166) that represent both a refusal of the contemporary world and a desire to impress the contemporary world through a ritual gesture. The pilgrim, in Turner's view, is a ritual paradox in action; a person who undertakes a pilgrimage is motivated by equal parts social obligation and "voluntariness" (175). Pilgrimages represent "an amplified symbol of the dilemma of choice versus obligation in the midst of a social order," which is perhaps best expressed by the pilgrim's concept that "it is meritorious to *choose one's duty*" (177; emphasis in original). The same conscientious choice of duty plays a strong role in the daughterly elegy, and Carson's prose poem is an excellent example.

Ian Rae notes that Carson consistently reminds readers that "the frameworks of myth, genre and gender are volatile" ("Dazzling" 38). She demonstrates that volatility in "The Anthropology of Water" by using the trope of the pilgrimage to test the tension between mourning and resistance read against the vicissitudes of filial devotion. However, Carson resists the simple equation of the labour of a journey with the work of mourning and is similarly resistant to consolation as a physical or psychic destination. The desperation of daughterly self-sacrifice is never far from the surface in this text, especially as the narrator's survival is accomplished, as is Macpherson's demanding mourner's, by a melancholic turn in her thwarted journey to consolation. Carson never loses sight of the dynamics of productive melancholia, and the daughter-elegist of "The Anthropology of Water" confronts the future with the wry knowledge that the worthiness of completing mourning may be forever undercut by the fundamental despair of daughterly existence.

"The Anthropology of Water" outlines the Oedipal and Antigonal tensions of father–daughter kinship, and such play with classical mythology establishes Carson's interest in all things joyous and tragic. It comes as no surprise that she begins "The Anthropology of Water" by addressing the central philosophical issue of determining "the truth." The search to determine "the truth" also begins the drama of *Oedipus the King*, and while Carson's results are less tragic, her text takes on the trappings of that tragedy from the beginning. Beginning "The Anthropology of Water" with the father's contention that some truths are "as obvious as a door in water" (119), Carson sets up the paternal function as both obvious and revelatory, positioning the father as bearer of Aristotelian logos. But this debilitated father has lost the capacity for rational speech; Alzheimer's-related dementia has "released some spring inside him, he babbles constantly in a language neurologists call 'word salad'" ("Anthropology" 120). This stream of indecipherable speech suggests paternal knowledge that has been codified by divinity as well as by disease: "Father had always been a private man. Now his mind was a sacred area where no one could enter or ask the way" (121). The father figure remains beyond the reach of the narrator's love, even as she strives to read him as an untranslated (and ultimately untranslatable) text that will not yield to traditional consolation. The father figure haunts various sections of "The Anthropology of Water"—"Kinds of Water," "Diving," "Thirst," "Very Narrow," and "Just for the Thrill"—but it is his influence on the pilgrimage featured in "Kinds of Water" that situates him as an elegiac figure. The narrator's pilgrimage to Santiago de Compostela is echoed twice in the text, in the narrator's trip across the continental United States with her lover in "Just for the Thrill," and also in her brother's journey around and through a lake in "Water Margins." Carson uses the trope of the pilgrimage to describe the tension between mourning and resistance, although her larger project concerns an epistemological inquiry into the vicissitudes of filial devotion by examining a daughter's duty to her dying father. The pilgrimage appeals to the narrator-daughter for its linearity and geographic certainty as much as for its spiritual dimensions; putatively freed from the frustrations of kinship, the pilgrim can seek answers on a higher plain, be that plain spiritual or critical. But the metaphor of the pilgrimage is itself a trap, for in Carson's prose poem, the endless road operates as an inscription of melancholia, emphasizing the tenacity of the narrator's grief against any arrival at consolation.

Early in female elegy studies, Celeste Schenck argued that the female elegist refuses consolation, and in doing so, she "deconstructs the genre's valorization of separation by means of apotheosis" (Schenck 18). Schenck's "Feminism and Deconstruction: Re-constructing the Elegy" deserves credit for raising issues of women's resistance to elegiac convention in 1986 when discussions of female-composed elegy were practically unheard of in literary criticism. However, Schenck's assertion that female elegists strive to criticize the apotheosis of the lost beloved and its attendant valorization is disproven by "The Anthropology of Water" because Carson's way of deconstructing the elegy springs partly from her attention to the daughter's longing after paternal apotheosis. Her protagonist's refusal of consolation is formed out of that longing rather than from refuting what Schenck calls "the absolute rupture that is death" (18). Carson does, as Schenck suggests, "deploy writing as a strategy for prolonging attachment" (22), but how that attachment is attenuated or severed is influenced by Carson's scholarly background as a classicist. "The Anthropology of Water" shows a daughter figure whose melancholia is strung upon her wish to write her dying father as a hero unmediated by the modern age even as she cannot resist noting that her portrait of him is a "blend of acids and sentiment" (170).

Kinship Terms: Anne Carson as Elegist

The limits of corporeal representation are a fundamental concern in any elegy, and one of the paths that female-written paternal elegies can follow is one of ambivalence towards filial piety, or a desire to delineate, and perhaps dismantle, the fidelity demanded by the father's death. Such delineation, as we have seen in previous chapters, may be critical of the father, or it may be aligned more with pleasing the father, or it may work with some combination of both. "The Anthropology of Water" is concerned with the daughter's desire to inherit her father's knowledge, but this inheritance is problematized by the fact that the father in question has Alzheimer's-related dementia. Nevertheless, Carson's prose poem depicts the father as a man whose attention the daughter craves despite his illness; in fact, her craving for his attention is so strong that the father's debilitation is presented as a parallel to the daughter-narrator's emotional stasis. She mirrors his distress, rocking her body as he rocks his, "making little lunges with [her] chest," and answering his dissociated utterances with a prompt "Yes, Father" (120). Although his single clear statement in this section of the text—"Death is a fifty-fifty thing, maybe forty-forty"—is bewilderingly full of import, she does not ask the "simple questions" that it inspires (120).

In an effort to negotiate her way through the unasked questions that crowd the father's presence, Carson makes her elegist both a pilgrim and a philosopher. Each of these tasks (elegizing, philosophizing, and walking the pilgrim's route to Compostela) offers the narrator a different way to answer the questions that seem to be her legacy. The narrator assumes the elegist's perspective in order to inquire into ways to live within the limits of the body. She assumes the role of a pilgrim in order to ask for penance, and she takes on the philosopher's persona in order to question the function of knowledge in a limited, sinful body. The roles of philosopher and pilgrim, devotees respectively of the brain and the soul, operate as disguises for the elegist, that devotee of the body. The pilgrim and the philosopher ask questions that the elegist forbids herself, just as she forbids herself "the unwary use of a kinship term" ("Anthropology" 190; 232).

Anne Carson's meteoric rise in Canadian poetry, along with her varied oeuvre of poetry, essays, opera ("Decreation"), novels in verse (*The Autobiography of Red, The Beauty of the Husband*), and translations of Greek poetry and plays, has brought her to a kind of prominence enjoyed by few Canadian writers. If Margaret Atwood is the Canadian writer whose reputation is most widespread within Canada, then it must be said that Anne Carson has replaced Atwood in recent years as the most polarizing figure in Canadian literature. The back cover of *The Autobiography of Red* bears an effusive recommendation from Michael Ondaatje, who praises Carson as "the most exciting poet writing in English today," while Montreal poet and critic David Solway denounces her writing as pretentious and overrated. She has become such a lightning rod figure that several scholars have written about Carson as a literary phenomenon in and of herself (in Ian Rae's *From Cohen to Carson*, Lee Upton's *Defensive Measures*, and Kevin McNeilly's introduction to a special issue of *Canadian Literature* dedicated to Carson, to name a few). While these writers have explored various ways to regard Carson's mystery and appeal, I cannot help but regard some of the more virulent criticisms leveled at Carson as anti-feminist in nature, for it is her independence that appears to drive her detractors to distraction. While Carson's feminism is definitely more implied than openly asserted, it cannot be denied that she operates as a writer who knows her own mind. She refuses to justify her choices, to capitulate to criticisms of her style, or to discuss her work under the terms other than the ones she brings to the work from her other studies.

Although Carson's subject matter varies widely, she has distinguished herself as a family elegist in several texts. The publication date of "The Anthropology of Water" (1995) makes it the earliest of Carson's family elegies to appear in print, and she echoes the subject of her father's dementia in her long poem (also from 1995) "The Glass Essay" published in *Glass, Irony and God*. The paternal elegy persists as a concern in Carson's work, and as late as June 2011, another of Carson's elegies for her father, "O Dad," appeared in *The New Yorker*. Her maternal epitaph in "Appendix to Ordinary Time" at the end of *Men in the Off Hours* appeared in 2000, and a series of elegies for her mother, Margaret Carson, appeared in *Decreation* in 2005. In 2010, *Nox*, Carson's book-length elegy for her brother, Michael, was reproduced by New Directions. It explores, among other things, her brother's estrangement from the family, a subject that she explores first in *Plainwater*, in "The Wishing Jewel" and "Water Margins," the final two sections of "The Anthropology of Water." By the time *Nox* was published, Carson was accomplished enough as a family elegist to admonish readers (and herself by implication) about the strictures of the elegiac mode: "If you are writing an elegy begin with the blush" (*Nox*). But fifteen years earlier in 1995, Carson was not as self-assured about elegiac form, and the blush that begins *Plainwater*, in "Mimnermos: The Brainsex Paintings" shows the same declarative style with a more tentative thesis: "the poet's task, Kafka says, is to lead the isolated human being into the infinite life, the contingent into the lawful" (12). The elegist's task is even more rigorous, then, for the elegist must lead the beings isolated by death into the "infinite life" of the elegy, and from the contingency of death back into the lawful space of the family.

This is no small task as a literary project or as a spiritual quest. The urgency with which contemporary theorists examine questions of loss and mourning underlines the danger of living with a mind that may be swallowed up by its thwarted desire. To situate the elegiac impulse at the intersection of mourning and critical theory is to observe the ways in which those two demanding and capacious practices are ravenous consumers of death and desire, poised at what Carson calls in *Eros the Bittersweet* the "blind point from which you watch the object of your desire disappear into itself" (145). Carson defines Eros as "the ground where *logos* takes root between two people who are having a conversation" (145; emphasis in original), and the broken ground of such conversation can be heard in the garbled speech between the father and daughter in "The Anthropology of Water": part mourning, part desire, part demand, a search for knowledge that is not so much thwarted as circular.

But, of course, even a passionate desire for the freedom from the limitations of structuralist kinship does not equal the attainment of that freedom. In *Antigone's Claim: Kinship Between Life and Death*, Judith Butler wonders: "Is structuralist kinship the curse that is upon contemporary critical theory as it tries to approach the question of sexual normativity, sociality, and the status of the law?" (66). Butler discusses Antigone as a victim of "kinship's fatal aberration" (15), emphasizing how Antigone's position as a female mourner for male family members (both her brother Polynices and her father Oedipus) complicates notions of cultural privilege and gender in mourning practices. When, in a 1997 interview for *Matrix*, Mary di Michele asks Carson about her view of Antigone's position in a just society, Carson asserts that Antigone operates as "an absolute insider, however radical that may be in any given time or place. It becomes very radical when other people value only outside things" (13). The "insider" nature of Antigone's devotion is the imperative against which Carson's daughter-narrator struggles to define her mourning practice in "The Anthropology of Water." The narrator "wakes up inside a question" (135) and cannot distinguish for herself the duties of mourning that Antigone takes up with passionate deference and absolute devotion. There is a definite possibility that Carson may be punning on Antigone's incestuous position as an "absolute insider" in that Antigone is both sister and daughter to Oedipus and so is doubly compelled to mourn his death: once after he is spirited away at Colonus and once again as a kind of echo in her pursuit of funeral rights for her brother Polynices.

Antigone, with her pure devotion and single-minded purpose, hardly seems a melancholic figure, but, rather, a woman determined to perform a ritual that will complete mourning. Who could follow the imperative to mourn with as much devotion as Antigone brings to the task? But Butler suggests that because Antigone represents an impossible model for mourning practice, the political urgency of melancholia has gone largely unexplored in female characters in Western literature: "melancholia [is] a performance that negotiates for power, proposing that autonomy is gained through the appropriation of the authoritative voice" (11). If the female-written paternal elegy pursues the father's knowledge as a function of mourning, then the appropriation of the father's voice is necessarily problematized by the search for feminine subjectivity. The narrator of "The Anthropology of Water" attempts to appropriate the father's authority through her manipulation of epistemology, but discovers that language becomes "an event of grievance" (Butler, *Antigone's* 80) rather than a mourning practice. How would a mourning language sound if it moved beyond the "event of grievance"? In "The Anthropology of Water," the acquisition of the father's knowledge demands a kind of dogged melancholia in which the daughter declares herself unwilling to repudiate the father's word despite his loss of rationality.

The emergence of epistemological concerns in women's contemporary paternal elegies is not surprising when considered alongside feminist psychoanalytic theories about the daughter's need to identify with the father. Jessica Benjamin claims a daughter's desire for her father's love is identificatory, "a homoerotic desire, a desire for likeness that often surfaces in the latency wish to be a buddy" (128), and asserts that "the complex nature of the father–daughter relationship has often been obscured by analytic acceptance of the fallacy that all opposite-sex love is heterosexual" (128). Jane Gallop proposes that the daughter's desire for the father yields an idealized fantasy of identification: "'Love' has always been sublimated, idealized desire, away from bodily specificity and towards dreams of complementarity, and the union of opposites, difference resolved into the One. 'Love' is tangled with the woman's complicity; it may be the bribe which has persuaded her to agree to her own exclusion" (79). The daughter's homosocial desires maintain the father's status as a desired subject while she remains excluded, even as his "buddy." Are contemporary female elegists writing out of a desire to acquire the intellectual privilege of logos or in order to dismantle privilege altogether? Carson seems to want both. In *Eros the Bittersweet*, she traces the epistophilic drive back to "an ancient analogy between the wooing of knowledge and the wooing of love," in which she claims that Socrates' knowledge was "*nothing but* a knowledge of 'erotic things'" (170; emphasis in original). In "The Anthropology of Water," the father's body and speech become an amalgam of knowledge and love that idealizes identificatory inheritance, though neither he nor his daughter can attain this ideal. The father's knowledge is trapped in his cryptic utterances; his eyes become the physical manifestation of his silence, emphasizing the white space surrounding the text of his disjointed words.

The daughter, for her part, is haunted by myths of demanding fathers and vengeful daughters. Early in "The Anthropology of Water," Carson retells the Greek myth of the daughters of Danaos, fifty women who "loved their father so much it was as if they were parts of his body. When Danaos stirred in his sleep they would awaken, each in her narrow bed, staring into the dark" (118). This beloved father marries off his fifty devoted daughters, all on the same day, to fifty bridegrooms, but the daughters' paternal loyalties are not so easily transferred. Wedding ritual or no wedding ritual, these daughters do not see themselves as objects in a male homosocial exchange, and the result is bloody: "at midnight on the wedding night, fifty bedroom doors clicked shut. Then a terrible encounter took place. Each of forty-nine of the daughters of Danaos drew a sword from alongside her thigh and stabbed her bridegroom to death" (118). The forty-nine murderous daughters are cast into the Underworld (which Carson calls "hell") to haul water in sieves as their punishment. Carson reserves special attention for the fiftieth daughter "who did not draw her sword. What happened to her remains to be discovered" (118). That which "remains to be discovered" concerns the agency of the fiftieth daughter, as well as her future. By allowing her husband to live, is she obeying or disobeying her father? Are her actions quiescent or defiant? Like Lear's Cordelia, the fiftieth daughter proves her love to her father by not proving it. She allows her husband to live and effectively to replace her father as her beloved. Is this devotion or betrayal? The murdering daughters are pathologically faithful; when the fiftieth daughter resists a fate in which she would remain "part of" her father's body, her filial piety is impugned. By refusing to behave dramatically or pathologically, the fiftieth daughter escapes banishment, but also refuses the only form of father–daughter kinship offered by the myth.

Carson uses the discipline of anthropology to form her questions about father–daughter relations, mindful of the dangers of claiming kinship and suggesting that "love makes you an anthropologist of your own life" (217). Butler asserts that female representations of the death of paternal figures are often problematically situated in sexual melancholy, and propose "a certain heterosexual fatality that remains to be read" (*Antigone's* 72). Between what "remains to be discovered" and "what remains to be read," Carson and Butler, in separate projects, are zeroing in on a gap in father–daughter kinship that is, as Carson writes, as dangerous as deep water. Butler suggests that female elegiac practices move towards a subjectivity in which "schemes of intelligibility make our loves legitimate and recognizable" (*Antigone's* 24). Assuming that questions of legitimacy in this context refer to love and not genetics, under what conditions could a daughter's love for her father be considered "illegitimate"? Such excursions into auto-anthropology are irrevocably challenged by the demands of filial piety. When the narrator of "Anthropology" admits that she is "afraid I don't love you enough to do this" (139), the ambiguous "you" suggests an expectant listener, an interiorized subject to whom she is obligated by love and/or kinship structure.

While the previous chapter in this study explored how Atwood solved the conundrum of melancholia by showing her daughter figure embracing alterity as a means to elegiac subjectivity, Carson's narrator engages fully with what Nancy Holland has identified as "the doubts and debts" of daughterly piety caught in the paternal hauntology (65). The subjectivity of Carson's daughter persona is formed largely by her engagement with what Butler would call "kinship's fatal aberration": the inability of the daughter to escape the father as an interiorized object. In "The Anthropology of Water," the narrating daughter's filial piety is more than paradoxical; it is concatenated to an imperative of loss. Paternal knowledge is denied to her no matter how true her mourning.

Sophoclean Daughters: The Problem of the Body

It could be said without much dispute that Carson's version of true mourning shows her stronger ties to Sophocles than to Freud. The narrating daughter of "The Anthropology of Water" is haunted by the ancient desire to be as devoted, and as satisfied to be devoted, as Antigone: an impossible task, but one that seems tantalizingly possible to the narrator. When Carson introduces the metaphor of men as water, an element in which women may swim or drown, she reminds readers that water is an element in which, historically, women have been asked to affect proofs of their virtuous femininity. Carson glosses the Salem witch trials when a male anthropologist figure tells the narrator about "a culture he had studied where true and false virgins are identified by ordeal of water. For an intact virgin can develop the skill of diving into deep water, but a woman who has known love will drown" (117). Women in Salem were determined to be witches if they floated and innocent (though drowned) if they sank. But in Carson's formulation, floating is not enough. Her juxtaposition of diving with drowning suggests a virgin with a hermetically sealed body, an untouchable Artemis figure whose virginity gives her power. Ordinary women, by contrast, are drowned by their weight of their romantic entanglements; to "know love," in this text, is to be made dangerously vulnerable.

Carson's virgin as the gold standard for whole womanhood questions the value of sexual experience. If a woman has "known love," would she not better understand the dangers of men as "deep water," and so increase her chances of survival? Carson emphasizes the dangers of men as water, warning that "[t]he mechanisms that keep us from drowning are so fragile" (128). When Carson writes that men are like water, she confirms women's vulnerability to drowning in the uncontrollable force of their own desire. This romantic motif of drowning in desire is intimately associated with elegiac transcendence, wherein the death by water acts as a deliverance from emotional and sexual frustration. Carson's "deep water" is as dangerous as the river or ocean of a traditional elegy, but water's masculine alliance with a Neptunian principle suggests that the danger of water threatens the female elegist as much as, or more than, the lost beloved. In elegizing her father, the elegist first invokes her own sacrifice to the elements and then implies that "anthropology," as the word is used in the text, means the study of men, rather than of humankind.

But if men are the water in which women may easily drown, what then can prevent a daughter's disaster? Carson's metaphor of the father as "a door in the water" (119) creates a hinge on which gender binaries swing back and forth, from solid to liquid, from male to female, from father to daughter. A psychoanalytic reading would suggest that the father stands for the door through which a daughter must pass in order to reach adult womanhood. The father-door is a solid form in the threatening sea of the Lacanian symbolic order, a paternal life raft for the drowning daughter. When the narrator's war-hero father succumbs to "madness," her discovery that dementia is "continuous with sanity" (121) can be read as an insistence upon making meaning from the father's cryptic utterances just as she constructs love from his smallest gesture.

The daughters of Danaos loved their father so obsessively "it was as if they were parts of his body" (118), and when dementia begins to manifest in the narrator's father, he loses "the use of some of the parts of his body" (119). The correlation suggests that the father's dementia becomes a mirror for the narrator's emotional stasis, and during a visit to the father in the hospital, the narrator matches her body movements to his, duplicating his compulsive rocking motion to gain access to his rhythm. The text's concern with his corporeal degeneration and cryptic utterance interrogates all the ways in which the "eye" of the daughter's gaze cannot be spoken through the "I" of narration. In *The Body in Pain*, Elaine Scarry asserts that the pressure of the gaze upon a body in pain reveals the process by which "other persons become visible to us, or cease to be visible to us" (22). In "The Anthropology of Water," the father's body clashes with the historical concept of the heroic male body and with his own history of military service. While memories of a strong healthy body are commonly used in elegiac writing in order to reify the body's waning prowess, in this text the father's military experience is punctuated by a wartime episode in which German soldiers find nylon stockings on his plane and question him "*Wo ist die Dame?*" ["Where is the woman?"] (209). As he does not speak the language, the father cannot reply; his silence and incomprehension parallel his tacit refusal to see, and accept, his daughter's increasingly feminine body as she sits with him in the text. "Where is the woman?" is the unanswered question. The narrator has difficulty in making her father visible to her questioning gaze, but the father, as a benighted Laius figure, has not recognized the reality of his daughter's physicality since her early adolescence.

The father's garbled speech presents as much a problem to the narrator as does his opaque body. As her father's dementia advances, his speech becomes increasingly cryptic and oracular. His inarticulate speech and uncontrolled body barely resemble his known love of order and masculine reserve: "Father was a man who knew the right way to do things" (198). But this love of order attempts expression even through his limitations, his "forty-forty" conception of death. The narrator offers no possible interpretation of this utterance, for as much as it demands explication, the daughter does not ask; because the father can barely control his speech, she cannot (or will not) speak her question. The father's uninterpretable speech acts as an elegiac prosopopeia, a voice from the edge of consciousness that echoes Holland's contention that the father's logos will remain forever out of the daughter's reach. If the Lacanian Law of the Father ushers all children into the symbolic order, then in "The Anthropology of Water," the daughter's struggle to find a key to "chang[ing] everything, all the meanings" (123) inscribes both a return to and a rejection of the father as the bearer of logos. The father's struggle against his illness and the daughter's struggle to receive the father's love are clearly physical efforts, but they also represent the family's attempts to assimilate multiple versions of reality into their quotidian existence: "To live with a mad person requires many small acts of genius—the reverse of the moment when Helen Keller shouts 'Water!'" (121). This "reverse discovery" of water as the logos of madness and genius reminds us that the daughter was looking for "a door in the water" that only the father could provide. His mad utterances are as garbled (or as gargled) as though he is speaking underwater, thematizing his madness as a genius that is extra-human, even oracular. His daughter must remake all the meanings, beginning with her father's puzzling speech, to which she attributes the gravity of prophecy and the weight of wisdom.

What Is It That Others Know?: Riddle as Wisdom

As the narrator gazes upon her father's body, her "eye" is intrinsically bound up with, and frustrated by, Carson's play upon the confessional "I." The act of riddling substitutes for the demands of the gaze and becomes the daughter's way to obey her own advice and "be gentle when we question our fathers" (122). Despite the questions that the father inspires, he is interrogated very little in this text; the narrator's refusal of consolation manifests itself as a refusal to ask the questions that haunt her, especially the poignant "What is it that others know?" (127). Adam Phillips speculates in an early article on Carson that she defines "the power of love as a craving for something—knowledge, a person, or the knowledge that another person exists—that makes the difference visible and by doing so intimates the possible infinity of such differences, the sheer horror and exhilaration of how different we can be from ourselves" (115). Such studied horror at the differences between father and daughter, and between the daughter's lived experience and her desire for love, examines the role that love and knowledge play in the desire for penance.

In "The Anthropology of Water," the legitimation of mourning is conflated with the legitimation of meaning. The text's use of riddles inscribes a melancholic mercuriality in the way it sets up the pilgrim as philosophizing clown. Her first riddles display a vaudevillian razzle-dazzle, as her initial witty answers facilitate her deferral of mourning even as she moves, geographically and psychically, down the road to the place of devotion. The pilgrim seeks meaning as part of her penance; she embarks upon her pilgrimage in order to "look for the simplest question, the most obvious facts, the doors that no one may close.... I was a strong soul. Look I will change everything, all the meanings! I thought" (123). The usual purpose of a pilgrimage to Compostela is to "ask St. James to change your life" (123), but the narrator wants "all the meanings" to change, and eschewing divine intervention, is determined to do it herself. However, a reconfigured meaning is very different from an answer. Her riddles represent an attempt to circumvent the rules of traditional philosophy, refashioning Socratic dialogue as a monologue that flirts with meaning while evading clear answers. The narrator's refusal of consolation echoes her refusal to ask the questions that haunt her, especially the plaintive "What is it that others know?" (127).

What "others" may or may not know is how to balance private grief with public affect, and the narrator's declaration that a successful pilgrimage (or a successful mourning practice) will be one that helps her to change "all the meanings" is a clue to the narrator's confusion with her role in this drama. For a drama it is, and gender becomes significant to the narrator's actions. Butler points out that Antigone, too, struggles with the tensions between the "breeding imperative" (*Antigone's* 76) and the "distinctly manly excess" of melancholy "hubris" (80) manifested in her insistent public grieving. Instead of manly excess, Carson takes her Antigonal character down the road to manly contemplation tinged with a quixotic bent. As the narrator nears Compostela and potential consolation, her riddles become more simple and, ironically, less answerable. Carson notes that the heroes of Kafka's texts are trapped in their own psychic nightmares because of their inability "to ask the simplest question" (119), and so situates her narrator as both she who questions and she who will not, or cannot, give a simple answer. In an unpredictable world, Carson reminds the reader that "it is already late when you wake up inside a question" (135), and she allows the questions to hang in the air, unanswered. The need to form and ask the simplest questions can impose order upon chaos, but even ordered, logical answers may bring about the pain that makes the most "alphabetical" ordered pilgrims "cry out" (143). "What is it that others know?" the narrator asks; how do others manage to love and not be destroyed by it? When the narrator suggests, "a pilgrim is like a Noh play. Each one has the same structure, a question mark" (148), she establishes the pilgrim as a philosopher who is also her own recalcitrant pupil.

Carson's inquiry cannot ignore the body's complicity in the structure of mourning. The riddles take on a corporeal concern, designed to "riddle" the human body full of epistemological holes: "When is a pilgrim like a sieve? When he riddles" (127). While this question cannot help but recall the punishment of the daughters of Danaos, its cheekiness also suggests subversive methods of survival, the fiftieth daughter's choice; Carson's pilgrim wishes for water (and men) to pass through her without drowning her. Riddling makes this particular trick of gender possible. She suggests the physical resistance to filial love and duty: "How is a pilgrim like a blacksmith? He bends iron. Love bends him" (176). The daughter bends towards her father's love (or the lack thereof), while the father fears bending to love his daughter. The father's illness softens him and confuses them both. Moving away from elaborate puns, the narrator begins to ask the simpler but ironically less answerable questions, the result being that she goads her own speech into seriousness. "What are we made of but hunger and rage?" (175), she asks, invoking the insatiable Sphinx. David Solway, perhaps Carson's harshest critic in Canada, has made much of his concern that Carson does not "radiate an impression of lexical authority" (24), but in doing so he misses the lexical inquiry that is central to Carson's work. Proposing a series of riddles as a philosophical inquiry positions the Sphinx as philosopher and, eventually, the Sphinx as Oedipus's challenging (and unacknowledged) daughter complete with riddles and a frightening, misbegotten body.

If the narrator acts as a Sphinx figure, the obvious Oedipus figure would be the father, and, good classicist that she is, Carson suffuses the text with images of blindness and madness, and frames the father as the embodiment of the Sphinx's riddle. Recall that the Sphinx's riddle concerns the aging body: the crawling infant Oedipus; the vigorous young man who kills Laius and governs Thebes; and the enfeebled blind Oedipus, a wanderer with his daughter, old before his time. Carson presents a parallel trio of vignettes about the father figure in "The Anthropology of Water." The father is a naïve young man who refuses to believe that his daughter will grow up to become a woman, then he is an older man who emphasizes a kind of righteous domestic order, and, finally, he is the enfeebled "madman" who speaks in cryptic utterances and, though not blind, is sightless. Like the cursed king of Thebes, whose physical blindness is paralleled with his despairing insight, the father in Carson's text experiences a dementia that is "continuous with sanity" (121). This disconcerting play of sanity and madness manifests in an interpretative crisis whenever the father speaks to curse himself with "a sound not human" that Carson likens to a bodily mutilation (121), an utterance reminiscent of Butler's caveat that "language carries a violence that brings it to the limits of speakability" (*Antigone's* 80). These limits on the father's self-condemnation continue even as he smiles: "You bastard, you stupid bastard you goddamn stupid bastard you goddamn stupid useless bastard you" (216). The cumulative quality of these curses suggests a more structured utterance than the "word salad" about which the doctors have warned the narrator. He curses himself and, and in so doing, robs her of the privilege.

The father's difficulty with answering questions impedes his function as an Oedipus figure, and a curious shift occurs about halfway through the text. Carson's contention that "a pilgrim is a person who is up to something" (145) should be taken as a caveat, for the pilgrimage seems to transform the narrator into an Oedipus figure. In asking the simplest but paradoxically most difficult questions, the narrator becomes a version of Oedipus in the grotto at Colonus, a wanderer whose knowledge of horror cannot satisfy the quest for meaning. Carson's reconfiguration of Oedipus as a young woman emphasizes the fundamental despair over gender that marks this text. Is this Butler's "heterosexual fatality that remains to be read?" When the narrator notes "My father and I shook hands on Christmas, birthdays and farewells" (211), her revelation of the controlled physical contact between father and daughter locates his fear of femininity in his daughter's body. The handshakes symbolize a stark, immobilizing fear of the physical body hidden behind a veneer of WASP politeness: "It wasn't until he went mad that I began to see I had always angered him. I never knew why. I did not ask" (122). The daughter is left with another "simple question" that is impossible to ask.

"The Anthropology of Water" is haunted by a persistent riddle about the location of femininity: Where is the woman? What is it about the daughter that "always angers" her father? She turns into a woman, and, even worse, she turns into what the father refers to as "one of those helpless women" (198) who cannot change a tire; her incompetence in outdoor living is painfully evident during the camping trip in "Just For the Thrill," a section of "The Anthropology of Water" in which the pilgrimage of "Kinds of Water" is repeated and perverted. But her adolescence was spent rejecting this kind of helpless femininity, presaged by her father's gloating, "Oh, she won't be like them" (188); that is, she won't grow up to be like other women, womanly, full of mysterious uncontrollable fluids. Upon hearing her father's comment, the daughter attempts to erase her gender. She grows into a body that is "hard and flat as the armour of Athena" (189) sprung metaphorically from her father's wish to keep his daughter in an angular pre-adolescent body.

But if the father does not want the daughter to become a woman, neither does he seek manly competition with her. The narrator's attempt at embodying a paternally pleasing androgyny reaches an ironic crisis as a direct result of the father's physical debilitation. When the daughter returns from the woods with a Christmas tree she has cut down herself, a task she and the father have always performed together, Carson explicitly figures the father as Laius and the daughter as Oedipus: "He was there in the kitchen. He looked at the tree and the saw and the ax. It was something perfectly quiet. 'I didn't think you could do that,' he said. Perfectly quiet. His hands hanging down. The tiny ticking kitchen. The snow-dark morning. It was draining from him into me. I had killed him" (205–6). The narrator's possession of phallic tools, the saw and the ax, plus the signifier of the freshly cut tree, strike the father as surely as Oedipus struck Laius. Her pseudo-masculine performance is read as a usurping action instead of a filial homage. As father and daughter stand devastated in the kitchen, she feels his masculine privilege "draining" from him into her, and this extension of the metaphor of watery exchange suggests that she is flooded with guilt over accessing her father's agency. She becomes a pilgrim in order to seek penance for her symbolic patricide.

The daughter acts as Sphinx and as Oedipus, a philosopher without answers, a mourner without a ritual to express loss, cut loose from Antigonal deliverance while still subject to the Antigonal imperative to mourn. Her body attempts to create an internal ritual of mourning; to appease her father's fear of femininity, the narrator does not menstruate for thirteen years (190). That "hard flat body" recalls descriptions of anorexic women who strive to maintain a boy-like body, accompanied by amenorrhea, a loss of the menstrual period brought on by maintaining a low body weight. The daughter's desire to "suppress the natural facts of 'woman' altogether" (189) becomes a bid for gender safety, as Susan Bordo asserts: "As [the anorexic's] body begins to lose its traditional feminine curves, its breasts and hips and rounded stomach, and begins to feel and look more like a spare, lanky male body, she begins to feel untouchable, out of reach of hurt... she has unexpectedly discovered an entry into the privileged male world, a way to become what is valued in our culture, a way to become safe, above it all" (23). In order to obtain the father's perpetually withheld approval, the daughter limits her female possibilities and attempts, with some success, to become asexual, "a young, strong, stingy person of no particular gender—all traits advantageous to the pilgrim" (123). Gender neutrality is another way for the daughter to try on the persona of the good son of father–son filiation.

However, female desire emerges in this text through the imagery of elemental fire. Phillips suggests that Carson is a Freudian, "if only in her sense that all language is the language of love, the language of self-betrayal" (116).

In "The Anthropology of Water," Carson's fire imagery speaks the desire for the father's love that overwhelms the daughter. One of the pilgrim's early questions concerns the heat of desire that longs to be spoken: "What is the fear inside language? No accident of the body can make it stop burning" (141). The fire worsens on the journey, prompting the pilgrim's self-definition: "Pilgrims were people who were glad to take off their clothing, which was on fire" (154). The burning pilgrim endures the fire of rejection by imagining her father's attention as soothing water, but his final utterance foregrounds the daughter's desire for paternal love to be unquenchable: "Fires are the furthest in you are and the worst you are" (240). The twisted syntax of this sentence, with its assonance of the half-rhymed "furthest" and "worst," is disturbingly lyrical. The "worst" and "furthest" fires in the human body are existential, and the "you" of the father's final utterance may be either self-referential or accusatory. In this anthropology, what does the daughter-elegist do with the questions she forms? Is it preferable to drown in love or burn with memory?

Much in the way that the narrator attempts to transcend femininity through her occupation of a body with "no particular gender," Carson writes the performance of penance as an attempt to go beyond pilgrimage. At the end of "Kinds of Water," the narrator travels past the cathedral that houses the bones of the apostle to arrive at Finisterre, the end of the earth (184). At this *ultima thule*, the text suggests a death as mysterious as that of *Oedipus at Colonus*, the corporeal vanishing that left no grave at which the distressed Antigone could mourn. The Sphinx throws herself into the sea when Oedipus answers her riddle, and "Kinds of Water" ends with the narrator lying, dead or dying, in the ocean off the rocks at Finisterre, a poetic death by water that suggests the drowning about which Carson warns readers at the beginning of the "The Anthropology of Water": "Clothe yourself, the water is deep" (118). The narrator's most difficult riddle remains: "What is it that others know?" (127). The assumption that others have knowledge that makes love less bewildering makes the pilgrim almost unbearably covetous of this knowledge.

While the grandiose gesture of throwing herself off a cliff affirms (and perhaps parodies) the tradition of the suicidal melancholic genius, the daughter acts out her monstrous self and becomes the Sphinx as an embodiment of frustration. Caught in the "fearful ashy light that falls on the end of the world" (187) the narrator's attempt to go beyond pilgrimage brings her not to transcendence but to a failure of the mind that echoes the father's madness. When Carson writes, "You take hold of my paws and cross them on my breast" (187), the daughter as dead Sphinx becomes a ceremonial representative of what Phillips calls Carson's "weird rationality of Eros that love is a ridiculous disfiguring" (115). The disfiguring Sphinx returns the mourner to abjection at the hands of Western mythology.

However, in this text, the daughter-narrator can sustain neither her Sphinx disguise nor her performance of self-sacrifice. She survives in the text to live Derrida's "unbearable paradox of fidelity" ("By Force" 159) as an insoluble riddle about father–daughter kinship that "remains to be read" in Butler's terms. Like the Sphinx's havoc-wreaking question, the paradox of fidelity remains, in this text, "a riddle too deep for common wits" ("Oedipus the King" 36). The narrator's attempt to go beyond the consolation of pilgrimage brings her not to transcendence but to a melancholic turn at the end of her thwarted journey to consolation, a turn that would suggest, according to Butler, that melancholia makes mourning possible (*Psychic* 170). The search for the fruition of logos and eros is ultimately thwarted in "The Anthropology of Water" as each section of the text repeats the journey that ends in frustration, whether the man fragments (as the father does in "Kinds of Water"), or withholds intimacy (as the lover does in the subsequent section, "Just For the Thrill"), or disappears (as the narrator's brother does in the final section of the prose poem, "Water Margins"). Though she is alive at the end of "Water Margins" and "does her best" on the advice of her father (258; 260), the daughter-elegist becomes a surviving Antigonal figure who is subject, as Carson suggests in "TV Men: Antigone" from *Men in the Off Hours*, to "too much memory" like her father before her. This is an Antigone who is so disconnected from her mourning practice that she claims, "I do not lament. / God's will is not some sort of physics, is it" ("TV Men: Antigone"). Here is "the unbearable paradox of fidelity" (Derrida, "By Force" 159) acted out on the body of a woman; she becomes dissociated from self, from family, from God, and from her grief.

As an elegy, "The Anthropology of Water" remains problematically obedient to the Antigonal imperative; the narrator's quest to change "all the meanings" (123) results in a reiteration of the historical idea of female filial piety as self-sacrifice. If works by Page and Macpherson situate the need for a commitment to a productive melancholia in order to question female subjectivity with the paternal elegy, Carson's text commits the mourning daughter to a riddle about father–daughter kinship that seems to challenge elegiac convention without the rigorous energy of anagnorisis. Discovery, in this text, is painful rather than invigorating. By maintaining relentless loyalty to her father, the narrator, like the forty-nine daughters of Danaos, sacrifices everything. Carson prophesies at the text's beginning that the "The Anthropology of Water" will tell the story of the fiftieth daughter of Danaos, she who did not kill her husband and whose story remains to be discovered. However, the daughter of "The Anthropology of Water" is not this fiftieth daughter but, rather, one of the forty-nine who demonstrated their desperate loyalty to their father. The narrator, instead of being condemned to "spend eternity gathering water in a sieve" (118), is condemned to articulate the anthropology of water—the ways in which men are water and women carry them, drown in them, or witness them slipping away.

When Carson writes that "a question can travel into an answer as water into thirst" (122), she intimates a performable penance and a drastic cure for dutiful daughterhood, both of which depend on a pilgrimage towards knowledge. Accepting her claim that "pilgrims love a good riddle" (125), this text proposes riddles that it refuses to answer, appearing to offer only the consolation of self-sacrifice, which is no consolation at all. But, curiously, a lack of consolation does not stop Carson from ending the daughter's pilgrimage with a declaration of faith, the kind of declaration that presupposes in good elegiac tradition that death presents no obstacle to devotion: "I am one who has been to the holy city and tasted its waters, its kinds. // Pilgrims were people who carried little. They carried it balanced on the heart" (187). What happens to that which is carried off-balance: the unasked question, the untranslatable speech, the deteriorating body? "The Anthropology of Water" carries forward an insoluble riddle about father–daughter kinship that refuses strategies of comprehension: "Where is the woman?" (209). The mourning daughter as a woman who cannot be located, on a pilgrim's map or in the father's eyes, remains a riddle she cannot, or will not, answer. The "strong soul" (123) who wished to change "all the meanings" (123) has been swallowed by her devotion to choosing her duty. Her melancholic turn grants her subjectivity, but it does not console her. The waters of the holy city remain, for this pilgrim, untasted.

7

Gateway Politics, Grief Poetics

West Meets West in Kristjana Gunnars's *Zero Hour*

> To write you this I have come to the Gateway to the West. Not because the West is intriguing. But because it is there: open, dry, with little culture and much politics. And beyond the West there is the ocean. The jungle. The rains. A place to long for. To think towards.
> — Kristjana Gunnars, *Zero Hour*

> Go west, young man, and grow up with the country.
> — John Soule, editorial, *Terre Haute Express* (attributed)

The Elegiac West

West as the space of opportunity, west as philosophical destination: the two quotations above suggest a dichotomy about ideas of the West as the great good place in North America and, more significantly, about the state of mind that accompanies the decision to travel west—into the sunset, towards the edge of the continent, and perhaps beyond everyday experience. Heading west in order to seek a new beginning—be that fresh start nationally inflected as John Soule asserts or spiritually aligned as Kristjana Gunnars implies—suggests an engagement with geography that is not limited to the physical act of traversing space, but also involves a choice to leave the centre for the relative wildness of the margins. Both Soule and Gunnars gesture to a preparatory moment before heading west, as though the West demands that the traveller transform into something other than the usual self. To stand at the "Gateway to the West" and prepare to enter the new frontier is to rethink the nature of being, selfhood, and change.

The advice attributed to an 1851 editorial in the *Terre Haute Express* by John Babson Lane Soule exhorting expansion into the western territories as an American opportunity for both adventure and financial gain seems worlds away from Kristjana Gunnars's allusive and genre-challenging non-fiction work *Zero Hour.* Soule's utterance is often attributed to Horace Greeley, founder and editor of the *New York Tribune*, who made the aphorism famous in his 1865 editorial. Debate rages on as to the original authorship, and as well it might, for the differences between Greeley's East Coast position and Soule's more liminal "gateway" position in the Mid-West are significant. The injunction to "go west" means something when uttered from the centre of the continent that it does not when uttered from the eastern seaboard. Soule's position as editor of the *Terre Haute Express* in the mid-nineteenth century indicates that he was acquainted with a gateway view, and spoke from a place that could be described, as Gunnars describes Manitoba, as "open, dry, with little culture and much politics" (9).

Beyond geography, the western edge of the continent is an effulgent symbol of freedom in both the American and Canadian imagination, and Soule's masculinist advice can be read alongside Gunnars's philosophical peregrinations as historically and geographically situated notions of paradise. Allan Pritchard's survey of paradise motifs in British Columbia literature, working with texts from the 1840s to the 1970s, has made the point that the West Coast has been written as an earthly paradise since the early days of its European explorers, and the metaphor continues to be ubiquitous. However, Pritchard also points out that those who encounter earthly paradise live in fear of their dispossession of that same paradise: "the image of paradise cannot be used without the apprehension of paradise lost" (36). Considering the position that paradise occupies in an elegiac text such as *Zero Hour*, a text that thinks towards the West rather than actually occupying it, is to consider paradise as a goal of completion, something that we should regard with some suspicion.

To read the West in *Zero Hour* as the locale of consolation means conflating consolation with paradise in a way that complicates the possibility of earthly consolation. In *Zero Hour*, as in "The Anthropology of Water," a geographical journey becomes part of the elegist's search for a mourning practice. While both Carson and Gunnars write daughter-protagonists who are driven by desperation, Gunnars's text references the national dream of a cross-country journey and folds into the mourner's journey a politics of peace that is larger than personal peace. The mourner's sojourn at "the Gateway to the West"—where she waits for mourning to overtake her and purge her before daring to traverse the prairies and enter the dreamscape of the West Coast—turns into a geographical project, as she uses the landscape to map the potential for mourning and, eventually, the progress of her mourning practice. Instead of a pilgrimage, then, as Carson writes in "The Anthropology of Water," Gunnars gives us a geography of mourning that situates global grief in a local context and considers histories of dispossession alongside those of personal mourning.

The literary tendency to imagine the West as both prosaically "there" and mythically "beyond" is neither frivolous nor contradictory, but, rather, a philosophical position that informs the Canadian metanarrative, as Robert Kroetsch suggests, as paradoxically defined by resistance to unity. Where Soule's gateway points to opportunity for growth as social maturity and financial gain in keeping with the American Dream, Gunnars's gateway is closer to the Kroetschian periphery, in which "doubt about our ability to know invades the narrative" (Kroetsch 23). In much of Canadian literature, Paradise West is "a place to long for" but not necessarily a place at which one may arrive. Decades of prairie literature affirm that Paradise cannot be found by rushing towards it, as Margaret Laurence's heroines—Stacey in *The Fire-Dwellers* and Hagar in *The Stone Angel*—discover upon arriving in Vancouver after years of hard-scrabble prairie life, and Laurence is by no means the only Canadian writer to construct the West Coast as an ambiguous paradise. Historical novels by Daphne Marlatt (*Ana Historic*) and SKY Lee (*Disappearing Moon Café*) suggest that the iconoclastic personal freedom of the West Coast was not available to female or Chinese immigrants to the coast in the late nineteenth century. Dorothy Livesay's 1944 long poem about Vancouver's industrial boom, "West Coast," notes that workers were "swept from farm and mine / drawn to the hungry suction of the sea," suggesting a rapacious capitalism in the heart of Paradise. In much Canadian literature, the West Coast is not so much Paradise found as it is Paradise deferred. Furthermore, Gunnars makes it clear that arriving at the West Coast is never just a matter of buying a plane ticket or driving over the mountains. The West as Paradise is a philosophical destination that must be thought towards, and in *Zero Hour*, Gunnars offers an unrepentant philosophy of desire that is all too aware of the effort that thinking takes.

Gunnars juxtaposes the stark prairie with the paradisal coast in a postmodern text that reaches beyond the nation-building ideals of "growing up with the country," and, instead, contemplates what it would mean to grow beyond the demands of time and space. Offering fragments of life writing, philosophy, literary theory, and a particular reading of the geography of the Canadian West, Gunnars arranges these shards in a shatter pattern by exploring the traditional elegiac mode through a very contemporary obsession with nuclear annihilation. Although the book's publication in 1991 technically disqualifies it from being part of Jon Paul Fiorentino and Robert Kroetsch's definition of twenty-century "post-prairie poetics," Gunnars's intense exploration of the ways in which "the anxiety of geography...reshapes the context" (Fiorentino and Kroetsch 9) of place suggests strongly that *Zero Hour* works within a similar post-prairie modality. Part prose poem, part elegy, part philosophical treatise, *Zero Hour* is the first-person account of a woman's attempt to establish a satisfying mourning ritual in the aftermath of her father's death. The text engages with elegiac conventions of pastoral renewal even as Gunnars casts a doubtful authorial eye on the Christian consolation on which such conventions lean. Her metaphor for the moment of her father's death is a nuclear explosion, the "zero hour" of her title, and the mourner must then travel through the emotional equivalent of a nuclear winter in search of a nurturing landscape. The narrator—who is explicitly identified in the text as a literary version of the author herself—describes an imaginative longing for that which lies "beyond the West" as a spiritual desire interlaced with a philosophical premise to move beyond her mourning self. But it is in Gunnars's inquiry into elegiac paradox that *Zero Hour* finds purchase as a text that rewrites the West as it rewrites mourning. The geographical west is only coincidentally located near to the consolatory West, beyond which lies Paradise. The impulse towards Paradise is far more significant than any actual movement towards it, for in this text, longing trumps doing, and *Zero Hour* proposes a West in which the impossibility of consolation is yoked to a mappable certitude. In true postmodern fashion, the Gateway defines the West by refusing to define it. Were the protagonist of Gunnars's *Zero Hour* to actually "go west, young woman" in order to keep the country (and all its messy postmodern disunity) at her back, her arrival would undo the premise of the Paradise that lies "beyond the West" (that is, beyond the space that mourning occupies).

The Gateway to the West as a philosophical space of preparation is wryly dismissed in Gunnars's initial description, but we cannot ignore that this dismissal echoes Northrop Frye's canon-defining question "where is here?" from his much-quoted "Conclusion" to *Literary History of Canada,* even as it reiterates George Mallory's claim about his reason for repeatedly climbing Mount Everest: "Because it's there." This claim is made doubly ironic in *Zero Hour* with the lugubrious implication that life in a Gateway city is a barely surmountable obstacle. Add to this a hint of Gertrude Stein's statement about her brief return to her hometown of Oakland, California, in *Everybody's Autobiography*: "There's no *there* there." All things considered, this West may not be intriguing, but it is most definitely there. But, to return to Frye's question, where in this text is there? Even a postmodern prose poem cannot entirely sidestep one of the most contentious points in working towards a thesis of the West in Canada: Where does the west begin? At the ocean, interior, mountains, foothills, prairie? And whose West is it: the West settled by pioneers from Europe, or the West of the indigenous peoples? Gunnars aligns notions of the West as stark prairie and lush coast as death and regeneration, and reconfigures what she calls "the disappointment, the heartbreak of the West" ("Was the West Ever One?" 118) into a post-prairie diasporic elegy. In *Zero Hour*, the father's death is conflated with the ends of the earth, the end of consciousness, and the end of meaning.

The Poetics of Zero

Writing beyond the limits of genre is a career-long aim for Gunnars. In an essay titled "On Writing Short Books" in her 2004 collection *Stranger at the Door: Writers on Writing*, Gunnars considers the popular expectation that novels must be lengthy tomes and argues instead for the appeal of the "brief, intensely written, poetic narrative" (86), citing Elizabeth Smart's *By Grand Central Station I Sat Down and Wept* as the ultimate Canadian example. Referring to another short book, Albert Camus' *The Outsider*, Gunnars observes that such books are often deeply allusive and "intergeneric" and furthermore, that the "brevity of narration is in itself a philosophical position" ("On Writing" 86–87), and that such books tend "towards the fragmented, the poetic and the theoretical" and demand "to be lived with rather than simply read and put aside for the next one" (86). Although she does not name her own text in her essay, it becomes clear that *Zero Hour* represents one of Gunnars's short books: a brief, intense and highly allusive narrative. *Zero Hour*'s use of fragmentation as a kind of shatter pattern, in keeping with Gunnars's explosion imagery, corresponds to Robert Kroetsch's idea that the postmodern novel treats the ongoing present as "the debris of something else" and any form of immediate experience as a digression from the "real" narrative of the past ("On Writing" 84). For Gunnars, this kind of book resists being consumed in the way that more realist texts are consumed: "Given that we cannot know the whole story, it would be absurd to try to master the narrative in all its parts and provide closure as well" ("On Writing" 85–86). Practising this liminal short book form that negotiates the space between a novella and a long poem, Gunnars uses the metaphor of the father's death as a bomb to convey the "sense of living on the margin of 'big' history"

("On Writing" 84): in this case, the "big history" of institutionalized and governmental violence that forms the subtext of *Zero Hour.*

The resistance to closure is important to reading *Zero Hour* as a contemporary elegy that considers the personal affect of mourning alongside the political implications of historical violence. Such explorations are not unknown in Canadian elegiac work, with Dennis Lee's *Civil Elegies* and Fred Wah's *Waiting for Saskatchewan* as two examples of long poetic sequences that fold the narrator-mourner's grief into troubled revelations of governmental policies of racism and war. However, the resistance to closure, and perhaps to consolation itself, is also a vital component of what Gunnars calls her own "poetry of belligerence" (183) in her essay "Avoidance and Confrontation: Excerpts from Notes on a Longpoem Poetics," published in *Trace: Prairie Writers on Writing* in 1986. Asserting that writers of her generation inherited "the post-war language of crisis that comes with the nuclear age" (183), Gunnars describes her struggle to write two kinds of psychological and linguistic estrangement: "the 'permanent' alienation of modernism" and a post-Hiroshima "social alienation [from] the company of the living" (180). Written with the fragmentation and the intergeneric allusiveness of the short book, *Zero Hour* presents social and geographical alienation estrangement through two central metaphors: grief as the emotional equivalent of nuclear winter, and the West as a Paradise that lies beyond consolation.

The major literary allusion in *Zero Hour* is to French philosopher and semiotician Roland Barthes's idea of "degree zero writing" from his 1953 text *Writing Degree Zero.* Barthes debates the possibilities for language use that extends beyond stale reference, possibilities that he claims are realized only in the dictionary or in poetry, where the written word may be "reduced to a sort of zero degree, pregnant with all past and future specifications," and, therefore, "contain simultaneously all the acceptations from which a relational discourse might have required it to choose" (48). Picking up on Barthes's idea of an encyclopaedic function of a word, Gunnars declares that *Zero Hour* will be her attempt at "ground zero writing... writing in which the author does not know what to do" because the "writing is enacted exactly where the bomb fell" (*Zero Hour* 10). Though the term "ground zero" was coined in the early days of the atomic age, Gunnars's use of the term to explore the literary practice of mourning predates the more recently popularized use of "Ground Zero" to indicate the site of the terrorist attacks on and destruction of the World Trade Center towers in New York City. *Zero Hour,* written in 1991, was published ten years before the implications of locating "ground zero" as a site of mourning and regeneration was made culturally explicit to the reading population of North America. The metaphor is fundamental to Gunnars's notion of entering a space with the intention of establishing a mourning practice. In *Zero Hour*, "ground zero" functions as a symbol of physical annihilation and of spiritual emptiness, as well as a statement of poetics: "If the mind were a nuclear reactor with a built-in safety shutdown mechanism, I could say my mind shuts down when thoughts of my father's decline and fall occur. All the meters instantly go down. All the arrows suddenly point to zero.... You are left with a story that is not a story. A novel that is not a novel, a poem no longer a poem" (*Zero Hour* 29).

Gunnars's concern with nuclear escalation and the need for nuclear disarmament has been a prominent feature in several of her texts. In "Avoidance and Confrontation," she vows to "write poetry that will help rechannel the ingredients of the Nuclear Age" (182). Nuclear disarmament acts as a major plot device in her 1989 novel, *The Prowler*, and is a prominent thematic concern in her 1985 volume of poetry, *The Night Workers of Ragnarök*. Given Gunnars's politics, the cameo appearance in *Zero Hour* of American physicist Richard Feynman as her father's dissertation supervisor at the California Institute of Technology is both highly appropriate and deeply ironic. Feynman worked on the Manhattan Project when he was a young man, and his image as a mentor figure to the narrator's father is an excellent example of Barthes's degree zero writing as writing that is all possibility. If the portrayal of that narrator's brilliant geophysicist father is largely given over to elegiac encomium, then the allusion to Feynman—even though he is mentioned in the text only as her father's dissertation supervisor—suggests a blip in paternal praise by referencing Feynman's historical legacy as a pioneer of the atomic age (*Zero Hour* 83).

Considering nuclear disaster as her most developed metaphor for violence, both historical and personal, the Icelandic-born Gunnars notes that "global nuclear escalation" is "an obsession in Scandinavia," but she is surprised to find the issue "woefully absent from Canadian letters": "There has been talk of making the Nordic countries a nuclear-free zone, and discussion is constantly taking place on issues of world peace. I could not help noticing the insidiousness of the situation where a nation [Iceland] without armed forces, dedicated to peace, nonetheless cannot escape the effects of nuclear escalation" (*Night Workers* 4). Gunnars's proposal to "think towards" a paradise in the West is as global as it is local and as political as it is personal. Her designation of the West Coast as paradise can be linked to the environmental and peace politics of that region as well; the cities of Vancouver and Victoria in British Columbia have passed ordinances declaring the regions to be nuclear-weapon-free zones, meaning that neither nuclear weaponry nor nuclear energy—including the materials for creating such technologies—are allowed within city limits, a law that the ports must enforce on a regular basis, especially with nuclear-powered American military vessels approaching their shores on a regular basis. The "effects of nuclear escalation" as Gunnars writes about them in *The Night Workers of Ragnarök* with its allusion to the Nordic concept of Apocalypse, are undeniably real, but in *Zero Hour*, these effects are metaphorically linked to the grief process. Far from offering an instructional narrative on how to get to Paradise, Gunnars contemplates what it is to live at the ground zero of affect, writing grief as an emotional annihilation equivalent to a nuclear disaster: "when a world disappears, it takes away with it everything you are up to that moment. Your past is erased within a few minutes and you no longer recognize it as your own. Suddenly you stand up and find you have to start over. There is no you" (*Zero Hour* 11). Declaring that she wants to write a book that demonstrates "loss without commentary" (25), the narrator offers a text that "steps outside of time" in order to get to the "zero" of grief (17). In *Zero Hour*, even the paradisal West Coast becomes vulnerable to denatured science and to human frailty. Gunnars offers an anti-pastoral symbolism that threatens Paradise West, emphasizing nuclear disaster as perverted entropy and suggesting fruitfully that her spirituality does align on some points with geography. In their shared vulnerability to despairing annihilation, West does meet west.

Gateway and Ground: The Politics of Mourning

Gunnars's "Gateway to the West" and, not coincidentally, the gateway to her state of mourning, is the city of Winnipeg. As Deborah Keahey notes in *Making It Home: Place in Canadian Prairie Literature,* Winnipeg acts as a "transformative site" in *Zero Hour*, as the narrator "makes home" (48) out of the strangeness of the city. The gateway function of Winnipeg, the fact that the city represents both west and not-west, emptied of "culture" yet filled with "politics," makes the city not only a transformative site, but also a philosophical trope: a gateway beyond the limitations of the self. Like a pushpin in the map of mourning, Winnipeg as Gateway to the West marks the West as an elegiac space of annihilation and regeneration, particularly as the Gateway's history of "much politics" forces the narrator to read a culture of profound mourning that lurks beneath her view of "little culture."

But before she can access the gateway, Gunnars's configuration of the West in her elegiac narrative begins as a declaration of intention and location of place that confounds the tradition of pastoral consolation. The death of the narrator's father takes place in the lush Willamette Valley in Oregon. Geographically, botanically, climate-wise, our narrator is already immersed in the paradisal pastoral beauty of the West Coast. But much depends upon how we view the west in this spiritual geography. The prairie and the coastal rainforest occupy positions on a map of mourning, points on a compass that we can read as Purgatorio and Paradiso, as though Gunnars is refashioning the opening of the Inferno portion of Dante's *The Divine Comedy*. Midway through her life's journey, she finds herself, not lost in "a dark wood of error" (Dante, Canto I), but, rather, in the stark landscape of grief. Moving east in order to think towards and eventually "beyond the West" is perhaps illogical, but *Zero Hour* configures the West as a spiritual destination, and the necessities of the mourning journey cannot be subject only to the force of logic. Spiritually and philosophically, this mourner's journey begins with the search for a space that reflects and even affirms her annihilated world. The Canadian prairies offer her a geographic demonstration of the paradoxical elegiac mode: space that appears empty but is historically and psychologically full and is evocative of a profound absence that bespeaks a presence. Much of *Zero Hour* is occupied with aligning the ethos of the prairies with the narrator's mythology of mourning. While the narrator's geographical route is undeniably circuitous, her emotional route follows the fractured logic of mourning. Grief is pure affect, but mourning is a process that demands ritual, and literary mourning loves a mythic symbol; for the narrator of *Zero Hour*, finding the Gateway to the other world is first an idea, then a ritual, and then finally a geographic space.

Historically, Winnipeg was dubbed the "Gateway to the West" during the nineteenth century when Ontario politicians advocated for Western expansion. In the United States, the same nickname was applied to both Fargo, North Dakota, and to St. Louis, Missouri, for similar reasons. The slogan is still used occasionally about Winnipeg, though the city's official slogan has become the non-historical, non-situated, giddily assertive "Winnipeg: One Great City!" This new slogan, blandly but vigorously proclaiming "greatness," does not reference the city's historical context or cultural milieu, but Gunnars's use of the old slogan in *Zero Hour* introduces a series of historical and cultural allusions to the city's past. As much as the narrating daughter claims that she desires a "blessedly empty and private place" (*Zero Hour* 27), it is the history of the region that teaches her about mourning. In fact, as the city of Winnipeg insinuates its history upon the text of *Zero Hour*, the city as entity and as historical site awakens the narrator's personal mourning to the role that mourning can play in inspiring political urgency. When the narrator holes up in the echoing empty rooms of an old mansion, adjacent to but safe from the floods and plagues of mosquitoes of Biblical proportions for which Winnipeg is infamous, her choice of mourning space is neither unmarked nor empty. Far from indulging in stereotypical regionalism that designates Ontario and British Columbia as great wealthy, fruit-bearing green provinces separated by a thousand miles of dust called the Canadian prairie, Gunnars's protagonist notes the unexpected greenness of the city, the gardens and lawns: beauty notable even in, or especially in, this supposedly purgatorial space. But Gunnars also notes that Winnipeg remains a "city of warehouses" (19), as it has been for more than a century: a storage and distribution centre for agricultural products of the prairies and for manufactured products from Eastern Canada. The idea that emotion may be stored and distributed at a later date has a great deal to do with rituals of mourning and could suggest that Gunnars's empty mansion is another kind of warehouse.

The mansion as metaphor becomes even more poignant and historically compromised as the narrator notes that the house was "built and owned by one of the owners of a warehouse during the heyday of the Exchange District" (20). The location of that mansion within the Gateway city says something about the guiding persona of the city of Winnipeg in this text. Despite the fact that she feels as though her own past has been wiped away by the enormity of her loss, the narrator finds that her search for a space that is unmarked by grief is impossible. She comes to understand that she cannot find a personal space for mourning without unearthing a politicized space of mourning. Such politicized space fans out from her personal space in historical waves, including her neighbourhood, the city, the surrounding prairies, the west that leads to the West: all spaces haunted by historical violence. The beautiful tree-lined neighbourhood in which the mansion is situated, described by Gunnars as "an old estate located in a park of such mansions, secluded by three enormous gates through which you pass" (20), is immediately recognizable to current or former Winnipeg residents as Armstrong's Point, on which the first mansion was built in 1845, and now more colloquially known as "the Gates." This neighbourhood in the Gateway to the West has its own internal gates and not everyone is welcome to enter. The original function of the metal gates was to lock out the undesirable working class that populated boomtown Winnipeg in the late nineteenth century, when the city limits began to creep towards the elaborate homes of Armstrong's Point. Ironically, since the 1950s, the Gates neighbourhood has shared an east–west boundary with one of the most poverty-stricken areas of Winnipeg. The gates still stand at the borders of the neighbourhood, but they are no longer locked, not because the spirit of solidarity has seized the residents of Armstrong's Point, but because the gates were ineffective in keeping the privileged space separate. (Current residents have found that active police surveillance does what the psychological barrier of stone gates could no longer accomplish.)

In *Zero Hour*, the empty mansion in which the narrator lives carries a legacy as ironic nostalgia for the city's commoditized glory days from the 1890s to the 1920s, and its riverside location in Armstrong's Point also suggests that the mansion sits on land that was much in demand by Metis and poor Scottish farmers from the 1840s to the 1860s, a site of contention in the Red River Rebellion of 1869–70. In the Manitoba Act of 1870, these peoples were issued "Manitoba Script" from the federal government, entitling the bearers to good farming lots lining the Red and Assiniboine Rivers. Such claims were never honoured, as the Manitoba Metis Federation reminded the Manitoba government in April 2006, when the Federation insisted that the province make good on its 135-year-old debt of river lot land. Located on the banks of the Assiniboine River, Armstrong's Point would come under the terms of those land claims, as would various communities in and surrounding Winnipeg. In the present day, the gateposts of Armstrong's Point indicate a socio-economic, class-based, and racialized border between the residents of the rooming houses on one side of the street (many of them of Aboriginal and Metis backgrounds) and the mostly white residents of the graciously aging mansions on the other. In the metaphor of the empty mansion, Gunnars's personal mourning practice runs up against historical echoes of mourned space that has already been stolen and recommodified.

Gunnars inscribes the Aboriginal subtext of *Zero Hour* through the narrator's two encounters with the Cree community. The narrator, invited to watch the dance of mourning performed by a Cree woman whose father has died, admires the indigenous culture's acceptance of and ritual to acknowledge "loss without commentary" (25). While she knows she can neither appropriate nor imitate the dance, she remembers and records it as evidence of mourning that does not "launder emotions" (17); the Cree woman's mourning dance lives in the narrator's memory as the example she admires but cannot follow. Later in the text, the narrator walks behind three Cree residents from the neighbourhood abutting the Gates and observes a teenage boy in the group beat a butterfly to death with his t-shirt. This is Winnipeg as Gateway: to an annihilated cultural past, to losses both personal and political, to pastoral consolation abutted onto the violence of poverty. The narrator realizes that the annihilation that she fears has already happened to indigenous populations in Canada: thousands of people have been institutionally and governmentally estranged from their families and their cultures, and communities have been usurped by despair and loss about which collective mourning has not yet finished.

Heartbreak of the West

It is possible to read the end of *Zero Hour* as quite conventional in terms of the elegiac consolation that it proposes. Completing the text as her ritual of mourning, Gunnars's narrator prepares to leave the mansion with the advent of fall; like Milton's swain in the final line of *Lycidas*, she will move on to "freshe fields and pastures new." However, as with many elegiac texts, *Zero Hour* debates the latitudes and paradoxes of consolation, and the narrator cherishes this definition sent in a friend's letter: "the only consolation I give you is that you will never get over it" (92). If the loss of her father is world-destroying, as Gunnars maintains throughout *Zero Hour*, to what fresh fields can the mourner realistically move? For the final unmaking of this world, Gunnars turns to Norse mythology for an alternate view of Paradise. Valhalla, the warrior's heaven, is understood to be merely a way station for warriors (albeit a very pleasant one) until the true paradise, Gimli, emerges after the climactic battle of Ragnarök. Gimli is also the name of a town on Lake Winnipeg, just north of the city, and the largest concentration of Icelanders outside of Iceland. The narrator attends a cultural festival there, presided over by the Viking statue that welcomes visitors to the town and by the not-dissimilar physical person of Icelandic-Canadian scholar and poet David Arnason. In *Zero Hour*, Arnason presides over Gimli like Odin after Ragnarök, reminding the crowd that it "must protect its own culture" (93). This is a different version of Paradise West, and the narrator's image of "many hundred pairs of hands ... clapping madly against the sun-laden blue sky" (93) seems to be the embodiment of heavenly approval, a surprise after the mournful tone of much of *Zero Hour*. It seems as though Ragnarök is over; we are in Gimli now.

But just as the repopulation of the west by immigrants from Scandinavia and all parts of Europe—those settler-invader populations—displaced but could not replace the Aboriginal peoples who originally hunted and lived on that land, so the making of the migrant's world, with its injunction to "protect its own culture," cannot quite dispel the politicized mourning to which the narrator has been awakened. In section 16 of *The Prowler*, Gunnars notes that a pejorative term for Icelanders is "white Inuit," connoting people who are foreign to both Iceland and Denmark, and yet claim a contested indigeneity to Iceland. While readers should take seriously Len Findlay's warning that many literary strategies to "self-Indigenize" in Canadian literature are doomed to merely "reinscribe diffusionist colonialism" (372), we should also consider the discussion between Gunnars, Marilyn Dumont, and Hiromi Goto in "Was the West Ever One?" about the parallels between the indigenous peoples who were removed from tribal hunting grounds on the prairies and the destitute Europeans who "were lured by false advertising" to farm the Canadian West (117). For Gunnars, these Europeans (including those "white Inuit" Icelanders) were so thoroughly "conquered by the West" that she notes "the disappointment, the heartbreak of the West is still in the air" (117–18). This similarity between those indigenous and immigrant populations who were "conquered" in different contexts by the project of western settlement suffuses *Zero Hour* with profound historical grief. Gunnars's protagonist knows it is her task to show "solidarity with the grieving" (25) she has found at the Gateway, and demonstrate respect to the mourning that remains unconsoled and largely unacknowledged when her ritual has been completed. She remains in spiritual debt to the example of the Cree woman dancing her grief for her father: the gift of observing "loss without commentary." The death of the narrator's father has reminded her that "*there is no zero on the clock.* To get to zero, you have to step outside time" (122; emphasis in original). The conflation of time and space, being at ground zero at zero hour, suggests that a history of annihilation, like a history of mourning, is always current and can never be fully consoled. It is loss without commentary, but it is always in need of commemoration.

It is towards such needful commemoration that the final pages of *Zero Hour* builds, for, on the level of story, the ending of the text is more indicative of Gunnars's "combining of harmony and disjuncture" ("Avoidance" 182) than a completion of mourning and more in line with a productive melancholia than consolation. Deborah Keahey suggests that the ending of *Zero Hour* is "massively confusing" with the sudden introduction of the narrator's son and his violin into what has been for most of the text a space of deep loneliness, as the beauty of the son's music suggests a final symbol of homemaking in a site that the protagonist is leaving (49). Appearing to offer familial consolation and a generational resolution of mourning, the narrator's son, the boy "in whom all [her] father's hopes are bound" (127) enters his mother's mansion apartment just as he appears earlier in the text at his grandfather's bedside to offer the gift of his youth and resiliency in the face of despair (110–11). When the boy plays his violin for his dying grandfather, he plays European music and American jazz, and the music is clearly a gift for the narrator's father who listens "raptly" (111). However, the key to reading the boy's appearance at the end of *Zero Hour* is also the key to reading the west (as prairie) as that space that both defines and refuses the West (as coastal paradise). When the boy appears again at the end of the text, the music seems to be a gift, but it actually functions to repay the narrator's debt to the Cree woman who showed her the dance of "loss without commentary."

In her reading of *Zero Hour*, Keahey discusses "Winnipeg's inscription as an empty present in which to recollect the past" (49), which is accurate as a description of personal mourning, but reading Winnipeg as both west and "Gateway" in Gunnars's narrative disunifies even the conventional mourning narrative, and instead suggests that one grief can recognize another grief more readily than people recognize their own histories.

Clearly, the Gateway is too bartered and betrayed a site to operate as a "place to think towards... to long for," but in the end, Paradise is indeed postponed for the harmony and disjuncture of west meeting West in Gunnars's poetry of belligerence. The story of the return gift begins with the narrator looking out of the windows of her now empty mansion, seated at an angle so she can "see out of the Gate and into the streets closer to downtown" and notes that "at five in the morning the streets of the Gates in Winnipeg are like a picture someone painted without people" (125–26). This "picture" refers to the unpeopling of early Canada as reflected in landscape paintings of the eighteenth and nineteenth century that paint out the Aboriginal presence. Thomas King parodies this artistic trope in his 1999 novel, *Truth and Bright Water*, in which indigenous painter Monroe Swimmer works as a museum restorer, restoring not the paintings themselves, but restoring images of Aboriginal people who have been painted out of colonial Canadian landscapes, literally and figuratively. Gunnars's evocation of the de-indigenized landscape that is re-indigenized, first by people "stumbling" and being helped by others into the various houses (126), and then by the figure of the narrator's son, is a reimagined acknowledgement of presence, again offered without commentary, like the mourning dance: at once unified by a past filled with grief and disunified by an uncertain present.

Even the boy's offering of music can read as an indigenous sign. The violin is, after all, an instrument adopted by displaced Metis peoples in Manitoba and Saskatchewan, and when the boy himself appears, wearing a "Peruvian hat" (127), he appears from the other side of the Gates, moving through the gated boundaries into that space of mourning for the west, that politicized, stolen, and commodified space, and offering in the music an art that describes loss without commentary, a parallel to the Cree woman's dance. Paradise is postponed again as the text ends without movement to the West. *Zero Hour*, as a post-prairie paternal elegy, positions the daughter-mourner as vulnerable to postmodern fears of the nuclear age, but she begins to move through the world—leaving for the West—newly awakened to the violent history of Canada's past. Arrested in her Gateway position, she enters into mourning at the very point at which "where" meets "there" in this place of "much politics." At the Gateway, postcolonial Canadian west meets the spiritual West, and the heartbreak of this history cannot and does not step outside of time.

Part Four

Furies and Filles de la Sagesse

Language and Difference at Century's End

8

Signature, Inheritance, Inquiry

Lola Lemire Tostevin's *Cartouches*

Inheritance is never a *given*, it is always a task.
— Jacques Derrida, *Specters of Marx*

a frog teeming
with recollection sang:
"I am the daughter,
I am the resurrection."
— Lola Lemire Tostevin, *Cartouches*

In *The English Elegy*, Peter Sacks cautions that an elegist must engage in "frequently combative struggles for inheritance," including the possibility that he may need to "wrest his inheritance from the dead" (37). When Jacques Derrida asserts in *Specters of Marx* that inheritance is a task, he stresses the performativity of inheritance: that work underwrites mourning. Derrida's reminder that inheritance is work that must be performed rather than an automatic privilege to be assumed is welcome to the task of reading daughteronomy and defiance in Canadian women's paternal elegies. As creative work that is undertaken on behalf of one person by another, elegies are conscious and deliberate undertakings that function to preserve memory (much the way other forms of inheritance preserve possessions or attributes), but at the same time, elegies as forms of inheritance do other important work in confirming the relationship between the granter and the inheritor. They preserve their cultural rectitude by balancing degrees of likeness against degrees of difference. Any prospective inheritor must prove him- or herself to be worthy of inheritance by demonstrating a dependence on the granter as a parental or mentor figure, yet also show an independence from the granter in terms of the inheritor's competence in the world, thus proving the inheritor's ability to use the inheritance in an appropriate manner. In other words, the inheritor must be enough *like* the granter to be named as inheritor, and enough *unlike* the granter to receive the inheritance in the proper cultural and social spirit.

Such derivations of dependence and independence are all very well in traditional father–son filiation, but how do such dynamics work across gender lines when the daughter is the inheritor-elegist? As Lynda E. Boose suggests, because a daughter is "set apart from the other members as the only one who does not participate in extending [the family's] integrity into history," she remains an "alien" in the filial system until such time that she can "change her sign" by giving birth to a son (22). However, the possibilities for a daughter's legacy to emerge outside of the bounds of patronymic inheritance are mediated by Derrida's assertion that inheritance involves labour and performance. The work represented by the elegy as an artifact of mourning offers hope for the reconfiguration of the daughter's ability to inherit from her father, if inheritance can be construed, as Derrida seems to suggest, as task-oriented work rather than a cultural given. This language of attentive labour suggests strongly that the work of mourning and the task of inheritance are contiguous, if not mutually inclusive.

In Lola Lemire Tostevin's 1995 book-length elegy, *Cartouches*, the daughter-elegist labours to inherit a transfiguring alterity, and, in doing so, she does not so much wrest inheritance from the father as forge subjectivity from the process of mourning him. Inheritance does a double duty in this text; the daughter transforms in order to inherit *and* she inherits in order to transform. Tostevin fashions the narrating daughter as the father's other and creates a poetic alter ego that is determinedly "other" to the narrating daughter herself. The mourning daughter of *Cartouches* locates the power of alterity in the multiple figures of the wise daughters of Egyption mythology, and reconfigures the act of naming as female transfiguration rather than reiteration of patronymic inheritance. In addition, a frog sings of daughterly resurrective power and so leads the mourning daughter away from grief and towards transfiguration. With such guides, Tostevin explores paternal elegies that not only enact the cultural imperative of a daughter's paternal mourning, but also consider the power of a daughter's alterity in the paternal elegy.

The alterity that Tostevin explores in *Cartouches* is a result of abjection; however, the daughter is not estranged by her encounter with otherness but, rather, transfigured and even enlarged by it. She remakes herself as a subject through an experience of otherness that proceeds from the father's death. The degree to which these poems assert alterity as an important component in a daughter's legacy is problematized by the absence of daughters from systems of filiation. In direct opposition to the son's implicit need to prove himself worthy of inheritance through his resemblance to his father, *Cartouches* proposes that a daughter's inheritance involves delineating her difference from her father.

The significance of filiation, as a system that accompanies and often defines the parameters of mourning, is of primary concern to rethinking the possibilities for daughterly inheritance from the father. Derrida's discussions on the work of mourning in Western culture are situated within, and problematized by, fidelity to a spectral father figure. In *Specters of Marx*, he identifies a ghostly figure that "conjures" (50) commitment from the living and demands responsibility in a constantly displaced space between the public and the private. In Derrida's criticism, this spectre is glossed as the ghost of a commanding father, and Nancy Holland points out that Derrida takes the ghost of Hamlet's father as his literary exemplar. *Specters of Marx* shows, not surprisingly, Derrida investigating Karl Marx as his critical "father," while in *The Gift of Death*, Derrida identifies the spectre as the biblical Abraham, and in "Archive Fever," Derrida works with the cultural patrimony of Moses, Sigmund Freud, and his own father.

This "spectralizing" element leads to Derrida's concept of a hauntology, that pun on a haunted ontology, ghostly tropes that have been historically predicated upon the idea of filial inheritance, specifically, "ontology, theology, positive or negative onto-theology" (*Specters* 51). But in his memorial essay for Louis Marin, "By Force of Mourning," Derrida takes hauntology to the level of paradox when remembering Marin's mentorship as a kind of paternal force. Derrida identifies a "fantastic force of the specter" that pushes mourners "beyond the alternative between presence and absence" (153). This tension between presence and absence, so common to the elegiac mode, is recast here by Derrida as "the force of mourning," a power that he attributes to the paternal specter's ability to endure—powerfully and sometimes terribly—in memory.

To begin to identify daughterly negotiations of inheritance, we must first consider how the daughter as inheritor may fit into or choose to reconfigure the dynamics of filial hauntology as Derrida has established them. We should recall as we do so that Derrida's strict assumption of a male mourner in elegiac work is old territory. However, the need to consider the female-written paternal elegy, with the possibility of a filiation that does not act out father–son dynamics of inheritance brings me to Nancy Holland's excellent question, taken from her article "Death of the Other/ Father": "what becomes of the daughter in [Derrida's] hauntology, the daughter for whom both the symbolic and the literal F/fathers, and thus also the duties and debts they engender, are always simply Other, beyond any possible filiation or inheritance?" (65).

Holland's question, like Juliana Schiesari's question about the silence surrounding a women's melancholic voice, pinpoints the necessity for an audacious discourse of feminist inquiry surrounding the assumptions of paternal inheritance. The growing body of female-written paternal elegies, particularly elegies that query the rhetoric of mourning as it defines and redefines memory, may be seen as textual evidence that daughters can and do negotiate actively to situate themselves as their fathers' rightful inheritors. The Otherness that Holland attributes to fathers may not be so simple after all, and their duties and debts may be integral to making a daughter's tropological bid for Otherness a central concern in the epistemological and kinship struggles inscribed in these elegies.

Inheritance and Interiorization: Another Other

Cartouches begins with a brief lyrical section titled "Small Amulets" that offers a comparatively traditional exploration of the elegiac mode funnelled through the tensions of daughteronomy. After this section in which each short lyric is topped by a tiny graphic of a funeral urn, Tostevin devotes the remainder of *Cartouches* to exploring the force of mourning through prose poems that imitate a travel journal charting a trip through modern-day Egypt, but like Carson's "The Anthropology of Water," these poems employ travel as a trope to explore the philosophy and rhetoric of mourning. The relationship between the short lyrics of "Small Amulets" and the longer lines and fragmented poetic prose of the Egypt sections suggests, in some ways, the relationship between mourning and melancholia: an organized modest exploration of personal grief versus a broad exploration of loss that emphasizes a search to articulate how loss lives in the world.

In proposing that alterity is the key to the daughter's inheritance, Tostevin sets the daughter-mourner to the task of exploring the otherness that the father's death precipitates. The Other, in this text, is a figure of absence that guides the daughter to subjectivity; though the Other is made available to the daughter through the catalyst of her father's death, the daughter's claim on alterity (and subsequent transfiguration) depends upon how she recognizes and embraces the Other as her own resurrection.

The Other is written unequivocally throughout *Cartouches* as a female force. This potential for alterity does not issue from the traditional sovereignty of the father, and Tostevin implies that attention to the death of a good father can precipitate a daughter's transfiguration into a larger subjectivity, in part because through her attention, he survives the crisis of paternity and is saved from what Kristeva calls the "erosion of a loving father" (*Tales* 378).

The distinction between mourner and elegist is crucial in *Cartouches*. The mourner functions as a character within the text, while the elegist engages the rhetoric of resurrection and transfiguration that Derrida asserts "stem from...the power of alterity that works over the being-to-death of every image" ("By Force" 150–51). The mourner remains subject to elegiac convention, while the elegist challenges and expands the generic concerns of the elegy. The mourner is placed at the service of the anagnorisis that the elegist pursues. The father's alterity as an elegiac object is "worked over" by the elegist in order to achieve deliverance after his death. Viewed this way, the "being-to-death" in Derrida's hauntology is not nihilistic but, rather, a belief in the power of "the imaginal representation" of the dead as a beloved and forceful memory that performs a kind of work even as it is itself "worked over" ("By Force" 151). Tostevin extends this power to the daughter figures of *Cartouches*. Reconfiguring the elegist as a transfigurative daughter rather than a dutiful supplicant to the paternal tropology of death, Tostevin challenges Derrida's claim that tropes of mourning succumb to "inevitable interiorization" ("By Force" 159). Far from maintaining a Derridean position as an "unbearable paradox of fidelity" ("By Force" 159), the force of mourning becomes instead a prompt to the mourning daughter to assert herself as the father's inheritor through her subject position as the Other.

In "By Force of Mourning," Derrida is frustrated by, yet insistent upon, the "imaginal representation" (151) of the dead beloved father figure that the mourning idealizes and re-forges into an internal image that gains force with time. Discussing his theories of mourning alongside Louis Marin's theories of the image, Derrida proposes an interiorized image of the dead as the gazer and the mourner as the person who is "gazed upon": "the force of the image has to do less with the fact that one sees something in it than with the fact that one is seen there in it. The image sees more than it is seen. The image looks at us" (160). The absence of the beloved father only underscores the power of his internalized gaze, capitalizing upon the play between absence and presence that is so central to the elegiac mode. For Derrida, the father's gaze is stronger after death, and this tenet not only describes the "unbearable paradox of fidelity," but also insists that such a paradox is served and strengthened through filiation. For female writers of paternal elegies this is a problem because the "unbearable paradox" is not necessarily one of fidelity but, rather, a paradox of daughterly duty that must demonstrate fidelity beyond filiation and without the certainty of any right to inheritance. Even as Derrida offers the interiorized gaze of the dead as a revelation about what a mourner inherits and how he deals with the implications of inheriting, it must be said that for a female mourner to consider herself the object of a male gaze—even one as idealized as the gaze of the lost beloved—hardly represents a new position for women. Significantly, there is a dearth of inevitable interiorization of the dead in Tostevin's work. This does not mean that such female-written interiorizations cannot be found in other texts, merely that they are not as inevitable as Derrida suggests.

For feminists who read Derrida's often persuasive discussions of mourning, images like his perpetually pregnant mourner or the internalized gaze of the Lacanian lawgiver may seem more like tropes of oppression than tropes of mourning. Kate Mehuron praises Derrida for "assuming an effeminate tropology" to "displace the aggressively phallogocentric tropes of exclusionary homosocial address that so often orchestrate men's encomia to men" (177), and Mehuron's reading assumes that a displacement of phallogocentric tropes will displace the homosocial address. Unfortunately, Derrida's choice to characterize the frustrated body of "impossible" and "necessary" mourning through metaphors of female reproduction manages to maintain homosociality while presenting yet another literary/critical example of a female body trapped by its physiology. However, there is hope for a feminist analysis of Derrida's paradox of fidelity, especially if we consider what may be bearable or unbearable about such fidelity. The condition of being beyond filiation could precipitate a model of inheritance that values alterity, as Tostevin suggest in *Cartouches*. If the daughter is as Other to the father as he is to her, her difference may become an argument for inheritance rather than against it, providing that she can appropriate the potential power of Otherness.

Inheriting the Father's Ghost: Other as Ideal Woman

If a daughter's inheritance requires her to embrace the power of her own alterity, what does this idea imply about the force of mourning in father–daughter kinship? Both Nancy Holland and Kelly Oliver identify possibilities for reading the daughter as the father's truest Other and, as such, his best inheritor. An heir is charged with creating a future for a father's memory and his legacy. His daughter, in Holland's and Oliver's formulations, is situated as the person most likely to build a future from the tension between her similarity to and difference from her father. The daughter's task of inheritance involves laying claim to an exchange of Otherness with her father that does not trap her in the crushing paradox between love and reason.

In *Subjectivity Without Subjects*, Oliver questions fatherhood as a "promise of ethics" that anticipates the future, and argues for the daughter's Otherness as a potential catalyst for inheritance: "How can the son be an absolute other if he is also the same?...Wouldn't the daughter be the stranger child? Because of sexual difference and the nonlinear cyclical effects of feminine time, wouldn't the daughter be other enough to open up an infinite future?" (35). Regarding a daughter as the future of the family has most often been construed as a generative metaphor, in which a daughter is valued for her reproductive capacity rather than for her ability to carry forward a moral or psychological legacy. However, Oliver contends that inheritance is less concerned with a child's gender than it is with paternal "election" of an heir, asking, "if fatherhood is a promise for the future, could this future be a daughter?"(35).

Like Oliver, Holland stresses a daughter's estrangement from her father as the key to defining her as a possible heir. To this end, Holland points out that a daughter is doubly estranged from her father. She fulfills the uncanny requirements of "another Other" as the most appropriate inheritor; because the daughter is "neither enough one's own to trust or include in the patrimony of full citizenship/personhood, nor enough other to exclude or to kill," she is, from the father's perspective, "an Other not one's own" (69). The ways in which Holland suggests that kinship implies ownership are problematic, for if the daughter is truly this kind of Other who is inevitably not the father's own, she seems equally likely to inherit everything or be completely erased from history. In an attempt to legitimate the daughter's loss of the father, Holland could be said to imperil the cause of daughterly inheritance as much as she argues for it.

However, Holland also proposes another formulation of the Other in the guise of an idealized female figure, a figure that becomes particularly pertinent to reading powerful female figures in Tostevin's *Cartouches*. If the daughter as inheritor is haunted by her own strangeness, Holland proposes that such an idea of strangeness can be both alleviated and promoted by the father's death. With a wry nod to the difficulties of her own formulation, Holland contends that the daughter's inheritance does not follow "the simple line of father to son or master to disciple, or even master to slave," but rather involves a triangulated relationship of father, daughter, and spectral Other (67). The spectral Other in Holland's formulation is not the ghost of the father, but rather the ghost by which the father himself is haunted, "the ghost of the perfect image of the Imaginary female... the ghost of a woman who never lived" (67). By inheriting the father's ghost of an ideal woman, Holland suggests, the daughter resurrects herself rather than resurrecting the figure of the father, using the father's ideal as a springboard to vault into her own version of the ideal woman.

It seems nearly impossible to ignore the similarities between Derrida's internalized, idealized paternal gaze and Holland's reading of the father's ghost. In both formulations, the daughter's mourning practice is dominated by the father's standards even after his death. Holland glosses Derrida's interiorized gaze when she asks "what if the ghostly apparition looks at us [and] sees not we ourselves, we daughters as we are, but only its own ghost, the spectral image of what it wants to see, desires to see, must see when it looks at a female form?" (67). The implications of this formulation are troubling, particularly the idea that the daughter is doomed to act out the father's desire as her task of inheritance. Holland's final question about this female rupture in Derrida's hauntology is poignant: "if one is haunted, not by the ghost of the father, but by the father's ghost, how could any salvation come out of that?" (68).

Salvation, such as it is, arrives when daughters seek to appropriate Otherness for themselves, and perform their own "paradox of fidelity." By acquiring and performing otherness, daughters become both other than and similar to their fathers. When Tostevin appropriates daughterly alterity, she also refigures the ideal woman as a female figure who leads the mourning daughter to transfiguration. This mediating ideal woman, as the father's ghost and tutelary Other to the daughter, lives in Tostevin's Filles de la Sagesse, or wise daughter figures, who act as guides to a transfigured subjectivity. Intriguingly, the mourning daughter figure in *Cartouches* regards the dead father as a parent who permits rather than forbids growth, contrary to Holland's warning that the father can only teach the daughter about the limits that the world will place upon her (65).

Cartouches defines the daughter's task of inheritance as a project of seeking alterity for both herself and her father's memory, a direction that is supported by Kelly Oliver's assertion that "paternity is a special case of alterity" in that it "is the only relation in which the self becomes other and survives" (31). Unsatisfied with tracing the father's illness and death through a traditional mode of panegyric, Tostevin's text offers a daughterly mourner who is enlarged by mourning rather than being diminished by it. In *Cartouches*, the female mourner makes of her mourning something more than a monument to the father alone, and proposes, in contrast to Oliver's formulation, that it is daughterly existence that forms a special case of alterity; the successful daughterly mourner takes on the "ideal woman" as her "father's ghost" and appropriates the power of otherness for herself.

Signature, Theft, Inheritance: Reading Cartouches

Popular wisdom has it that all elegies begin at the end, so perhaps it is not so strange to begin an examination of *Cartouches* by looking at its ending. The final page of the text is blank except for five words: "for Achilles Lemire / in memory." This is Tostevin's dedication of the book to her father, whose illness and death from cancer are the subjects of the "Small Amulets" section. On the penultimate page of this defiantly unpaginated text, "Acknowledgements," Tostevin outlines the origins of her interest in the cartouche—"an oval frame with hieroglyphic symbols depicting the name of a ruler"—both as a cultural artifact of ancient Egypt and as a system of naming. Tostevin uses the feminine possessive to describe ownership of the cartouche, despite its immediate association with the male authority of the Egyptian pharaohs; besides being emblazoned on the tombs of the pharaohs, a cartouche also "was worn on the body so the wearer wouldn't forget *her* name, wouldn't forget who *she* was" (emphases added). Although Tostevin does invoke the female pharaoh Hatshepsut as one of the wise daughter figures in *Cartouches*, her appropriation and regendering of the cartouche for female use is not just a reference to Hatshepsut, but also relate directly to what Tostevin cites as the next subject of the Acknowledgements page: "the intricacies of the history of the written word, of naming, and how, historically it was connected to death."

Considering writing as a signatory act, Tostevin goes on to acknowledge writers who influenced *Cartouches*, though she notes that she intentionally does "not always identify them by name" on the Acknowledgement page, nor even within the text of *Cartouches*. The one writer whom she does name on the Acknowledgements pages is Canadian experimental poet and artist bpNichol, who emerges as a second lost beloved figure within the travel journal section of *Cartouches*. Tostevin's choice to name Nichol openly in a text so allusive of the works of other writers is certainly significant, not the least because it recalls her article about Nichol, "Paternal Body as Outlaw." In that article, published in *Open Letter* in 1986, two years before Nichol's untimely death and almost a decade before *Cartouches*, Tostevin discusses the ways that Nichol's experiments with language seek to displace "the privilege of authoritative speech" with the result that Nichol's poetry may be read as "less phallic and more oral, moving towards what the French call *écriture féminine*" (78). Regarding the paternal as outlaw in his work, Tostevin sets Nichol up as a mentor figure whose death parallels that of her father, and she dedicates a poem to him ("In ancient Egypt, the sign for H was shelter") in *Cartouches*. These two dedicatory presences and elegiac absences—Achilles Lemire and bpNichol—appear in the text as lost beloved men who promote naming through their encouragement of the narrator's writing. The father admires his daughter's "facility with words";

in the poem for Nichol, the male writer "reassures" his female colleague that her small poems are worthy beginnings, or "little underpinnings" that are "open-ended...to escape being locked in place like tombstones." Both men are encouraging forces who declare that the "privilege of authoritative speech" is already available to the daughter-poet, and Tostevin's acknowledgements and dedication make it clear that she is grateful for such support. The presence of the father as the addressed subject of "Small Amulets," and Nichol as the addressee of "In ancient Egypt, the sign for H was shelter" in the centre of the text lend *Cartouches* a structural frame, as though the book itself is constructed like the box of resurrective memory that Isis keeps.

But the metaphor of the box is not complete, for Tostevin refers to another influence on her writing on the Acknowledgements page: a third, shadowy father figure whom she resists naming but whom she describes as "that other master-name who gave me the definition of a cartouche that best describes the nature of this book." The definition, when Tostevin quotes it, is not credited with a name, but its syntax and style are nearly unmistakable as those of the writings of Jacques Derrida. (Perhaps Derrida's writing style is not so unmistakeable; Thomas M. F. Gerry has written about Tostevin's use of the "master-name" concept without identifying the master's name.) The quotation is from Derrida's essay, also titled "Cartouches," in which he discusses "the coffin as father" in response to Gérard Titus-Carmel's art project "The Pocket Size Tlingit Coffin." Derrida's essay appears in *The Truth in Painting*, and contains the quotation that defines cartouche: "I not only have a cartouche, I am it. This is my cartouche, I'm the one who's stolen it. This is my body, the body of my name" (232). It is this quotation, wrested from Derrida's text and given an enforced but not unbreakable anonymity by Tostevin, that appears on the Acknowledgements page, crystallizing the central concerns of daughterly mourning practice in her *Cartouches*: the patronym, the politics of theft, and the tensions of inheritance. Tostevin's refusal to declare the "master-name" cheekily implies that Derrida's writing style, not to mention his ideas, acts as its own signature. In this way, Tostevin acknowledges Derrida *and* denies him a name in a book that questions the power and ownership of names, and engages specifically with what it might mean for women to inherit a name through elegizing the father. Tostevin's willingness to name two beloved men in this text (Achilles Lemire and bpNichol) only emphasizes the purposeful absence of Derrida's name and places the idea of acknowledging the "Name of the Father" defiantly *sous rature*. In this text, if Achilles Lemire is the individual, biological, familial father, and bpNichol is a fraternal figure whom Tostevin appreciates for his ability to challenge linguistic gender norms, with her phrase "paternal as outlaw" making Nichol into some version of a literary father, then the unnamed Derrida is the "critical father" in every sense that this term implies. Tostevin's choice to quote Derrida's cartouche definition as a signatory act that invokes "the body of my name" emphasizes the kind of presence in absence discussed in "By Force of Mourning," but Tostevin's strategy sidesteps both idealization and interiorization. Truly, Derrida is present "in theory" and absent "in name" from this text.

There is, undeniably, a certain feminist joy in the act of stealing from Derrida, especially when the theft remains a secret—a locked box within a locked box—and I am a little chagrined that I must reveal Tostevin's theft in order to acknowledge her audacity. This theft and the sly silence surrounding it is hard-won indeed; Tostevin's critical relationship with Derrida has been made public in Tostevin's own writing, first in her essay "Breaking the Hold on the Story: The Feminine Economy of Language" in Smaro Kamboureli and Shirley Newman's 1986 critical anthology *A Mazing Space: Writing Canadian Women Writing*, and then in a published series of letters exchanged with Kamboureli, published in 1988 as "Women of Letters: Envois Between Victoria and Toronto." Tostevin's fascination with Derrida's theory has been matched by her frustration with his public behaviour towards women as she witnessed in 1987 when she attended a series of lectures given by Derrida at the International Summer Institute for Semiotic and Structural Studies at the University of Toronto. Responding to Derrida's lecture in a prose piece titled "by the smallest possible margin" in her 1988 book *'sophie*, Tostevin considers Derrida's refusal to engage with feminist perspectives in philosophy: "when asked by one woman why women are so conspicuously absent from his material, he says that perhaps the best way to answer that question is to suppress it. This is of course the perfect answer and the woman never shows up again but another woman claims that he is the greatest mind of the 20th century so most of us hang on" (45). In *Cartouches*, Tostevin may be said to be suppressing Derrida while he hangs on to his influence until his non-naming at the book's end.

Derrida is never really far from discussions of Tostevin's poetics in Canadian criticism. I have titled this section to allude to two critical texts that are already parallel texts: Derrida's essay "Signature Event Context" from *The Margins of Philosophy* and Stephen Scobie's book, *Signature Event Cantext* published in the "Writer as Critic" series by NeWest Press in 1989. (It is worth noting that Scobie's book is also dedicated to bpNichol, with the addendum "in memory of his name.") Derrida's essay explores the ways in which the notion of "*différance* instigates... subversion" of all received desires for authority (21–22), while Scobie's book considers a group of

Derridean terms as "intertexts for the study of Canadian writing" (7) including that of Tostevin. The influence of one text upon another, or of one writer on another, is a function of the context of Scobie's "Cantext" as it is constitutive of the context of reading the rhetoric of these texts through philosophy or critical theory. To apply this to *Cartouches*, we can read the Derridean context against Tostevin's production of a "Cantext" that offers itself as an amorce—that is, to use Scobie's phrase, as a fuse to explode Derrida's context of master–student discourse. What are the ways in which a mourning text named *Cartouches* can engage with an essay about mourning named "Cartouches" without overt reference to this second text? What is being inherited and what refused in this context and in this Cantext? The three major terms of Derrida's "Signature Event Context" resonate throughout Tostevin's *Cartouches* to suggest that the event of inheritance may be predicated by how the living signs herself in relation to the lost beloved, but it must engage with the ways that the text shares signs with other texts, be they cultural or literary.

"Cartouche" is, as Derrida is careful to point out, the name of a legendary French thief whose name has passed into common usage ("Cartouches" 231). The name implies someone who works in situations when fine calibration is necessary: someone who works *car touche*, or by touch. And this fine touch describes the light-fingered work of creative and critical theft. In the quotation as it exists in Tostevin's "Acknowledgements," Derrida appears to claim to have stolen the cartouche as a repository for the body, but in his essay in *The Truth in Painting*, Derrida seems to steal this very declaration from the mouth of Titus-Carmel. Although no quotation marks actually attribute these words to the artist, Derrida writes, "This is a cartouche. *Says he.* I not only have a cartouche, I am it" (232; emphasis added). Additionally, the idea of reading the coffin as cartouche comes from Titus-Carmel's "theft" of his "pocket size" (that is, pickpocketable) coffin from the Tlingit tribes of the British Columbian Northwest Coast, what Derrida calls a "double violent insertion, by colonization" (232). In a long line of performances of creative thievery, it is clear that Tostevin's theft of Derrida's quotation is only the most recent. Derrida, as well as Tostevin, also glosses the slippage between "cartouche" and "cartridge," with Derrida considering the "box within a box" as a "supplementary cartridge" and Tostevin using the word "bullet" instead of "cartouche" in an earlier published draft of a poem that later appears in *Cartouches*: "a bullet / puts into play / the bodies / of my name" ("from Cartouches" 281). These cascading acts of thievery underline the significance of theft as a complex (and sometimes violent) element in the performance of creation, appropriation, and inheritance.

Tostevin takes up this heritage of thievery as a feminist act of stealing the language of power as part of a daughterly mourning practice, and in doing so, she appropriates the history of writing in order to redefine or rework the function of naming. When Derrida calls the cartouche "the body of [his] name," Tostevin asserts her right to the cartouche as written artifact and to the name as a way to inherit the spirit of the father. Stressing the function of the cartouche as "both title and signature" carved onto the outside of a tomb, Derrida notes that the cartouche speaks for the "mute" coffin that would otherwise "keep the last word" (209–14). As the daughterly signature upon the text, Tostevin's cartouche marks the text with her first name—Lola—rather than her surname or the first name of her father and thereby suggests that while the text mourns his passing, the text remains hers, in title and signature.

The gold cartouche that "puts into play / the bodies / of [her] name" adorns the cover of the book: a set of four hieroglyphics—"a lion / a dove / a lion / a vulture" as Tostevin writes in the text—one image for each letter of her first name. The naming cartouche makes an amulet of the book, a way to guard against forgetting, just as the poems of the "Small Amulets" section ward off the chilliness of consolation, that detachment from the loved one that completes the Freudian work of mourning. In this section, Tostevin enters the daughter's chaos of "exaggeration" as "the summit / of every living image," released from the father's "[m]emory arranged / in neat rows." This exaggeration in itself may be read as a manifestation of Derrida's influence on the text, as is the animal featured in the cartouche that is often associated with Derrida: the lion. Stephen Scobie, among other critics, has suggested that Derrida "looked like a lion, the shock of white hair carried with the pride of a mane" and even goes so far to say that Derrida "was writing [the text] with his hair" (*Ghosts* 22). Tostevin writes that her cartouche shows "all I am and all I want to be"; she usurps Derrida in the trace of the lion's head.

Tostevin's dedication of *Cartouches* to her father performs this paradoxical act of theft by writing the name of the dead (Achilles Lemire) on the "outside" of the coffin that is the text (i.e., the text's final dedication page), creating a bookend with Tostevin's given name in hieroglyphics on the front cover. As Derrida suggests, the cartouche as theft, naming, and mourning encompasses the text: "The dedication belongs to the book's cartouche. Like the title and the signature, the exergue, the epigraph, the epitaph. Where does a cartouche end?" ("Cartouches" 228). The cartouche is offered as a construction in this book, an object Tostevin has made for herself and an artifact for which she has paid; it is not glossed as an inheritance so much as a declaration. As one of the book's epigraphs, Tostevin's choice of Anne Hébert's lines from *Le tombeau des rois* is telling: "*Les signes du monde / Sont gravés à meme ses doigts*." Tostevin engraves her own sign—her name, her poems—onto the world with *Cartouches*. She chooses her second epigraph from H. D.'s *Helen in Egypt*, suggesting that a woman whose name is partially erased by history may be read as "a hieroglyph."

Proceeding from her assertion earlier in *Cartouches* that "[a] name is as much / a part of a person / as the soul," Tostevin affirms on her Acknowledgements page that a cartouche "decorated a pharaoh's temple walls and was worn on the body so the wearer wouldn't forget her name, wouldn't forget who she was." The implication that the pharaoh was female is borne out by Tostevin's inclusion of one of Egypt's most well-known female pharaohs, Queen Hatshepsut, as one of the "daughters of wisdom" that Tostevin names throughout the text. She calls the Sphinx "Fille de la Sagesse," invoking the order of Catholic nuns who work in service of the poor at the same time as the Sphinx as a wise daughter will mentor the narrating woman. Tostevin even tweaks Genesis when she writes, in the poem that begins "From the Aga Khan's Mausoleum," of buying a picture of a bird in the "tree of life. Or is it the tree of knowledge?" Egyptian deities included in this company of wise daughters are the resurrective goddess Isis and a daughterly version of Thoth, the god of writing that Derrida discusses in *Of Grammatology*. Tostevin proposes an alternative to Thoth in the goddess figure Seshat, the "Mistress of the House of Books" and "true inventor of letters and numbers." In emphasizing the resurrective potential of a wise daughter, Tostevin's mourning moves away from obedience to the father as a manifestation of the Law, and instead demonstrates the daughter's task of inheritance: to resurrect the father as memory and the daughter as subject through her "facility with words."

Derrida warns that a cartouche yields an "autobiographical performative of the signatory" ("Cartouches" 219) in ways that may intentionally "disconcert" the reader, "like that of a narration the site of which would remain improbable" (220). As a paternal elegist, Tostevin performs a disconcerting daughter. In the "Small Amulets" section, she notes that her father is "a man of few words" who is "intimidated" by his daughter's intelligence, and he worries about her tendency to "exaggerate everything." Even as she counters with the argument that "exaggeration is the summit of every living image," she struggles with the elegiac concern that her words, be they description or encomium, will never be adequate:

> I know. This order of language is not easy
> to accede to. Sentiment, they'll say.
> Yet these words also lie in the realm

of my other, father, and you are not just
another arbitrary sign.

In asserting "my other" as both father and not-father, Tostevin talks back to the theorists, agreeing with Lacan and Derrida that the father is a powerful cultural symbol, but resisting characterizing him as a dread *nom du père*, or a Name of the Father figure.

What is at stake in these lines is Lacan's contention that filial patricide "is the fruitful moment of debt through which the subject binds himself for life to the Law," the result being that "the symbolic Father is, in so far as he signifies this Law, the dead Father" (*Écrits* 199). But why must the f/Father signify the Law of the filial "murder"? If anything, in Tostevin's text, the father represents parental devotion. He is "a father who never abused his daughter" but who worries about her enough to be angrily relieved when he finds her after believing she may have drowned; a father who shows his fear; a father who fixes the child's doll when God does not. The father in the poems is more admiring than forbidding, a "good father" in love and in punishment.

Lacan's reliance on the alpha father's dominance over, and eventual murder by, a primal horde of sons in Freud's *Totem and Taboo* presages a strange gender twist on Derrida's insistence on mourning as a pregnancy or abortion. Derrida's iteration of the lost beloved as an invasive force, not unlike an inner primal horde, glosses Freud's take on the primal horde as a violent physical force that cannot be stopped. However, Tostevin, in writing this particular father–daughter kinship as "unmediated by concept or mastery," proposes a filial connection rather than rivalry or divide:

These poems
are of a body that links us, inescapable,
given. This amulet is but a small conjunction
to compensate for this afternoon when you sighed
for the last time, and, slowly, your hands
took on the temperature of the room.

Tostevin designates the elegies as a "conjunction" that links the bodies of beloved and mourner, as well as linking the "Small Amulets" to the Egypt section, the work of mourning to the search for wisdom, and ultimately the father to the daughter as inheriting Other. Kristjana Gunnars finds that Tostevin's contrast between the "dour silent bedside" of the "Small Amulets" section and the dynamism of the Egypt section emphasizes a "self-consciousness" in the text that "keeps the poems from losing their ground," even when bombarded by an "environment of dead things" that only "thicken[s]" as the text progresses (Rev. of *Cartouches* 134–35). Examining both "the tourist as a consumer of dead culture" and "the scholar as purveyor of that which is no longer there," Gunnars reads *Cartouches* as Tostevin's investigation of "the strange present" (134). However, "the strange present" cannot be separated from the familiar absence of the dead father, so the Egypt section becomes a peripatetic search for new metaphors for recollection and inheritance. Karen I. Press speculates that Tostevin explores Egypt in the second half of *Cartouches* partly "because of her interest in foreignness, in not-belonging or lack of place," but Press also notes that "[t]he non-place of the desert... facilitates creation rather than prevents it" (136). Tostevin begins the Egypt section by asserting the fear of and possible benefits to being lost amid one's own inability to make meaning, an admission that echoes the father's lack of facility with language, or as Tostevin writes in "We've rented a room at Midan Tahrir": "In a country where you can't always read the signs you can't always measure the extent to which you are lost."

The choice of a frog as the daughter's resurrective alter ego glosses the title of Tostevin's novel *Frog Moon*, and brings to mind the associations of being "frog-voiced" and "tone-deaf" that Tostevin brings to light in her novel (*Frog* 15). However, in *Cartouches*, the frog sings in the morning, signaling an end to mourning. Her voice is "teeming / with recollection" as she sings her song of transfiguration: "'I am the daughter, / I am the resurrection.'" Tostevin's "gender trick on Jesus" (Press 133) in the frog's reconfiguration of John 11:25 is not a direct or complete reversal. Jesus' promise to raise Lazarus from the dead—"I am the resurrection and the life"—is not quite the same resurrective declaration as the frog's reflection on the daughter's powers. The daughter, as frog and Tostevin's speaking persona, claims the Son's privilege of resurrection, but does not claim to be able to bring the father back to earthly life. Instead, Tostevin's narrator first declares herself "the daughter" and then a force of "resurrection." Thomas M. F. Gerry's article on *Cartouches* claims that "the poet's father is resurrected through the powers of language" (198), but this is not true even in metaphoric sense. An elegy may mourn the loss of the beloved in the most profound terms possible, and it may constitute ongoing affectionate relations with the dead, but it does not resurrect the dead. Tostevin's daughter-narrator knows that she cannot bring her father back to life, but she can recollect him—as Isis actually re-collected the scattered pieces of Osiris's body—through "transmuting elements of reality into the shining, enduring element of fiction," that which Tostevin calls "the magical art of transfiguration" (*Frog* 161).

For the wise daughter, the task of inheritance includes getting lost in order to steal the name and stealing words in order to declare who she is. The ironic paradox of needing to steal what one already owns may be said to sum up many of the tensions of daughterly mourning. The wise daughter does not take on her father's voice but discovers her own. In recollecting her father, the frog-daughter resurrects herself and enacts the tendency for a cartouche, as a site of theft, to "steal itself" (Derrida, "Cartouches" 220). Nancy Holland considers the daughter's role in inheriting the father's name, and quotes Derrida on the incredulity of patriarchs who "do not cease to be surprised and to remain skeptical about the possibility that the daughter could speak in her own name" (66). As Holland asks, "[d]oes the daughter have a name of her own?" (66). The daughter's inherited patronymic surname may or may not be construed as her own. When Derrida asserts that "paternity... is always inferred from a sentence, a declaration in the form of a judgment" ("Cartouches" 222), he implies that the name, as a declaration of paternity, may be withheld from a son or a daughter. But Tostevin challenges this assumption when she begins her text with her own act of naming; urging young writers to give a name to death and love, she reveals by the end of the first short poem of the "Small Amulets" section that, for her, "each word, / each awkward line invokes one name / and one name only. My father. My father." The narrator already knows that naming does not rekindle life or love, nor does it necessarily create kinship, but it does challenge the daughter to consider the parameters of paternal love and parental death.

Tostevin does not debate whether or not the patronym belongs to or even represents the daughter. Stephen Scobie points out that in *Double Standards* Tostevin puns on the name she shares with her father in a poem titled "*les trois ailes de mon nom.*" The poem's final words are "*le monde où je le mire*"—the world where I reflect it—and Tostevin's use of the first-person pronoun "*je*" with the broken syllables of her last name comprising both verb and object can also be read as "*je le mire,*" or "I Lemire" (*Signature* 77). But it is her first name—Lola—that is inscribed on the cartouche and on the cover of *Cartouches*, Derrida's "title and signature": "All I am and want to be: at the same time lion, dove and vulture." The animal bodies inscribed on the cartouche as name signify courage, peace, and an acknowledgement of physical death. In *Of Grammatology*, Derrida reminds us that proper names are "always caught in a chain or systems of differences," and that the figuration of a name is as important as its pronunciation: "Metaphor shapes and undermines the proper name" (89). Tostevin demonstrates with equal conviction that names can shape metaphor, when she invokes Isis as a resurrective goddess. Tostevin locates the daughter's power of alterity in the image of Isis, a goddess with the power to "bewitch the heavens" and raise the dead. "If only I were Isis," she writes during her father's illness: "I would transform myself into a swallow / and fan you with my wings." The figure of Isis draws the text towards the peripatetic journey of mourning, a trip into the past in which Tostevin's daughter figure inherits the future by transfiguring herself: "Time and space, / water and desert, every / woman knows you by her name." Isis is a poet figure who "fashion[s] words into perfect bodies" in her "effort to recapture Yesterday." Even the name of Isis can be read as an ontological statement, her name a repeated verb of existence: "is is," an insistent assertion of female being.

But even Isis cannot grant the daughter access to "the box of silver and gold" which holds the "book whose words disappear into thin air," the box and book that Tostevin introduces towards the end of the "Small Amulets" section. This box of disintegrating memory, like a sarcophagus, holds the fragmenting corpse of written discourse. Tostevin conflates it with the "marble box" that contains the father's ashes, suggesting that "the trace of a lingering story" hovers in place of the disappearing words. Recalling Derrida's idea of the cartouche as Titus-Carmel's tiny coffin, the daughter's trip to Egypt becomes part of retrieving the box of disappearing words; the book becomes the cartouche as wordbox. The trip is nearly thwarted by the realization that, despite Isis's power, all the narrating daughter can do is "continue to cling to" the engraved hieroglyphs "on either side of [Isis's] forehead"; the goddess's resurrective powers will not be granted merely by request. To embrace her own alterity, the daughter must transcend "time and space, / water and desert" and understand that "every / woman knows you by her name." The ambiguous possessive of this last line implies that for a woman to know Isis means to know her own name, and the woman's own name becomes the apostrophe that asserts presence. Working with the elegiac impulse to tell that trace of story, asserting her own name into a story that begins with the father but ends with the daughter, Tostevin implies that Isis's gift to the narrating daughter is not eternal life but "*a writing down*, a new becoming, ongoing till the end" (emphasis in original).

The final poem of the Egypt section, in the form of a journal entry, notes that the "traces" of the two beloved men, bpNichol and Achilles Lemire, linger on in two separate public memorials. Nichol's memorial is a poem carved into the concrete pavement of a lane now named after him behind the Coach House Press building in Toronto. Achilles Lemire's name is carved into a plaque at the base of a tree in a conservation area, an allusion to the Canadian forest in which he worked as a young boy. In *Frog Moon*, the narrator claims the daughter's voice joins the father's story to "establish their proximities and their differences" (*Frog* 152). In *Cartouches*, Lemire and Nichol are memorialized with literal signs in which their names are inscribed, and "continue to sidetrack" off the authoritative paternal pattern, "at least as far as two names can."

When Derrida calls a cartouche a "descriptive or definitional utterance" that is also "a *performance without presence*," he emphasizes how the deviations of such a performance "dislocate" from its own self-production ("Cartouches" 236; emphasis in original). Such a dislocation is fundamental in an elegy in which mourning may be enacted or inscribed in deviation from tradition. But this "performance without presence" retains an elegiac quality. Early in *Cartouches*, Tostevin notes the Egyptian hieroglyphic symbols specified in *The Book of the Dead*. The heart is rendered as an AB, "represented by an inkwell in the shape of a heart," and the soul as a BA in the shape of "a human-headed hawk / that bears the words 'Let me be true of voice.'" She goes on to offer the text as "[h]ieroglyphs in lieu of a heart, / an engraved stone to weigh the body down," suggesting that words can be both ephemeral and weighty.

But it is her final question that *Cartouches* attempts to answer: "What other part for an ABC?" This enquiry implies that something is lacking from the formulation of the dead person as heart and soul. The daughter, as "Other," supplies the "other part" without substituting herself in sacrifice to the father. Instead, she initiates "a new beginning" that relies upon the power of her own resurrective abilities. In an interview with Barbara Carey, Tostevin declares "[w]riting is a kind of burial," and compares *Frog Moon* to a "tombstone," a "concretized inscription of memory" ("Distance" 5). Tostevin's eschatological metaphors for books as tombstones or cartouches point to her play upon the name as an expression of absence, a concept she proposes to a "shrugging" Derrida in *'sophie* (47). After reporting Derrida's assertion that "God as name is the origin of the law and he can only maintain his role if he remains hidden, which means he can only be experienced as absence" (46), Tostevin proposes that "the absence of God and the absence of woman" could be "the same thing" (47). Derrida's disinterested answer, despite being in the affirmative, only reinforces Tostevin's conviction that a woman writer's narrative "I" "can only differ from nothing by the smallest possible margin" (47). With the "smallest possible sign," a woman's name may find purchase on the language: "even an apostrophe in addressing absence turns that absence into presence. *'sophie*. Name of a woman, title of a book. On its own, a title has no meaning, which must be very uncomfortable for philosophers in search of meaning, but a title is at least a promise. Lives up to its promise by giving voice to words in which a figure is described" (47–48). While the title to which Tostevin refers in this passage is *'sophie*, *Cartouches* also hides a woman's name on the cover, in the hieroglyph made from representative symbols for the author's name. Writing is not always a burial; *Cartouches* resembles an archaeological dig, where the ancient treasure of the daughter's name is rediscovered and asserted as a sign. The resurrected daughter, concealed yet revealed on the book's cover, turns her absence into presence in *Cartouches*, and asserts her subjectivity by becoming a promise: to the text and to the strength of her own frog-like voice.

Some of the work of that transfiguration is accomplished by tracing the mourning practice of the daughter as a parallel to the father's death journey, while resisting the traditional mythic descent pattern. Certainly the Christian apotheosis of the lost beloved is a common enough elegiac convention, but the transfigured spirit within an elegy is traditionally the lost beloved. Recall Milton's Lycidas who is "mounted high, / Through the dear might of Him that walked the waves" (lines 172–73) or Shelley's Adonais, whose "soul... like a star" ascends "burning through the inmost veil of Heaven" (lines 493–94). But in *Cartouches*, the transfigured spirit is that of the mourning daughter, not that of the dead father. The father is equipped for the journey toward death in conventional elegiac terms, though Tostevin does not allow anything as grandiose as an apotheosis. In the final poem of "Small Amulets," Tostevin makes her poem a gift to accompany her father on his spiritual journey:

> So with these words, father, I make you a pillow
> to cradle your head towards the horizon.
>
> With these words I give you a cake to eat
> on the eastern side of the Lake of Flowers.
>
> With these words I give you a heart
> of lapis lazuli—a stone heart maybe,
> but, nonetheless, everlasting.

Notably, the convention of equipping the beloved for transformative travel does not console completely, and Tostevin spends a significant portion of *Cartouches* working out the terms of the daughter's transfiguration as a parallel journey. This transfiguration does imply a kind of consolation and an elegiac remaking of the world after death, with female subjectivity at the core of that remaking.

The key to discovering "what becomes of the daughter" in a hauntology is in Nancy Holland's apt choice of verb: the daughter *becomes*. She sidesteps Derrida's "tendency to accept incomprehension" ("Mnemosyne" 31) in mourning, and instead aligns herself with the Otherness that her father's death has emphasized for her. Favouring alterity might mean refusing Derrida's inescapable tropes of interiorization, but it does not mean refusing mourning. Tostevin shows that a feminine filiation and inheritance is not necessarily attached to Derrida's "unbearable paradox of fidelity," but rather works within that paradox, using the force of mourning to imply enhanced subjectivity for the daughters, a subjectivity that is neither vengeful nor neglectful, but grows nonetheless from the father's departure. This elegiac performance includes refusing the rhetoric of mourning while exploring the elegiac impulse. The injunction for female elegists to mourn without inheritance is itself paradoxical, and any ventures into the possibilities of female inheritance require an audacious assumption of filial right. In proposing daughterly mourning that does not bury the daughter beneath her duty to her father, but rather proposes mourning as a trope of female inheritance, Tostevin situates her mourning daughter figure as a productive inheritor rather than a supplicant.

9

Elegy of Refusal

Erin Mouré's *Furious*

> Poetry, I think, is the *structuration* (the action or condition of structuring, the rendering visible, audible) of *memory* that can undo the Law of the City, because it both precedes and transgresses the Law. *Transgresses*, for even poetry can't avoid the Law. Even memory can't.
> — Erin Mouré, "Poetry, Memory and the Polis"

> Where certain male philosophers and writers see death... women imagine, instead, the death of patriarchy.
> — Gail Scott, "A Feminist at the Carnival"

Reading Lola Lemire Tostevin's *Cartouches* as a text that is seriously mischievous in its defiance of Derrida as the master/father while seriously devoted to grieving the loss of Achilles Lemire introduces ways to think about the female elegy in the context of experimental poetics. The "prismatic publics" of such poetry, according to Kate Eichhorn and Heather Milne's latest anthology on innovative poetry written by Canadian women, signify their intention to investigate language's properties and political uses by noting how it may be bent or fractured, as light is bent through a prism: in short, "working out the problems *in* rather than simply *with* language" (14; emphases in original). With this prismatic metaphor in mind, perhaps it is not so unusual to read Erin Mouré's 1988 Governor General's Award–winning *Furious* as the final text in this study, although it may seem to be an unlikely choice. But *Furious*, as Mouré's breakout work of feminist defiance of the anaesthetic use of language, deserves attention for its rigorous feminist politics against the ubiquitous force of the patriarchal rhetoric of mourning. Among other actions, the text challenges the male body's position as a traditional elegiac object/object of desire and emphasizes the dynamics of elegiac convention as a social structure in literature and language. Mouré's interrogation of memory as a structure that is regulated by tradition and by language suggests, audaciously, that the structures of language devalue the structures of women's memories and favour a rigid set of conventions that confirm the patriarchal status quo. *Furious* is a text that is haunted by elegiac convention but is equally appropriative of elegiac convention in order to demonstrate how such conventions might be dismantled, even on a provisional basis.

If we read *Furious* as a text that refuses elegy in order to reinfuse elegy with the force of female memory, we must consider the ways in which Mouré uses the anxiety of language to showcase the ways that elegiac convention values the male body over the female body. A return to a model of mourning from the first chapter of this volume is useful here: Gillian Rose's conception of mourning as a law that trades in "difficulties and injustices" (36) and cannot be separated from the inaugural and, in Mouré's work, the social function of mourning. Filtering a righteous daughter figure as Fury—one that recalls Macpherson's demanding daughters—through an anxiety that resembles Rose's "perennial anxiety" (36) of mourning, Mouré's strategy of "getting out of the ending" (*Furious* 101) promotes a politically disobedient melancholia that reinvigorates political life, or in this case, re-enlivens a genre that is still in the process of defining its political life in a national literary community.

Mouré begins *Furious* with a poem that alludes to the rustic swain as elegiac protagonist, but immediately casts doubt upon how the image and its attendant conventions work in a feminist context. Without denying the historical and literary power of elegiac convention, Mouré reveals the elegy's debt to and support of a patriarchal social system. In "Whose," the opening poem of *Furious*, a first-person speaker declares herself (or himself: the gender is not specified) to be "sleeping perfectly" in a neglected garden, dressed in pajamas and lying among the flowers and vegetables. This deceptively whimsical image accrues a sense of vulnerability with the flora as the poem progresses; a carrot is not merely "rooted in the earth," but is also "a pointed microphone listening for water." The zinnias are "ragged" and the garden is surrounded by "slug-dust on the outer border." This garden is addicted to the "drug of topsoil." The image is neither of an idyllic nor a ruined garden, but one that has been pulled askew, productive but not quite balanced. Even more strangely, the sleeper professes an innocence that does not seem questionable until it is professed: "It is true that I am only sleeping / it is true that my fingers are uncurled & bothering no one." Why should sleeping, such a passive act of "bothering no one," need to be defined as harmless and what does this augur? The final line, in italics in the text, reveals the key to unpacking the poem's determined collision of absurdity and threat, of colloquialism and convention, and potentially, of female memory and male-focused elegiac tradition: "my knees pulled up and feet splayed outward, / in whose garden, / *refusing a few years to abandon my despair.*"

The elegiac setting of the garden contrasts with the resistance of the sleeping speaker who is "bothering no one" even as she refuses the abandonment of a politically conscious despair. Abandoning despair means admitting the efficacy of consolation; it also means abandoning the political perspective of despair or melancholia as a mode of productive trouble-making. The final two lines of the poem question ownership of the garden and ownership of despair, emphasizing the political dimensions of "owning" despair for all of the female elegists discussed in this volume of essays: exactly *whose* despair is legitimized through elegy? Whose memories are honoured publically? While Mouré does not specify the gender of the speaker in "Whose," she sets readers to the task of considering the historical dismissal of women's grief outside social parameters of approved mourning practice as a very good reason for a woman to refuse to abandon her despair.

To read *Furious* as a feminist text demands attention to its politics; to read the text's elegiac interlocutions of love and reason means locating female fury as political and textual necessity. The title of "Whose" questions the garden's ownership; is it the garden of a Christian God—Eden or Gethsemane—or the realm of a vegetation goddess? Within what tradition is this garden situated? The speaker's description of her physical position, with "knees pulled up & feet splayed outward" indicates resistance, despite her sleeping posture. When the speaker declares that she "refuses... to abandon [her] despair," this line, borrowed from John Newlove's poem "And the Dead Rose Up from the Water," plays upon Bloomian anxiety of influence without quite legitimizing it:

> Coming alive at the age of thirty,
> refusing a few years
> to abandon my despair,
> and the dead rose up from the water,
> their heads buoys in front of my love;
> I tried to kiss them alone
> but the water moved their pale fleshy faces.

Newlove's mourner sees the bodies of the dead emerge from the water, but the dead refuse tactile contact with the living. The movement of the water makes their faces inaccessible to the elegist's devotional (and possibly necrophilic) kiss. In good elegiac tradition, Newlove's poem offers several drowned bodies and an elegist who longs for consolation. In "Whose," Mouré resists the pressure to produce a human body other than that of the speaker, situating the poem's inquiry in melancholia rather than mourning. *Furious* is not a despairing text but, rather, a text that consciously regards the furious energy that despair masks. Is the sleeper the mourner or the beloved? Who or what is being mourned? "Whose" is an elegy without a beloved, a poem that invokes convention only to flout it: an elegy in which despair masquerades as sleep.

More traces of elegiac convention and resistance crop up throughout *Furious*. The poems "Betty" and "Surface" re-examine the dangerous but potentially transformative properties of water, invoking the drowned youth's "wat'ry bier" and the elegist's "melodious tear" in Milton ("Lycidas" 12; 14). Anne Carson invokes the daughter's self-sacrifice by asserting that men are the substance in which women drown, but Mouré reconfigures the trope of watery death as a passage for the female elegist, an emergence into a politicized consciousness. Using water as a metaphor for language, Mouré regards both the surface and depth of language as a substance in which subjects are socially immersed. Like Adrienne Rich's woman who "dives into the wreck" in order to retrieve "the thing itself and not the myth" ("Diving Into the Wreck"), Mouré enters the pool of language through a conversation with and a definite resistance to the elegiac convention of drowning in sorrow while lamenting the drowned beloved. In *Furious*, the drowned body of the lost beloved becomes the intentionally submerged body of the elegiac subject, who then "breaks the surface" to emerge into a feminist consciousness ("Betty"). Jahan Ramazani has noted Rich's refusal of "the elegiac metahistory in which much poetry by her male counterparts is embedded" in an effort to "distance herself from male modernist nostalgia" (311). Mouré's poetry takes feminist refusal a step further by using elegiac convention to show the limitations that have been placed on the rhetoric of mourning. By adopting a melancholic but adamantly political position throughout *Furious*, Mouré's strategy is one of resistance to the cultural prescription of organizing women's grief around the trope of the dutiful daughter. Her anagnorisis reveals ways to write about women's sorrow and women's desire that do not reference filial piety, and she begins her project by revealing the enormous social influence of elegiac convention as the accepted literary rhetoric of mourning, and ultimately how such conventions restrict women's access to what Mouré calls "the civic house of memory" ("The Acts 7").

Questioning Convention: Despair and the Refusing Daughter

Mouré's reconfiguration of the drowned-beloved trope is characteristic of how she uses *Furious* to challenge the elegy's discourse of privilege, and to draw attention to a feminist elegiac mode that is written in the fissures of an authoritative language system. Mouré has commented that the risk of writing from a feminist perspective is often usurped by the way social hierarchies absorb and nullify the language of rebellion: "The word 'risk' only protects the hierarchy in us from its own loss, *because it is made of 'loss,'* the loss of women" ("To Speak" 135; emphasis in original). By defining a "loss of women" that includes women's social, sexual, and political desires as elegiac objects, Mouré risks writing these losses in a social system that traditionally exalts the transcendent male subject.

Mouré offers a poetic narrator who refuses to abandon despair in order to claim the city as a place of "collective memory" (201), as she states in "Poetry, Memory and the Polis," and notes that the polis—cities and their organizing systems—is a dichotomous space. The city houses collective memory, yet it privileges male discourse in "the civic house of memory." Calling the modern city "one of the crucial factors in the social production of (sexed) corporeality" (242), Elizabeth Grosz proposes that civic space is the site "where the body is representationally re-explored, transformed, contested, reinscribed" (249). But the city's potential to act as a site of subversion of social norms should not be ignored, and, indeed, critical discussion about the city as a place for female subversiveness, and for lesbians in particular, is brisk. Dianne Chisholm suggests that for lesbians and gay men, an urban metropolis represents "the most promising site of emancipation from capitalist mass deception that still has us catastrophically spellbound," and writes the city as a space in which subversions of the patriarchal mainstream can, and often do, proliferate (198). Lesbians who "see themselves arising and enduring within urban culture without the traditional means of social reproduction afforded by family, ethnicity, nationality, and religion" may be the first citizens to question the social parameters and limits on civic speech imposed by the modern urban metropolis, and eventually write a "genealogy of their own telling" (Chisholm 195). Chisholm and Grosz appear to be speaking back to feminist theorist Luc Irigaray, who, in *Speculum of the Other Woman*, warns that it is a patriarchal commonplace to insist that a woman must "give up the specificity of her gender if she is to take part in public life" (308n). It is exactly this specificity of the female gender in civic space that Mouré advocates in *Furious*. Identifying the Law as the structure of "Western social organization" that "underlies the Polis, the city" ("Poetry" 201), Mouré's version of the polis is as a structured social organization that claims democratic ideals while making democratic action impossible, not unlike John

Ralston Saul's concept of the unconscious civilization as a "corporatist society with soft pretensions to democracy" (34–35).

In her 1995 article, "The Anti-Anaesthetic," Mouré warns "the Polis absorbs into itself as marginal something it calls poetry, which invariably supports the dominant order" (14–15). However, because *Furious* functions as criticism of the social structure supported by elegiac convention, Mouré's conception that "the entry into the symbolic order is the entry into sign, syntax, *La Loi du Père* (the Social Order, the Republic, the Polis)" ("Anti-Anaesthetic" 15) is played out in the challenge she offers to the dominant order. *Furious*, and Mouré's work taken as a whole, draws attention to the ways that questions of meaning rely on a set of conventions that act as a literary "anaesthesia" to painful experience and strive to "inject us with the comfortable" ("The Acts 5"). To suggest that language can resonate both within and outside of literary convention, Mouré uses sound, syntax, and intertext to disturb the anesthetic effect of literary convention and reading expectation and, in the gap created by such disturbance, to draw the reader's attention to the structures of power within language. Working with the play among memory, desire, and language, Mouré debates the relations between speaker and subject, men and women, absence and privilege, and logic and reason, reminding readers that "[t]he discourse of privilege is infinitely absorptive" ("Anti-Anaesthetic" 13). Writing poetry, for Mouré, is a political project designed to awaken readers to the limitations and possibilities of language, or, as she phrases it, to "mak[e] people feel prickly heat in the bomb shelter" of poetic convention ("Acknowledging" 129).

But no one will feel that "prickly heat" unless poetic conventions are emphasized as conventions: literary constructions that are mediated versions of social reality. This is the place from which Mouré's project of dismantling convention begins. Each section of *Furious* re-explores the female body's experience of loss while advancing an argument for the value of women's speech in Western social organization, first by refusing elegiac convention and eventually by proposing a feminist syntax of mourning. In the first section of the text, "Pure Reason," Mouré contrasts the "logic" of social sacrifice with a reason that exists "beyond all logic, and beyond the signs," advocating that all reason "must have to do with love, at its root" ("The Acts 3"). The next section, "Visible Affection," concentrates upon making female love visible outside of the sexual economy of male desire, opposing what Teresa de Lauretis calls "sexual indifference to lesbian representation" (17). In the text's eponymous third section, Mouré focuses upon breaking the surface of language in order to live "furiously," with the right to mourn losses and celebrate love in civic space. In the text's final section, "The Acts," a series of numbered prose poems masked as footnotes (or vice versa) elaborate upon what the refusal to abandon despair might mean for female and lesbian subjectivity. In "Surface," the prose-poem that finishes the section titled "The Acts," Mouré proposes ways to "get out of the ending," which includes refusing the consolation that elegiac convention proposes and defying a daughteronomy of self-sacrifice.

At the core of Mouré's inquiry is the role of the female citizen in accessing the "civic house of memory." When Gillian Rose declares that "all meaning and all mourning belong to the city" (103), it is hard to know whether she intends this as a caveat against or a prescription for participation in the polis. I believe Rose's "all meaning and all mourning belong to the city" is a confirmation that the authority of patriarchal social organization decrees all meaning, and that the language law of Western social organization subsequently regulates mourning practices. For instance, Mouré's poem "Wearing the Map of Africa" asserts that a government, as the active representative of the citizenry, justifies shooting citizens at a funeral because they "have gone beyond mourning the dead." The judgment of excess in this poem, of "going beyond" the prescribed parameters of mourning, recalls Freud's pathologizing of melancholia, but the violent results in Mouré's poem are anything but theoretical. This most violent and horrific regulation of mourning practices stands as a demonstration of power as the polis defines and enforces appropriate behaviour: that which does not "go beyond."

What is inaugural in this instance is not justice, but rather, injustice disguised as prudence and backed up by judicial law that condones violence against difference. On the strength of this evidence, Mouré can only emphasize that "[m]emory creates the City, collective memory, and women are still kept out of this memory" ("Poetry" 201). In terms of the poem's appeal to the rhetoric of mourning, the problem becomes one of practice; how can the practice of making meaning and the practice of mourning create a space for those who are kept out of that "civic house of memory"? Acknowledging that "even poetry can't avoid the Law," Mouré advocates attempting to recognize patriarchal power as a conscious construction rather than as a "natural" cultural and linguistic arbitrator ("Poetry" 201).

Mouré's concern with the elided bodies of women manifests itself in a reversal on the elegiac tradition; she elides the male body only to have it reappear in spectacular elegiac style, a submerged body whose symbolic power will not be denied. *Furious* traces the influence of a paternal imperative implicit in the production of language and in elegiac convention but instead of searching for the undiscovered female body as Carson does in "The Anthropology of Water" ("where is the woman?"), Mouré places the women at the centre of her discourse and the men on the margins. By refusing the male body as an elegiac subject and sidelining patriarchal authority, Mouré draws attention to the commanding father and the mournful young man as figures of epistemological and social convention. The father of "Pure Reason: Having" is so distant that the poem reveals only the back of his head in his car, heading "[w]herever we are going. / Wherever parents drive." Though Mouré treats the family as a social microcosm for the larger world, *Furious* has little in common with a confessional family elegy. The psychologically distant father is usurped early in the text by social patriarchs like the colleagues of "Snow Door" and the "friend of the family" of "Fifteen Years." More overtly political paternal forces are figured as restrictive social authority (in "Patron"), as public figures that exert overt political authority (in "Breakneck Speed"), or as manifestations of Western social organization in Mouré's multiple figurations of law and language. The good fathers imagined by other female elegists do not appear in *Furious*, and the death of the authoritative father is less mourned than it is anticipated. Gail Scott sums up this unsentimental attitude in her 1988 essay, "A Feminist at the Carnival," when she writes that "where certain male philosophers and writers see death... women imagine, instead, the death of patriarchy" (135).

It is unusual to read *Furious* as a text that comments on the power of paternal elegy, yet the text makes it clear that any re-imagination of female citizenship must first debate the traditions and tensions of father–daughter kinship. Mouré reminds readers that patriarchy involves not only the faceless force of the Law, but can also include the everyday faces of fathers, uncles, and co-workers. In "The Acts 7," she writes that men "do not have to put themselves at risk, which women have always had to do, to exist, to speak, to have their existence affirmed by others." Though she does not repudiate kinship with men, Mouré's inscription of lesbian resistance to heterosexuality—women who "walked away, from the word *cock, & ravishment*" ("Speaking of Which")—suggests something other than a refusal of male relationship; it suggests that relationships with men are not central to female subjectivity.

Mouré pinpoints an important difference between writing the father and writing *for* the father that produces the characteristic social tension of women's paternal elegies. The tension of the daughter's elegy acknowledges the possibility that the energy of her anagnorisis could be defused by the poem's reception as exclusively affective. The challenge, then, is to speak within the elegy of daughterly experience as part of an emerging rhetoric of mourning that is more directed towards female citizenship than daughterly duty. Primed by the sleeping figure in "Whose," *Furious* moves through a series of feminist awakenings that expose the "drug of topsoil" in the garden of elegiac tradition. The sleeping figure, anaesthetized perhaps by her own acquiescence, earns her place in the elegiac garden by "bothering no one," but because she refuses to abandon her despair, she cannot stay asleep for long and will be troublesome.

Like Macpherson's more traditionally presented texts, *Furious* addresses the conundrum of daughterly subjectivity in the face of authoritative constructions of meaning. Lacan unequivocally characterizes the Law of the Father as inescapable, and it is this discourse against which Mouré pits the fury of female subjectivity. The sleeping poet of "Whose" refuses to abandon her despair, for to do so would mean abandoning comprehension of her oppression. Despair in this context, as in much of elegiac tradition, is necessary for discovery; the source of grief in *Furious* is the personal and political comprehension that neither the Father's language nor his Law can represent female joy or female grief. In working with the tropes and conditions of elegiac convention to serve a larger political purpose, Mouré's refusal to abandon despair defies the Law of the Father that values completed mourning as a form of transcendence and the signification of the male body as meaning. A woman who writes a paternal elegy may already be considered "in excess of the Law" (Mouré, "Poetry" 204). The anxiety inherent in defying convention, elegiac or social, emphasizes that female memory is rarely honoured in conventional literary and social forms.

Operating out of this anxiety, *Furious* negotiates between anger and elegiac grief, and Mouré's interest in the dynamics of relationality reveals itself through her frequent shifts between the speaking positions of elegist and beloved. In "Speaking of Which," Mouré voices her speaking subject as the lost beloved, the elegiac object that is "thrown up into the scarce air" with her "first-born stars." The speaker becomes the female beloved, initially lost but filling with the heat of fury throughout the poem until she is fully embodied, alive but no longer sacrificial. In "Miss Chatelaine" and "Betty," the speaker returns as the furious elegist who actively refuses the social imperative to attend to male bodies with either grief or desire. Mouré's shift of subject positions, with a corresponding shift in speaker positions, unmakes the paternal world and suggests that relations between elegist and lost beloved cannot always be defined by social prescription. Part of the intrigue of unmaking the elegy in *Furious* exists in the possibilities implied by relationality, primarily lesbian desire, but also by friendships between women and relations with men that are run neither by heterosexual desire nor by a commitment to Western social structures. Indeed, the text's many positive references to brother figures suggest hope for male–female relations, and suggest that Mouré's target is not the male sex but belief in exclusive structures of power.

"Terribly, Terrifyingly Alive": The Fury of *Furious*

Judith Butler warns that Lacanian readings of the Oedipus/Antigone legend insist on "freezing the social arrangements of kinship as something intact and intractable," indicating a "crisis in kinship" that has yet to be resolved (*Antigone's* 14). Any question of legitimating women's loss has been, in Butler's view, systematically "suppressed by those who seek to make normative versions of kinship essential to the working of culture" (25). In *Furious*, Mouré proposes a figure that speaks back to these normative versions of kinship, a narrator that manifests her own brand of reason that challenges the limits of Western logic. If the sacrificial daughter pays for the sins of the father, then the defiant daughter must perform a corresponding task: to point out the crisis in kinship and suggest possibilities for a new and more functional relationality.

How can female resistance to consolation (recalling the violence of Sacks's substitutive consoling artifact) be recuperated as a constructive force? The text offers the central image of a female figure whom Mouré calls "terribly, terrifyingly alive" in desire and language, using a "rapport with rage" to advance her argument ("my existence" 216–17). This is the Fury as a figure of female recuperation. Mouré writes the resistant woman as a Fury who maintains her right to perform a work of melancholia. In her 2002 study, *Beyond Fate*, Margaret Visser reminds readers that since the Furies were inevitably called up by crimes of extreme social transgression, "typically... incest and kin murder," it should be no surprise that "the family was the special province of the Furies" (52–53). The Furies were unregenerate and unforgiving, and the punishment they inflicted included insanity and exile—social deaths perhaps worse than physical death: "The Furies might... drive the transgressor mad, chasing him away from sheltering city walls, away from the map of streets and all the city's other structures, and out across a featureless plain. Madness was confusion, a loss of all points of reference. The punishments of the Furies were claustrophobia and agoraphobia" (95). Visser warns that the Furies rule the realm of Moira, where "laws are... shorn of transcendent dimension" and obey a "pattern pure and simple, the imprisoning outline of the universe, policed in our nightmares by the Furies" (53). However, Mouré uses the figure of the Fury to expand the possibilities for legitimate love outside of that "imprisoning outline" of patriarchy. In "A Feminist at the Carnival," Gail Scott proposes a version of the mythical Fury as a figure of discursive strength and political acuity. Suggesting that history could "come full circle" if myth were read from a feminist perspective, Scott reconfigures the death of Oedipus and, with it, the imperative of daughterly duty: "In the myth, Erinyes (the Furies) hounded Oedipus to death at Colonus in Attica. His crime? Perhaps society was punishing him for unconsciously trying to substitute the matrilineal for the patrilineal line. I like to think that the Furies were furious at his failure, [and were] ready to upset the power on which the whole Oedipal drama is based" (122–23). Scott's revisionist Furies, with their politics of matrilineal descent, find a counterpart in a younger figure of a girl as a potentially heroic figure whose "bittersweet mixture of eroticism and foreboding" could introduce "a new heroine who is not merely the feminine of hero," a heroine who would "uncover the matrilineal traces buried in the folds of classical drama" (123). This heroine, Scott proposes, would be "both grandiose and humble, miserable and angry," embodying binary contradictions "without shame" (124). Scott warns of the difficulties that may befall the Fury as heroine, situating her, as does Mouré, in a struggle with language and Western social structure: "the heroine cannot close that gap between word (usage), body and the father's law, unless she becomes a parody of herself (a little man). Or a fragment (the cliché of mother, lover, prostitute)" (132). This parody or situation of being a "fragment" creates a nearly untenable subject position, or rather a non-subject position, for women. Scott calls the struggle towards subjectivity a heroine's "tragic journey" that recalls the rhetorical standoff between love and reason (132). But Mouré uses her Fury to revive the possibility of female discourse in civic space. The daughter-as-Fury becomes a figure that is driven by perspicacity rather than by rage, the kind of figure Mouré introduces by warning that "not reproducing... hierarchies" within a community of women is "not easy. And it's anxious. And it takes attentiveness" ("Poetry" 203).

In the poems in the section "Pure Reason," Mouré challenges the contrast between love and reason by blurring the Kantian distinction between the empirical individual and the critical agent, and, in doing so, she reveals the insidious sacrificial economy that governs dutiful daughterly mourning. The poems "Snow Door," "Pure Reason: Femininity," and "Fifteen Years" reveal the terms of a daughter's sacrifice to the "paternal" authority of logic, that "same old interrelated logic of signs" that "makes [Mouré's speaker] furious" ("The Acts 2"). Proposing that "pure reason" must reach beyond an "imposed" logic ("The Acts 3"), Mouré counters theories of the *pharmakon* proposed by René Girard, Jacques Derrida, and others. Working with recurring images of animals being sacrificed for human consumption in "Goodbye to Beef" and "Cure," Mouré suggests a parallel medical and linguistic sacrifice of women's bodies in the paired poems "Pure Reason: Science" and "Pure Reason: Femininity." These two poems, identical in structure, feature both animals and women launching a radio protest against their treatment by science and by patriarchy, respectively.

Mouré's use of animal experimentation as a metaphor for gender oppression captures the despair that the narrator has refused to abandon. Playing up the Kantian irony that "reason only perceives that which it produces after its own design" (Kant 10), Mouré lets her analogy dramatize the horror by comparing women to the laboratory animals. By demonstrating that a being's critical agency cannot be separated from its empirical circumstances, Mouré lampoons "pure reason" by inviting comparisons between the poems. Locating a political consciousness in mutilated animal bodies and disempowered female human bodies, Mouré shows us resistance in midst of victimhood: "As if you could dream like we dream and be cured" both groups say, as they "push back the announcer" to gain better access to the microphone ("Pure Reason: Science"; "Pure Reason: Femininity").

Like the preceding set of paired poems, "Fifteen Years" and "Thirteen Years" (also in the "Pure Reason" section) work by echoing each other, but this time Mouré sets a woman's memory of a single event in opposition to a family story about the same event. A sacrificial daughter narrates these poems, both of which begin with the same image: "a daydream of my uncle, / his shirt out at his daughter's wedding." Where "Fifteen Years" remembers a series of disjointed images about the wedding reception, "Thirteen Years" draws the dread of those images into the memory of a thirteen-year-old girl who is sacrificed to a lecherous "*friend of the family* touching [her] new chest" (emphasis in original). The two poems are echoes rather than juxtapositions; the sacrificial narrative of "Thirteen Years" is veiled by the disjointed images of "Fifteen Years." By revealing the terms of female sacrifice to male authority and discourse in "Pure Reason," Mouré notes the valuation of the female body as an adjunct to female memory.

Asserting the right to women's memory as manifested in bodily experience and rendered, however problematically, in women's language, the next section of *Furious*, "Visible Affection," concentrates upon making female love visible outside of the sexual economy of male desire. Lesbian sexuality is one way to embody female desire, but while the affection referred to in this section is indeed "visible," Mouré suggests the importance of acknowledging female friendship, mentorship, and supportive community as much as she touts the importance of lesbian textual representation. Mouré suggests that love *is* solidarity, or solidarity in the making, and that otherness, instead of calling up abjection, implies the strength found in a heterogeneous community.

The strength of Mouré's rebellious women reflects Kristeva's concept of the powerful role played by the semiotic chora, a prelinguistic, pre-symbolic state experienced in the first few months of life. Mouré's designation of the maternal semiotic as a precursor of the paternal symbolic originates in Kristeva's *Revolution in Poetic Language*, and it is no surprise that Mouré endeavours to write what Kristeva herself suggests: "poetry that is a not a form of murder" (*Revolution* 72). Mouré echoes the sound of the word "chora" to link the maternal daughter to the Fury, particularly in "Speaking of Which," the key poem in the "Visible Affection" section of *Furious*. Establishing a resurrective anger in the chora as prelinguistic experience, Mouré suggests a homonymic echo of the word as the personification of fury: "this fury is our hardest core." Mouré layers the text with such homonyms, claiming in "The Acts 7" that "[t]he resurrection of the woman's body is of Kore, not of the phallic king-dom." Mouré chooses Kore the maiden as her semiotic daughter figure, much as Gail Scott re-imagines a Fury figure as a girl, not yet a woman. Though the fury of "Speaking of Which" represents the "hardest core" of the female psyche, like the diamonds and stars that appear throughout the poem, the figure of the Fury also lives as a "rivulet / of anger" in the women's lungs, a source that they can "touch & keep warm." Mouré combines these images, resonant of the apparently contradictory notions of a maiden's innocence and a supernatural Fury, to locate lesbian desire as it has been underrepresented in language. The fiery "rivulet / of anger" is kept alive by "clear globes of oxygen," implying that breath keeps anger alive as air keeps fire alive. At the end of "Speaking of Which," Mouré returns to the resurrected daughter figure with the phrase "by these signs you shall know us," echoing Biblical phraseology in a way that is reminiscent of Macpherson's work with surviving daughter figures. The resurrected daughter is configured as Kore, Persephone's state before Zeus sacrificed her to be the bride of Hades.

To "speak of which" indicates a demand for a place in the symbolic order for women who "walked away from" the male body as desirable object and from the male affirmation of female existence, as "The Acts 7" asserts. The impulse to walk away, though such an action is rebellious in a heterosexist culture, is glossed in the poem as sustenance, as the air that sustains those globes of oxygen in the women's lungs. Mouré's poetry works within the symbolic order to call attention to the violence of that order, particularly the sacrifice of daughter figures by their fathers. Fury seeks articulation in the air, and finds community by refusing paternal patterns of desire, rejecting with them the reign of the Underworld, the worship of death, and the conventions of elegy. "Speaking of Which" both speaks and does not speak its subject; it refuses to speak the subject in symbolic terms that do not affirm the existence of the "which" under consideration. The unnamed referent acquires significance through its absence. The melancholic turn of the poem, pivoting upon the undesignated "which," suggests that the resurrection asserted by these poems is not of language but of female presence in the gaps between language. The poem shows an apprehension associated with naming a desire that may be diminished through naming. Such words seek inclusion in "the civic house of memory" but have struggled to maintain their promise and integrity in a social system that remains hostile towards women who refuse normative heterosexual desire and its potential violence or, as Mouré writes, women who want to "name what our own tongues will call *something*" ("Speaking of Which"; emphasis in original). That "something" signifies the space for love in the civic order, an overarching concern in Mouré's text that plays out as the struggle for lesbian representation of "Visible Affection" and the reconfiguration of fury as passion in the "Furious" section.

Mouré ends "Visible Affection" by locating a female homosocial desire for community that operates outside of the heterosexual economy of desire. In "Miss Chatelaine," Mouré creates a community where "[f]inally there are no men between us." But even in this originary moment of female community, the patriarchy hovers at the edge of women's consciousness. The elegiac convention that values the vanished male body as transcendent and beautiful haunts this poem. By invoking a girl-and-her-horse film as an image of pre-adolescent female sexual desire, Mouré suggests a poignant look at the development of a female sexuality that is not necessarily lesbian, but does not include heterosexual power dynamics. The poem situates women at the moment of discovering points of shared subjectivity through their memory of the film, especially the relationship between the girl and the horse:

> we are fifteen years older, serious
> about women, these images:
> the girl running at night between the house & the barn,
> & the noise of the horse's fear mixed in with the rain

The space between the house and the barn, between the "feminine" domestic space and "masculine" agricultural space, is also featured in the poems "Hooked" and "Pure Writing is a Notion Beyond the Pen," and "Miss Chatelaine" suggests that passing through such a space is the work of a heroine, the young Fury as rebellious daughter. The girl's caring attention to the horse's fear and her need to act beyond reason to aid the horse locates her as a heroine; she saves the horse (significantly gendered male in the poem) from "some parasite" by making an incision in his side, draining the poison from his body, and calming him.

The girl's task of cutting open a loved (and living) body to expel an invasive toxicity suggests the operation that Mouré performs on language—

creating a gap to allow new resonance. The girl's risk in passing through the space between genders is heroic; she acts out of her love for the horse and, in the morning, "the space between the house & barn is just a space again." The girl, ironically a protagonist in a movie considered "a classic for children," offers a model for the women who "are all feminist" fifteen years after graduating from high school. The speaker acknowledges the social conditions that create the moment of community among the women:

> Finally there are no men between us.
> Finally none of us are passing or failing according to
> *Miss Chatelaine.*
> I wish I could tell you how much I love you,
> my friends with your odd looks, our odd looks,
> our nervousness with each other,
> the girl crying out as she runs in the darkness,
> our decoration we wore, so many years ago, high school
> boys watching from another table.

Mouré matches the boys' "watching" attitude with the women's "odd looks," referring to their physical appearance and their "nervousness with each other." Earlier in the section, the women in "Hooked" exchange "furious glances" in an erotically charged situation, while the "odd looks" in "Miss Chatelaine" gloss the idea of queerness as well as suggesting that the looks exchanged by these women are unusual, in that they are women looking at women while not being observed by men.

But the gaze of the high school boys is a manifestation not only of compulsory heterosexuality, but also of a patriarchal culture that doubts the seriousness of the girl-heroine. Mouré's invocation of "our true tenderness" makes "Miss Chatelaine" a poem of community as well as a poem of erotic potential. Her penchant for punning titles suggests that "Miss Chatelaine" may refer not only to the Canadian fashion magazine, but alternatively to a "chatelaine" as the mistress of the house, implying that a woman could be unmarried ("miss") and a woman of property ("chatelaine"), making the title ironically suggestive of independence rather than decoration. (Whether or not k. d. lang's song "Miss Chatelaine" references Mouré's poem is another question. The poem's publication in *Furious* predates by four years the song's 1992 release.) "Finally I can love you," writes Mouré in the final stanza, but, though tenderness emerges between the women, the language of love remains in possession of the boys at the other table. The speaker is left with the chance to "meet with you & talk this over" without the ultimately desirable language of love ("I wish I could tell you how much I love you"). Implying that to be tender with other women in a heterosexist culture requires great courage, Mouré conflates the tender woman with the rebellious heroine of the next section of *Furious*, in which she explores how such tenderness must be buoyed up by the energy of fury.

In the text's third section, "Furious," Mouré concentrates upon the overt refusal of the male body as a compulsory love object for women. Mouré synthesizes the anger needed to sustain her project of breaking the surface of language and law, while continuously referring to love between women as the force that saves women from despair. It may seem ironic that in a society so greatly reliant on (and presumptive of) men's heterosexual desire for women and homosocial desire for other men, that Mouré would pinpoint women's "compulsory heterosexuality" (to use Adrienne Rich's term) as the idea upon which Western society predicates power inequities. The male body is honoured, admired, presumed to be important, valiant, redeemable, clean, and consequently grieved as a loss in Western social organization. If this valuation relies upon women's sexual desire for men, or the cultural presumption of the masochism of female desire, Mouré's ambiguous but resonant insistence of the "loss of women" as the touchstone for grief has currency for both lesbian and heterosexual women. Part of what lurks in this ambiguity is the uncomfortable suggestion that when women concentrate on the value of the male body as powerful, erotic, or of particular social significance, they lose women as social support and political allies.

With several poems that take feminist refusal of patriarchal power structures as their subject, Mouré suggests the pervasiveness of patriarchal power, in overt and covert political relations. "Patron," "Breakneck Speed," and "Wearing the Map of Africa" use the syntax of feminist resistance. The tightly repetitive diction of "Patron" suggests an atmosphere of sexual harassment, all innuendo and presumption in an "office tower" that remains "airless," devoid of life for the speaker. The syntax, too, displaying the man's "hands / up on his face push the slow skin dissolve frame over sunlight," suggests a surreal dissolve into non-contextual reference. The "patron" of the title is an individual and a representation of social authority: a patron of the patriarchal social organization and a participant in the inherent social presumptions of male power. By titling the poem with a word that has different connotations in English and in French, Mouré conveys the systemic use of power and the culture of male authority, combining the English resonance of "patron" as a consumer of services with the French connotation of the "patron" as the proprietor of a business. The man in the poem is patronizing in the sense that he assumes authority over the woman, relying upon a gendered power differential to support his right to comment on her emotional state as well as the quality of her work.

But if the loss of points of reference seems indicative of the Furies' presence in the poem, it is very clearly the Fury who speaks at the poem's end to free the woman from her social/professional confinement and confusion: "I will not, she said / I will/not." Mouré's play upon the force of will presents a variety of possibilities. The slash in "I will/not" functions as punctuation and as pause, a formal resistance to the man's will and a determination of the woman's will. She refuses his rhetoric of power along with his assumption that she will "learn the hierarchy" and "do this work so calmly." But the slash in the second statement of "I will/not" implies difficulties in resistance in the form of a stutter, implying that refusal is not always a matter of exerting one's personal will, and that what a woman wills to happen, or what she does not will, is not the only factor at work in power. The law may be refused, but this refusal is not an instantaneous solution to oppression.

"Breakneck Speed," with its image of the "disgraced American president Nixon / in our history books," moves from the toxic power portrayed in "Patron" to draw a distinction between "what we think we know, & / what happened. / Nothing happened." The photo of Nixon with sheet-music hymns displayed on his piano in the background depicts a bland innocence that contrasts sharply with the former president's political disgrace. In the "history book" of "Breakneck Speed," Nixon sings for the Christian Rock of Ages to "stand by him" in his moment of crisis, to support him in his unearned righteousness. So when Mouré's narrator says "Nothing happened. / Take my word for it," she is pointing to the lack of change in governmental ideology that neither "hides" corruption nor exposes it, but rather stands by it in implicit approval. Corruption is uncovered, but nothing changes. The poem lists other public figures who would support the claim of "nothing" happening: "Krushchev, Eisenhower... Roosevelt, Stalin. Or ask General Patton," moving backwards through twentieth-century history to name other men who performed acts of public disgrace while maintaining righteous reputations within their own ideologies. With "General Patton" appearing so soon after "Patron," the eye could be forgiven for creating a visual equivalency between the names. The poem ends with a rejection that draws attention to its frustration: "If you ask me, I'm getting / outa here at breakneck speed." The idea of "getting out of" Western discourse and politics, out of the complicity of being a middle-class white person in North America, recurs in *Furious* with the frequency and ferocity of a Fury who has lost the power to punish but who can still see that the boundaries of the polis are transgressed with impunity by its own government.

"Wearing the Map of Africa" addresses the political insurgency of public grief and the complicity or hope in "trying to dream" in a violent world.

The riot in South Africa over the funeral processions of "the rioted dead," those killed in previous protests or police riots, points to a perpetuation of violence, especially when "the ruling party" declares: "These funerals have to stop… / they've gone past mourning the dead." Once again, the limits of mourning are enforced, this time by a patriarchal government against people of colour. The irony of "the government" that attempts "to restore calm" with "policemen / with peaked caps & rifles who look like the army" and "tear gas bombs" thrown into the crowd of mourners makes the speaker question the importance of diction in news reportage: "Does the word *restore* mean anything? / The word *calm*?" (emphases in original). Positioning her own whiteness as a condition of unavoidable complicity, the speaker comes to the following conclusion:

> The word calm means suppressed anger
> The word calm means implode.
> The word restore means suppress anger.
> The word means where does the anger go to when its beak is
>   shut, forcibly
> Where does the anger go to it doesn't go anywhere

The Fury as heroine resituates the anger without attempting to control it, noting that the word has "gone beyond mourning the dead. / It is honouring the living. / It is honouring the mouth, hurt, / trying to dream." This is the same fury that refuses to keep "its beak… shut" about loss and the same force of anger that is "still dancing" at the poem's end. "Wearing the Map of Africa" demonstrates the labour of mourning as a force of solidarity, acted out by the crowd and reiterated in the speaker's final injunction in "trying to dream" the "indescribable… colour of sweetness." That search for sweetness, in the oranges from South Africa that were part of the Western world's sanctions on exportation, implies the irony of "honouring the living" through capitalist principles. Once again, as in "Patron," the oppressors require and admire "calmness" as a condition of victimhood. These poems display individual, social, and political resistance to oppression, beginning by situating the male body as powerful and ending by refusing the ideology proposed by that "body" of thought.

Mouré resists the social valuation of the gendered body, and offers an alternative homosocial, if not always homosexual, affection for women as embodied presences, tracing the struggle for women's presence in language as a condition of the desiring subject. In "Salt: Condition," the speaker struggles with the condition of speech, holding her "still wriggling" tongue in her hands, and retreating to the female space of the girls' bathroom "which was / huge and white as in high school, where the young women / smoke together & feel their bodies growing." On the heels of "Miss Chatelaine," this nostalgia for the bartered gynotopia of the high school bathroom echoes the tenderness and promise of female friendship of that poem's ending. But Mouré suggests that such a world is fragile, for the girls are not only growing into women, but also "growing, / apart from each other, secretly, alone." The secrecy and isolation of these young developing bodies presages their disappearance, another tragic loss of women in this text. The female friends who were so welcomed in "Miss Chatelaine" reappear in "Salt: Condition" in younger guises, only to disappear, trapped early by male sexual desire and perhaps by the unexpected product of their own desires: "That year, two of my high school friends cried & said they were / pregnant, then vanished, / the washroom left empty." The boys who "watched from another table" in "Miss Chatelaine" exert the influence of their bodies in "Salt: Condition," and these girls, who unlike the girls in "Speaking of Which" did not "walk away, from the word *cock, & ravishment,*" vanish from the female community.

"Salt: Condition," with the title's reference to tears and the domesticity of "salt upon the table in its cellar," as well as the element that "is poured onto the chests of the newly dead to / *taketh away their sins,*" is the female condition; the pillar of salt that is Lot's disobedient wife is a strong unspoken presence in this poem. The placement of the tongue outside the speaker's mouth and in her own hands corporealizes the separation between female speech and power. Mouré writes the disembodied tongue's panicked struggle as "a bird / whose nest was touched by humans, its eggs pecked / ragged in its fright, / the young leaked out and ruined." The words which the tongue might have engendered are "ruined," an ironic counterpoint to the girls' fecundity as another kind of ruin. Mouré finishes "Salt: Condition" with a single phrase isolated by a stanza break: "Where the mouth is." The singularity of the line emphasizes the tongue's distance from the mouth with its inability to speak, even as the tongue's frantic flutter in her hands implies desperation. The "tongue" as language is literally separate from the girl's experience.

The opening lines of "Betty" revisit this desperate separation, and show speech encouraged by community. By writing "women / speaking light words into the cups of each other's fingers," Mouré indicates lips and digits as two halves of a whole system of speech. Later, women's hands are "frozen, without fingers" but with "strange sprung words leaking // into our sentences." The "strange" words "sprung," like poetic invocations of Gerard Manley Hopkins's "sprung rhythm," surprise in their suddenness; when holy words at last leave the mouths of the women in *Furious*, they are spoken by a two-year-old girl who, with the infinitely logical play of a new language learner, asserts the pun "A-girls" as a blessing instead of "Amen." The girl's declaration is joyous; she "called out at the supper table" like a holy fool, "Let's not say 'Grace' again... let's say 'Betty.'"

But the child's exuberance only reminds the speaker of the lack of language freedom experienced by adult women and the gargoyle-like presence of adolescent boys who watch over the memories of the women:

> Why are so many women lonely, empty as the insides of bicycles, as
> the mouths using all the room,
> the boys in their tight jeans &
> slimness that will leave them in their 22nd year,
> the boys & their hard laugh who is tougher,
> boys getting at each other's love, thru the inside
> of women, their intermediary, their confessional.

The appearance of beautiful young men as an echo of the traditional elegiac lost beloved, "in their tight jeans & / slimness that will leave them in their 22nd year," reminds readers that patriarchy also limits the ways a male body is honoured or valued. "Betty" suggests that even homosocial (or homosexual) love must be funnelled like a "confession" through women's bodies as "intermediary" devices of exchange value. The "inside of women" refers to physical penetration, but also to women's work as the bearers of grief.

The final stanza of "Betty" declares the sexual ethic of *Furious*: "I want to speak sexually of one thing—not male love / but physical knowing." By distinguishing between the Western tradition of "male love" (implying in this context both love *from* men and love *for* men) as a social convention and the apparent certainty of "physical knowing," Mouré proposes a philosophical conundrum. "Physical knowing" in "Betty" becomes "the distance / between the breastbone and the palm, the two / important parts of the body," an epistemological metaphor for the blend of corporeality and speech. Mouré's use of a female breastbone as a place of love often torn by violence reaches back to the women's "soft chests / torn open" in "Pure Reason: Femininity." The distance between chest and hand acts out the distance between love and language; this distance becomes fluid at the end of "Betty," as "the water runs in the long veins" and the palm becomes a pool "where you can dive in & drink & never come up again." Women's language becomes a pool into which women may dive—surely an allusion to Rich—in order to redefine subjectivity. The feminist refusal to abandon despair becomes a way of breaking the surface of the water like the surface of the grand elegiac narrative. The apparent contradiction of the diving heroine as someone who "never come[s] up again" and someone who "break[s] the surface" plays out this journey into the watery body of discourse as an exhortation to live furiously. The protagonist surfaces from her dive into the pool of consciousness, her "head wet, smelling faintly of milk or oranges," and here Mouré's birth imagery contrasts with her use of head and hair as images of control in "Pure Reason." The head of this Cixousian "newly born woman" is both out of control—"streaming" water—and perfectly in control—slicked down and smelling of mother's milk or the fruit of paradise. The narrator no longer needs the ironic device of the "small comb" ("With a Small Comb"); the water transforms her head into a place of "physical knowing."

From this epistemological position, Mouré begins the poem "Gorgeous" on a note of doubt with a phrase that imitates the syntax of a question without its interrogative mark: "what are our chances." The idea of chance informs the poem's movement, and Mouré's coiled self-contained images contrast with the free-flowing liquid imagery that leads the reader through the poem. This body is a place of paradox, featured as coiled and invulnerable at the same time as it is flowing and possessed of a powerful beauty. In the lover's body, "small coils of the chromosomes" inside "cells... inscribed with the secret code given her at birth" describe a lover's genetic code: her female sex and her "possible range" of longevity. The lover's body is both vital and infirm: she lies listless upon a bed; she bleeds; she is invaded by cancer. Mouré's repetition of "I river, I river, I river" is sweetly and ironically elegiac, as the river that has traditionally drowned the beloved and soothed the elegist becomes a verb resonant with the word "lover."

The elegiac body in "Gorgeous" is definitely that of a woman, and she is most definitely not dead; she leaves the bed in the poem, despite the fact that her blood "gorges the bed." *Furious* has been directed towards rejecting the male body as the ultimate object of worship and grief, and "Gorgeous" completes this action with its ambiguous and highly resonant iterations of violence and love. When Mouré draws the reader's attention to "[t]his expiation of the body, not petty, but, *critical,*" the expiation to which she refers is the menstruation in the preceding line ("Who touches, every month, her own blood"). But this expiation of the body also refers to the lost or threatened body as an elegiac object, the body as a mortally vulnerable entity in the elegiac mode. The speaker's declaration of love is followed by a declaration about the text: "I love you. The book is ended," as though the declaration of love will make the beloved less vulnerable.

One of the lessons of the elegy is that arguments against death are valuable for the revelations they may yield about living, but neither love nor argument has ever been successful at warding off death. Mouré's declaration, in true (reclaimed) elegiac fashion, does not stop the terrifying final line: "The blood gorges gorges gorges the bed." The conflation of death and beauty (the homonymic pun on "gorgeous" and "gorges") suggests the intractability of life and death, the strength of the elegiac contract, and the strength of reason predicated upon love. Is there another homonymic pun on "gorge" as the French word for throat? Mouré demonstrates how the body may "speak" in its own blood, and how "trusting the verb" means maintaining a flow that is free of the tight confines of the coiled insides.

Of course, the book has not actually ended, for "The Acts" appear as the last section of *Furious*, performing as Mouré's ending that is not an ending. As designated in the Table of Contents, "The Acts" perform as footnotes for each of the poems, explicating but not explaining the theoretical basis of the poems. But by scattering "the acts" throughout the body of the text, while also placing them in the last part of the book, Mouré implies a tension between the author's privilege of the last word while also "getting out of the ending" in "Surface." Resistance to the ending has been a feminist strategy at least since Rachel Blau Duplessis's 1985 *Writing Beyond the Ending*, her text on women's narrative strategies that "express critical dissent from dominant narrative" and create a text that "denies or reconstructs seductive patterns of feeling that are culturally mandated, internally policed, hegemonically poised" (5). Though Mouré claims that the function of "The Acts" is to "free memory and desire" ("The Acts 14") by supplying a critical context for the poems, the rhythm of these prose poems suggest an impatient exhortation to action. "The Acts" may refer to the Acts of the Apostles; both texts are adjuncts to a previous "text"—the life of Christ and the life of the female heroine—and both celebrate a resurrection of the disallowed body: in *Furious*, the female body as the object of love and elegy.

Mouré exhorts women to "refuse to restrain ourselves" ("The Acts 14"), and this refusal emerges as a performance in the final pages of "The Acts," with "Surface," not coincidentally the only "Act" with a title instead of a number. The reiteration of refusal in "Surface" describes the formation of a literary aesthetic and a political consciousness in a narrative that relates the changes in the speaker's perspective undergone in a single evening. The speaker declares the surface is too familiar: "After a while it becomes too easy, that surface you know so well. As if the animals could jump off coins, their antlers burnished. Into the street, where you put *palm trees*. The line suffers from you. You don't want the ragged edge anymore" ("Surface"). The speaker's declaration that "the line suffers from you" is reminiscent of the conventional complaint of the Wildean aesthete, who suggests that a lack of talent is an affront to the page. But Mouré's syntax also implies the converse of her statement, that the poet suffers from the line. By the next stanza, dissatisfaction has become desire; as "the surface folds up into its mathematical planes," the speaker discovers her own aesthetic: "You want to write only the gaps, between the eyelids of the letters." The sea returns as the subject of the only picture the speaker has ever painted, and her self-admonition that "[w]e are what we paint" refers back to the transformative qualities of water as a corollary for a woman's body. Because "[t]ranscribing the view has become impossible," the speaker must rely upon locating what she names "the female imaginary." The poem needs a female politics expansive enough to address the quotidian, including the designation of "pierced and unpierced spoons" as "male and female." By the fourth stanza, the speaker has discovered the possibility of a new aesthetic: "The line ends where it wants to. The surface is thirsty."

Refusal returns on the book's final page: "Each note of the page was a refusal, of the end of the line, a refusal of 'title,' & a refusal of the 'middle' of the poem. You will write again & give up your claim to the surface." Giving up the need to remain on the surface, to obey standard rules of form and syntax, is a tension throughout *Furious*, but also apparent in the speaker's need to give up her claim *unto* the surface, to walk away from the limitations of the surface. Mouré's final lines recall images from the collection, such as the brightly lit kitchen of "Hooked," the ocean of "Ocean Poem," and the "small door" of "Snow Door." All these images involve lesbian desire as an unspoken presence beneath the surface of a compulsory heterosexual Western culture. In the final words of the text, the speaker adopts a position familiar to us from Carson's "The Anthropology of Water": "You will get out of ending by falling fully-clothed into the sea." Mouré has commented on how she wants to use the ending of a poem to inspire thought rather than closure: "[t]he poet pushes it [the poem] off the page and into the reader. Real thoughts do reverberate. To add an 'end' is a figment of the head. (Not the imagination)" (Interview with Peter O'Brien 246). "Falling fully-clothed into the sea" echoes the diving action of "Betty," in which the dive becomes an immersion in a new aesthetic, or, to compare *Furious* with "The Anthropology of Water," Mouré's narrator begins where the Sphinx saw only an end. The surface of the poem becomes a new narrative thirsty for revelation, proposing that reading must involve a resonant immersion into possibility, a willingness to dive beneath meaning.

Reading the fall into the sea as an intentional act of escape, "Surface" traces the creation of a poetic and political consciousness. The female elegist confronts water's potentially transformative power along with the patriarchal ideology of femininity as a fluid concept that defies subjectivity.

If the "female imaginary exists," it is beneath the surface. Mouré matches the physical vulnerability that haunts the socio-political oppression of women with the elegiac convention of transformative fluidity, and asserts the female self as both elegist and elegized. She chooses who to mourn and how (or if) to write the self as a lost beloved. If "[e]ach note on the page" is "a refusal," then getting out of the ending is one more refusal to abdicate the force of female melancholia.

Proposing 'Activity Beyond Activity': Rose's Meaning and Mouré's Mourning

Mouré asserts the necessity of a politicized "fury," which is not the same as the aberrant anger about which Gillian Rose warns in *Mourning Becomes the Law.* Mouré recasts her Fury as the energy of anxiety, a socially responsible power of assertion and refusal, and is willing to forge an anger that demands a responsible political address. Part of the responsibility taken on by "The Acts" is that of urgent reconfiguration, which Mouré defines through a quotation from Jerome Rothenberg's study of postcolonial poetics, *Technicians of the Sacred*: "images that 'act within a context but do not refer to it'" ("The Acts 5").

Campaigning against melancholia, Rose claims that the anger inherent in unexamined mourning will cripple the mourner as citizen, and Mouré might argue that aberrated mourning already limits the discourse of women in Western social organization. Mouré, despite the text's title, does not create a toxic rant but, rather, a text in which women remain furiously alive to the possibilities of love and grief. Rose asserts quite boldly that the law has no other ethical choice but to acknowledge that "acts of justice" by female mourners "reinvent the political life of the community" (35), yet Antigone's fate convinces us otherwise, and Mouré remains less certain than Rose about the inevitability of justice. For the first three sections of *Furious*, Mouré eschews the use of the question mark, allowing the syntax to suggest both interrogative and complete assertion. This formal choice emphasizes relationality and proximity in language, prompting a syntactical "stutter that replicate[s] surfaces imperfectly" ("The Acts 14"). The stutter is the vehicle that brings language to the edge of what the speaker knows, and Mouré's artful truncation invokes "a stutter at the edge of" without identifying the edge.

Disregarding the elegy's social efficacy can disempower mourning as a political force and expunge the possibility of discovery. Mouré's search for a "new surface as a reflex for emotional depth and power" ("Changes" 44) is the project of anagnorisis: the revelation achieved through an examination of "false reference or intended deceit" (37) of which Abby Findlay Potts writes. By suggesting that Western social organization molds the language of grief and desire, Mouré inquires into the risks of assuming a subjectivity that is not yet included in "the civic house of memory": "What is key to this desire: To have one's existence affirmed by others. Or, put oneself at risk forever (a panic at the cell's edge). Or is it affirmation, first, that then makes the risk possible?" ("The Acts 7"). While the risk in this quotation is a declarative and demonstrative lesbian desire, desire is also undeniably epistemological: a desire to know and be known. Mouré's "panic at the cell's edge" is enlivened by her refusal to be consoled by a system that perpetuates oppression.

This has been the paradoxical project of all of the female-authored elegies of this study: to mourn loss while criticizing the rhetoric of mourning. If the melancholic turn in *Furious* means using a traditional mode to turn from one form of subjectivity (the consoled male elegist) to another (the resolute and demanding female elegist), then trends in the female elegy towards speaking the unspeakable cannot be ignored. Mouré asserts that "poetry is, in its nature, protest, because it opposes, even as it uses, ordinary speech.... Its context is a disruption of order" ("Anti-Anaesthetic" 20). Poetry in this context does not mean poetry "which invariably supports the dominant order" but, rather, poetry that presents itself as "a knot made out of the world" ("Anti-Anaesthetic" 14). The knot composed of the loss of women demands an exploration of the elegiac convention as a social structure, and takes seriously Butler's claim that "where there is no public recognition or discourse through which such a loss might be named and mourned, then melancholia takes on cultural dimensions of contemporary consequence" (*Psychic* 139). These "cultural dimensions" include the paradox of female duty and female subjectivity when the cultural duty of mourning meets the social anxiety of female melancholia. The female elegist is also the female hero, by virtue of her anxiety, not despite it. Butler's melancholic turn is generated from an anxious impulse—to recognize, to reply, to remember—in an anxiously gendered body.

This thought itself produces some anxiety. In "The Anti-Anaesthetic," Mouré is wary about simplifying the discourse of female subjectivity through the "radically unstable" ways by which patriarchy glosses the state of being female: "[i]t's hard to make identity-discourse out of women's desire, because its *terms* slip" (18; emphasis in original). To speak, to write, or to exert a political presence in the world means to practise a legitimate mourning and an anxiety about language. Mouré's "stutter inside us" ("To Speak" 132) may be the elegy's most socially responsible bid for subjectivity, and her anti-anaesthetic poetics demonstrate Rose's "*activity beyond activity*...the relinquishing of and *taking up again* of activity which requires the fullest acknowledgement of active complicity" (122; emphases in original). Rose assures us that this activity strives towards a worthy outcome: "The work of mourning is difficult but not interminable; beginnings may be made in the middle. This work of mourning is the spiritual-political kingdom—the difficulty sustained, the transcendence of *actual* justice" (122; emphasis in original). Though *Furious* is more a work of furious melancholia than of mourning, describing the text as "difficulty sustained" seems particularly apt. In "The Acts 15," when Mouré writes "Grief, now; the hand prevents me," the symbol of the hand, which has served throughout *Furious* as the portal to women's language, supports through its prevention of grief the female elegiac mode as melancholic fragmentation. The bodily tension between hand, mouth, and breastbone performs a stutter of the body, an attempt at physical knowing outside of speech. In her refusal to speak a single truth out of an elegiac utterance at the same time as she asserts the value of a politicized subjectivity of fury, Mouré's "stutter at the edge of" becomes Rose's "activity beyond activity": the anxious political work of mourning, unrelieved by anaesthetic language.

Conclusion

From the Water

The painting by Canadian artist Erica Grimm-Vance that appears on the cover of this volume is titled *Whatever you hear from the water, remember.* It is part of a series of paintings called *Metaxu*, and from the moment I saw it, I was struck by how the painting shows productive melancholia at work. The painting's visual language is very precise in its depiction of a moment of elegiac revelation. From the woman's feminine yet quasi-androgynous appearance, to the water streaming off her head, to the way the image of her head is bisected between morning and mourning, to her upturned face, so calm and yet so unconsoled, Grimm-Vance's painting captures so many of the contradictions of daughterly mourning. The title, too, bears an allusion to the watery death of the beloved and to the female elegist who struggles to keep from drowning in tradition. The injunction in the title, not yet knowing that what she will "hear from the water"—that site of transformation—and yet certain that it will be worth remembering, suggests a receptivity and a burgeoning subjectivity. Even the name of the group of paintings is strangely appropriate: *metaxu* from Plato, meaning "between" or "meanwhile" and used in the twentieth century by activist and mystic Simone Weil to refer to an object that connects even as it separates, gestures to paradox and to affectionate relations with the dead.

Exactly what the woman has heard from the water remains mysterious, or perhaps primarily affective and not discursive, but the woman's upturned face shows her beginning the work of remembering. Her expression is not serene, and neither is it greatly disturbed. She is calm as she focuses on a point beyond the frame—a frame that, in turn, encloses our frame for the ways that we may understand her. Divided between grief and something that is not yet hope, she looks up. Note how her expression is not quite supplication, unlike many depictions of female saints or martyrs. She is not offering up her pain; she is keeping the pain, but the shift between the grey world of grief and the brightness of discovery has just happened in the world of this painting. The line down the centre is the line of anagnorisis; here we see the mourner in the moment after discovery, when revelation has almost completely cleared away her pain, but not quite. This is *metaxu*—that which happens between: the mourning that happens meanwhile.

That "meanwhile" is read on the body, waiting for the next moment. In the painting, the woman's head is tipped back so that water still streams from it in the dark side of the painting, like phosphorescent rain that drips onto her shoulders and back, smearing them with the strange glow of grief. The light she looks towards in the left side of the painting is also long and vertical; discovery mirrors grief. But the difference with the light is its surprising weight: it pulls rather than spatters; it draws itself down her face like gravity. The woman's head just fits the frame with the tip of her chin and flat of her forehead in perfect alignment with the edges of the painting, and yet she doesn't look trapped or boxed in. She looks as though she is thinking; she looks as though she is seeing something beyond the frame. The elegy is a performance in which the acting mourner must look up. Looking up becomes the act of remembering.

* * *

This book began with Jay Macpherson's poetic assertion that the nightingale, that ambiguously interpreted bird, sang for "no man." Either grieving or rejoicing, or some version of both, Macpherson's nightingale defines herself by four words that speak the subjectivity of the surviving daughter: "I sing and thrive." In the spirit of such a song, Macpherson's nightingale is one of the images we could take forward in answer to Judith Butler's call for "new schemes of intelligibility" that would "make our loves legitimate and recognizable, our losses true losses" (*Antigone's* 24) in the coming years of the twenty-first century. The female-written paternal elegy is fuelled by the quest for such schemes of intelligibility, such ways of looking up to remember, and retell, what the water has told. Risking a redefinition of filial piety through female engagement with creative melancholia makes the elegists under discussion into examples of what Juliana Schiesari imagined in *The Gendering of Melancholia*: women writers as "disagreeable but justified rebel[s]" (50).

The appeal of elegies has endured throughout literary history not only because death is inevitable or because the human capacity for grief is huge, though both of these facts are true. Elegies linger in our public fascination and literary study because they demand attention but will not easily yield up their secrets or the terms of their struggle. They are driven by an epistemological impulse and enlivened by a long tradition of affective contradiction. The energy necessary to sustain an elegiac series of poems is considerable, and while it is not a bad idea to think of elegies as Wordsworthian recollections of emotion in tranquility, what is recollected—and reformulated—in such tranquility is as rhetorical as it is emotive. The death of the patriarch remains a powerful cultural experience, and postmodern North America is no exception. Poetry that strives to capture that strange dynamic of enormous grief abutted onto a shift in power must be considered one way to ask about, and sometimes reify, the changes that death brings to the cultural and economic fortunes of family life.

This book deliberately places the work of poets of different generations, styles, and politics beside one another for comparison, though my intention is not to lump these women writers together intellectually or ideologically, or to otherwise efface their differences. There is a certain risk in considering Macpherson in the same book as Mouré, placing Atwood next to Carson, or even including sometime rivals Page and Livesay as poets grappling with similar problems. By describing an arc of female paternal elegiacs in Canadian literature, the essays in this volume resist the history of group identification and re-identification that has been especially prominent in the history of Canadian poetry. These poetic silos and their accompanying declarations and ideologies are undeniably fascinating in themselves, and the aim of this book has not been to convince anyone to abandon them. But the pervasiveness of the concern with establishing poetic subjectivity through paternal loss speaks for itself, demonstrating how thoroughly this idea has occupied Canadian female poets of different generations and political outlooks.

Like funereal rituals that act out—and facilitate—the mourner's grief, elegies perform an inquiry into the ineffable from the inquisitor's position: the bereaved are especially empowered to demand answers in a way that the rest of us are not, or cannot be, until we too move into the mourner's position. The elegy's greatest task is to make conscious the inquiry awakened by grief: an inquiry that may have lingered in the background, throbbing with energy but buried by affect. A demanding reader will not diminish an elegy by reading it with attention; the rigorous application of theory will not bruise an elegy. The most enduring elegies have affective resilience because of their energy of inquiry: Livesay's lifelong argument with her father, Page's steady gaze, Macpherson's bloody-minded determination, Atwood's refusal to simplify, Carson's long classical reach, Gunnars's robust longing, Tostevin's audacity, and Mouré's furious looks.

* * *

Partway through my research into female-written paternal elegies, my father was diagnosed with cancer and died five months later. What had begun in curiosity became more urgently situated in the quotidian functioning of my existence. With a determination that I could not help but recognize as equal parts scholarly direction and my own brand of bloody-mindedness, I continued with the research. Freud's metaphor seemed even more resonantly odd after my father's death, for while the work of research was clearly work as I understood it—effortful and directed, something I did and did not do as the tasks produced themselves—mourning was not work as I construed work. It was effortful to be sure, but it was not task-oriented; I could no more refuse to mourn than I could refuse to breathe. But life and the page have a strange relationship. I was not so naïve as to think that my research into elegy, even father–daughter elegy, would grant me perspective on my own grief, and indeed it did not. However, the death of a parent changes the family dynamic, for good or for ill. It changes the frame on the world. It made me an adult—the way nothing up to that time had made me an adult—in one fell swoop.

As for productive melancholia, I cannot be sure that I am finished with it even yet. A poet as well as a professor, I wrote elegies for my father: self-consciously, compulsively, resisting some days, and entering into the spirit of anagnorisis on others. I did not find solace in doing so, but I found something else: community and kinship, a way of marking my place in time the way that others have also done, by remembering what I heard from the water.

Works Cited

Alighieri, Dante. *The Divine Comedy: The Inferno.* Trans. John Ciardi. New York: Penguin, 1982.

Allott, Kenneth, ed. *The Poems of Matthew Arnold.* London: Longmans, 1965. Print.

Arnason, David. "Dorothy Livesay and the Rise of Modernism in Canada." *A Public and Private Voice: Essays on the Life and Work of Dorothy Livesay.* Ed. Lindsay Dorney, Gerald Noonan, and Paul Tiessen. Waterloo: U of Waterloo P, 1986. 5–18. Print.

Arnold, Matthew. "The Forsaken Merman." 1849. Allott 95–100.

———. "The Scholar Gipsy." 1853. Allott 331–44.

———. "Thyrsis." 1865. Allott 496–508.

Atwood, Margaret. "Bored." *Morning* 91–92.

———. *Cat's Eye.* Toronto: McClelland, 1988. Print.

———. *The Circle Game.* Toronto: Contact P, 1964. Print.

———. "Dire Things: An Interview with Margaret Atwood." *Poetry Canada Review* 15.2 (1995): 1–3, 28–29. Print.

———. "Down." *Morning* 72–75.

———. "A Fire Place." *Morning* 116–17.

———. "Four Small Elegies." *Two-Headed Poems.* Toronto: Oxford UP, 1978. 52–55. Print.

———. "Girl Without Hands." *Morning* 112–13.

———. "Half-Hanged Mary." *Morning* 58–69.

———. "Jay Macpherson: *Poems Twice Told.*" *Books in Canada* 11.4 (1982): 14–15. Rpt. in *Second Words: Selected Critical Prose.* Toronto: Anansi, 1982. 407–11. Print.

———. *The Labrador Fiasco.* London: Bloomsbury, 1996. Print.

———. "Man in a Glacier." *Morning* 81–82.

———. "Morning in the Burned House." *Morning* 126–27.

———. *Morning in the Burned House*. Toronto: McClelland, 1995. Print.
———. *Negotiating with the Dead: A Writer on Writing*. Cambridge UP, 2002. Print.
———. "The Ottawa River by Night." *Morning* 103–4.
———. "A Pink Hotel in California." *Morning* 76–77.
———. *Power Politics*. Toronto: Anansi, 1971. Print.
———. *Procedures for Underground*. Toronto: McClelland, 1970. Print.
———. "The Signer." *Morning* 115–16.
———. "Shapechangers in Winter." *Morning* 120–25.
———. "Statuary." *Morning* 118–19.
———. *Surfacing*. Toronto: McClelland, 1972. Print.
———. *Two-Headed Poems*. Toronto: McClelland, 1978. Print.
———. "Up." *Morning* 110–11.
———. "Vermilion Flycatcher, San Pedro River, Arizona." *Morning* 107–8.
———. "Wave." *Morning* 83–84.
———. *You Are Happy*. Toronto: Oxford UP, 1974. Print.
Auden, W. H. "Song of Master and Boatswain: The Sea and the Mirror." *For the Time Being*. London: Faber, 1945. 26. Print.
Babcock, Barbara A. *The Reversible World: Symbolic Inversion in Art and Society*. Ithaca: Cornell UP, 1978. Print.
Baird, Jean and George Bowering, eds. *The Heart Does Break: Canadian Writers on Grief and Mourning*. Toronto: Random, 2009. Print.
Banting, Pamela. "Daddy's Girl: Dorothy Livesay's Correspondence with her Father." *Canadian Poetry* 22 (1988): 10–21. Print.
Barber, Paul. *Vampires, Burial and Death: Folklore and Reality*. New Haven: Yale UP, 1988. Print.
Barthes, Roland. *Writing Degree Zero*. 1953. Trans. Annette Lavers and Colin Smith. New York: Hill, 1977. Print.
Bayer-Berenbaum, Linda. *The Gothic Imagination: Expansion in Gothic Literature and Art*. London: Associated UP, 1982. Print.
Benjamin, Jessica. *Like Subjects, Love Objects: Essays on Recognition and Difference*. New Haven: Yale UP, 1995. Print.
Benjamin, Walter. *The Origin of German Tragic Drama*. Trans. John Osborne. London: NLB, 1977. Print.
Beyer, Charlotte. "Feminist Revisionary Mythology and Female Identity in Margaret Atwood's Recent Poetry." *Literature and Theology* 14.3 (2000): 276–98. Print.
Bloom, Harold. *The Anxiety of Influence: A Theory of Poetry*. New York: Oxford UP, 1973. Print.
Boose, Lynda E. "The Father's House and the Daughter in It: The Structures of Western Culture's Daughter–Father Relationship." *Daughters and Fathers*. Ed. Boose and Betty S. Flowers. Baltimore: Johns Hopkins UP, 1989. 19–74. Print.
———. and Betty S. Flowers. "Cultural Filialogy." *Daughters and Fathers*. Ed. Boose and Flowers. Baltimore: Johns Hopkins UP, 1989. 9–18. Print.

Bordo, Susan R. "The Body and the Reproduction of Femininity: A Feminist Appropriation of Foucault." *Gender/Body/ Knowledge: Feminist Reconstructions of Being and Knowing*. Ed. Alison M. Jaggar and Bordo. London: Rutgers UP, 1989. 13–33. Print.

Botting, Fred. *Gothic*. London: Routledge, 1996. Print.

Brabon, Benjamin A. and Stéphanie Genz. Introduction. *Postfeminist Gothic: Critical Interventions in Contemporary Culture*. Ed. Brabon and Genz. Houndsmills: Macmillan, 2007. 1–15. Print.

Brandt, Di. "The happiest reader in the world: David Arnason's revisionary stories." *So this is the world and here I am in it*. Edmonton: NeWest, 2007. 55–71. Print.

———. *mother, not mother*. Toronto: Mercury P, 1992. Print.

———. *Wild Mother Dancing: Maternal Narrative in Canadian Literature*. Winnipeg: U of Manitoba P, 1993. Print.

Bromwich, David. "Parody, Pastiche, Allusion." *Lyric Poetry: Beyond New Criticism*. Ed. Chavia Hosek and Patricia Parker. Ithaca: Cornell UP, 1985. 328–44. Print.

Brontë, Emily. *Wuthering Heights*. 1847. New York: Oxford UP, 1995. Print.

Brossard, Nicole. *These Our Mothers or: The Disintegrating Chapter*. 1977. Trans. Barbara Godard. Toronto: Coach House, 1983. Print.

Butler, Judith. *Antigone's Claim: Kinship Between Life and Death*. New York: Columbia UP, 2000. Print.

———. *The Psychic Life of Power: Theories in Subjection*. Stanford: Stanford UP, 1997. Print.

Camus, Albert. *The Outsider (L'Étranger)*. 1942. Trans. Stuart Gilbert. London: Hamish Hamilton, 1946. Print.

Carson, Anne. "The Anthropology of Water." *Plainwater* 113–260.

———. *Autobiography of Red: A Novel in Verse*. Toronto: Random, 1999. Print.

———. *Decreation: Poetry, Essays, Opera*. New York: Knopf, 2005. 153–81. Print.

———. *Eros the Bittersweet*. Normal: Dalkey Archive P, 1998. Print.

———. *Glass, Irony and God*. New York: New Directions, 1995. Print.

———. "The Matrix Interview." *Matrix* 49 (1997): 10–17. Print.

———. *Men in the Off Hours*. New York: Knopf, 2000. Print.

———. "Mimnermos: The Brainsex Paintings." *Plainwater* 3–26.

———. *Nox*. New York: New Directions, 2010. Print.

———. "O Dad." *New Yorker*. 12 June, 2011: 102. Print.

———. *Plainwater: Essays and Poetry*. New York: Knopf, 1995. Print.

———. "TV Men: Antigone." *Men in the Off Hours*. New York: Knopf, 2000. 100–1. Print.

Cavitch, Max. *American Elegy: The Poetry of Mourning from the Puritans to Whitman*. Minneapolis: U of Minnesota P, 2007. Print.

Chisholm, Dianne. "The City of Collective Memory." *GLQ* 7.2 (2001): 195–243. Print.

Cixous, Hélène, and Catherine Clément. *The Newly Born Woman*. Trans. Betsy Wing. Minneapolis: U of Minnesota P, 1975. Print.

Clemens, Valdine. *The Return of the Repressed: Gothic Horror from* The Castle of Otranto *to* Alien. Albany: SUNY P, 1999. Print.

Coleridge, Samuel Taylor. "The Nightingale: A Conversation Poem." 1798. *Samuel Taylor Coleridge: A Critical Edition of the Major Works*. Ed. H. J. Jackson. Oxford: Oxford UP, 1985. 99–101. Print.

Crozier, Lorna. *Inventing the Hawk*. Toronto: McClelland, 1992. Print.

Davey, Frank. *Canadian Literary Power*. Edmonton: NeWest, 1994. Print.

de Lauretis, Teresa. "Sexual Indifference and Lesbian Representation." *Performing Feminisms: Feminist Critical Theory and Theatre*. Ed. Sue-Ellen Case. Baltimore: Johns Hopkins UP, 1990. 17–30. Print.

de Man, Paul. "Autobiography as De-Facement." *The Rhetoric of Romanticism*. New York: Columbia UP, 1984. 67–82. Print.

Derrida, Jacques. *Archive Fever: A Freudian Impression*. Trans. Eric Prenowitz. Chicago: U of Chicago P, 1998. Print.

———. "By Force of Mourning." *The Work of Mourning*. Ed. Pascale-Anne Brault and Michael Naas. Chicago: U of Chicago P, 2001. 142–64. Print.

———. "Cartouches." *The Truth in Painting*. 1978. Trans. Geoff Bennington and Ian McLeod. Chicago: U of Chicago P, 1987. 183–254. Print.

———. *The Gift of Death*. Trans. David Wills. Chicago: U of Chicago P, 1995. Print.

———. "Mnemosyne." *Mémoires for Paul de Man*. Trans. Cecile Lindsay, Jonathan Culler, and Eduardo Cadava. New York: Columbia UP, 1986. 5–43. Print.

———. *Of Grammatology*. Trans. Gayatri Chakavorty Spivak. Baltimore: Johns Hopkins UP, 1998. Print.

———. "Signature Event Context." *Margins of Philosophy*. Trans. Alan Bass. Chicago: U of Chicago P, 1984. 307–30. Print.

———. *Specters of Marx: The State of the Debt, the Work of Mourning, and the New International*. Trans. Peggy Kamuf. New York: Routledge, 1994. Print.

Diehl-Jones, Charlene. "Knowing That Survives." *Books in Canada* 24.2 (1995): 29–31. Print.

Diogenes Laertius. "Chilo." *The Lives and Opinions of Eminent Philosophers*. Trans. C. D. Yonge. London: Bohm, 1853. 31–34. Print.

DuPlessis, Rachel Blau. *Writing Beyond the Ending*. Bloomington: Indiana UP, 1985. Print.

Edwards, Justin D. *Gothic Canada: Reading the Spectre of a National Literature*. Edmonton: U of Alberta P, 2005. Print.

Eichhorn, Kate and Heather Milne, eds. *Prismatic Publics: Innovative Canadian Women's Poetry and Poetics*. Toronto: Coach House, 2009. Print.

Enright, Robert. "Maestro Margaret." Rev. of *Morning in the Burned House*, by Margaret Atwood. *Border Crossings* 14.2 (1995). 58–60. Print.

Fiamengo, Janice. "'A Last Time for This Also': Margaret Atwood's Texts of Mourning." *Canadian Literature* 166 (2000): 145–64. Print.

Finlay, Len. "Always Indigenize!: The Radical Humanities in the Postcolonial Canadian University." *Unhomely States: Theorizing English-Canadian Postcolonialism*. Ed. Cynthia Sugars. Peterborough: Broadview P, 2004. 367–82. Print.

Fiorentino, Jon Paul, and Robert Kroetsch. "Post-Prairie Poetics: A Dialogue." *Post-Prairie: An Anthology of New Poetry*. Vancouver: Talonbooks, 2005. 9–13. Print.

Foucault, Michel. *The History of Sexuality*. Vol. 1. Trans. Robert Hurley. New York: Random, 1978. Print.

Freake, Douglas. "The Multiple Self in the Poetry of P. K. Page." *Studies in Canadian Literature* 19.1 (1994): 94–114. Print.

Freud, Sigmund. *Beyond the Pleasure Principle*. 1920. Trans. C. J. M. Hubback. London: International Psycho-Analytical P, 1922. Print.

———. *The Ego and the Id*. 1923. Trans. James Strachey. New York: Norton, 1962. Print.

———. "Mourning and Melancholia." 1917. *A General Selection from the Works of Sigmund Freud*. Ed. John Rickman. London: Hogarth P, 1937. 142–61. Print.

Frye, Northrop. *Anatomy of Criticism: Four Essays*. Princeton UP, 1957. Print.

———. "Conclusion." *Literary History of Canada*. Ed. Carl F. Klinck. Toronto: U of Toronto P, 1965. 821–49. Print.

———. "Letters in Canada: 1957." Rev. of *The Boatman*, by Jay Macpherson. *U of Toronto Quarterly* 27 (1958): 434–38. Print.

Fussell, Paul. *The Great War and Modern Memory*. Oxford UP, 1975. Print.

Gallagher, Jean. *The World Wars Through the Female Gaze*. Carbondale: Southern Illinois UP, 1998. Print.

Gallop, Jane. *The Daughter's Seduction: Feminism and Psychoanalysis*. London: Macmillan, 1982. Print.

Gerry, Thomas M. F. "'If Only I Were Isis': Remembrance, Ritual and Writing in Lola Lemire Tostevin's *Cartouches*." *Response to Death: The Literary Work of Mourning*. Ed. Christian Riegel. Edmonton: U of Alberta P, 2003. 179–99. Print.

Gerson, Carole. "The Canon Between the Wars: Field Notes of a Feminist Literary Archaeologist." *Canadian Canons: Essays in Literary Value*. Ed. Robert Lecker. Toronto: U of Toronto P, 1992. 46–56. Print.

———. "The Most Canadian of All Canadian Poets: Pauline Johnson and the Construction of a National Literature." *Canadian Literature* 158 (1998): 90–107. Print.

Gilbert, Sandra M. *Inventions of Farewell: A Book of Elegies*. New York: Norton, 2001. Print.

———. "Life's Empty Pack: Notes Toward a Literary Daughteronomy." *Critical Inquiry* 11.3 (1985): 355–84. Print.

———, and Susan Gubar. *The War of the Words*. New Haven: Yale UP, 1988. Vol. 1 of *No Man's Land: The Place of the Woman Writer in the Twentieth Century*. 3 vols. 1988–94. Print.

Grant, George. *Lament for a Nation: The Defeat of Canadian Nationalism*. Toronto: McClelland, 1965. Print.

Greenfield, Susan. *Mothering Daughters: Novels and the Politics of Family Romance, Frances Burney to Jane Austen*. Detroit: Wayne State UP, 2002. Print.

Grosz, Elizabeth. "Bodies-Cities." *Sexuality and Space*. Ed. Beatriz Colomina. Princeton: Princeton Architectural P, 1992. 241–53. Print.

Gunnars, Kristjana. "Avoidance and Confrontation: Excerpts from Notes on a Longpoem Poetics." *Trace: Prairie Writers on Writing*. Ed. Birk Sproxton. Winnipeg: Turnstone P, 1986. 179–86. Print.

———. *The Night Workers of Ragnarök*. Victoria: Press Porcépic, 1985. Print.

———. "On Writing Short Books." *Stranger at the Door: Writers and the Act of Writing*. Waterloo: Wilfrid Laurier UP, 2004. 81–92. Print.

———. *The Prowler*. Red Deer, AB: Red Deer College P, 1989. Print.

———. Rev. of *Cartouches*, by Lola Lemire Tostevin. *Journal of Canadian Poetry* 11 (1996): 133–35. Print.

———, Marilyn Dumont and Hiromi Goto. "Was the West Ever One?" *Open Letter* 10.2 (1998): 101–21. Print.

———. *Zero Hour*. Red Deer, AB: Red Deer College P, 1991. Print.

H. D. *Helen in Egypt*. New York: New Directions, 1961. Print.

Hébert, Anne. *The Tomb of the Kings/Le Tombeau des Rois*. Trans. Peter Miller. Toronto: Contact P, 1967. Print.

Heiland, Donna. *Gothic and Gender: An Introduction*. Malden: Blackwell, 2004. Print.

Hiebert, Paul. *Sarah Binks*. Toronto: McClelland, 1947. Print.

Holland, Nancy J. "The Death of the Other/Father: A Feminist Reading of Derrida's Hauntology." *Hypatia* 16.1 (2001): 64–71. Print.

Hornyansky, Michael. Rev. of *Welcoming Disaster*, by Jay Macpherson. *U of Toronto Quarterly* 44 (1975): 336–38. Print.

Howells, Coral Ann. "*Morning in the Burned House*: At Home in the Wilderness." *The Contact and the Culmination*. Ed. Benedicte Ledent and Marc Delrez. Liege, Belgium: Language and Literature, 1997. 69–78. Print.

Huggan, Graham. *The Postcolonial Exotic: Marketing the Margins*. London: Routledge, 2001. Print.

Irigaray, Luce. *Speculum of the Other Woman*. Trans. Gillian C. Gill. Ithaca, NY: Cornell UP, 1985. Print.

Jacobs, Dale. Rev. of *Morning in the Burned House*, by Margaret Atwood. *Prairie Schooner* 72.1 (1988): 183–85. Print.

Jamieson, Sara. "Mourning in the Burned House: Margaret Atwood and the Modern Elegy." *Canadian Poetry* 48 (2001): 38–68. Print.

Jardine, Alice A. *Gynesis: Configurations of Woman and Modernity*. Ithaca, NY: Cornell UP, 1985. Print.

Johnson, Samuel. "Milton." *The Lives of the Most Eminent English Poets: With Critical Observations on Their Works*. Vol. I. London: Rivington, 1790. 123–271. Print.

Kahane, Claire. "The Gothic Mirror." *The (M)other Tongue: Essays in Feminist Psychoanalytic Interpretation*. Ed. Shirley Nelson Gordon, Claire Kahane, and Madelon Sprengnether. Ithaca, NY: Cornell UP, 1985. 334–51. Print.

Kant, Immanuel. *Critique of Pure Reason*. 2nd ed. 1787. London: Dent, 1934. Print.

Keahey, Deborah. *Making It Home: Place in Canadian Prairie Literature*. Winnipeg: U of Manitoba P, 1998. Print.

Keats, John. "Ode to a Nightingale." 1819. *The Poetical Works of John Keats*. Ed. H. W. Garrod. Oxford: Clarendon P, 1958. 257–60. Print.

———. "This Living Hand." 1819. *The Poetical Works of John Keats*. Ed. H. W. Garrod. Oxford: Clarendon P, 1958. 553. Print.

Keith, W. J. "Jay Macpherson's *Welcoming Disaster*: A Reconsideration." *Canadian Poetry* 36 (1995): 32–43. Print.

Kertzer, Jonathan. *Worrying the Nation: Imagining a National Literature in English Canada*. Toronto: U of Toronto P, 1998. Print.

Killian, Laura. "Poetry and the Modern Woman: P. K. Page and the Gender of Impersonality." *Canadian Literature* 150 (1996): 86–105. Print.

King, Thomas. *Truth and Bright Water*. Toronto: Harper, 1999. Print.

Kristeva, Julia. *Black Sun: Depression and Melancholia*. Trans. Leon S. Roudiez. New York: Columbia UP, 1989. Print.

———. *Powers of Horror: An Essay on Abjection*. Trans. Leon S. Roudiez. New York: Columbia UP, 1982. Print.

———. *Revolution in Poetic Language*. Trans. Margaret Waller. New York: Columbia UP, 1984. Print.

———. *Tales of Love*. Trans. Leon S. Roudiez. New York: Columbia UP, 1987. Print.

Kroetsch, Robert. "Disunity as Unity: A Canadian Strategy." *The Lovely Treachery of Words: Essays Selected and New*. Toronto: Oxford UP, 1989. 21–33. Print.

Lacan, Jacques. *Écrits: A Selection*. Trans. Alan Sheridan. London: Tavistock, 1977. Print.

———. "The Splendour of Antigone." *The Seminars of Jacques Lacan, Book VII: The Ethics of Psychoanalysis*, 1959–1960. Ed. Jacques-Alain Miller. Trans. Dennis Porter. New York: Norton, 1982. Print.

Lane, Travis. "Hologram Dimensions: The Poetry of P. K. Page." *P. K. Page: Essays on Her Works*. Ed. Linda Rogers and Barbara Colebrook Peace. Toronto: Guernica, 2001. 99–109. Print.

lang, k. d. [Kathryn Dawn]. "Miss Chatelaine." By Ben Mink and lang. *Ingenue*. Warner Brothers, 1992. CD.

Laurence, Margaret. *The Fire-Dwellers*. New York: Knopf, 1969. Print.

———. *The Stone Angel*. Toronto: McClelland, 1964. Print.

Lee, Dennis. *Civil Elegies and Other Poems*. Concord, ON: Anansi, 1972. Print.

Lee, SKY. *Disappearing Moon Café*. Vancouver: Douglas, 1993. Print.

Leed, Eric. *No Man's Land: Combat and Identity in World War I*. London: Cambridge UP, 1979. Print.

Livesay, Dorothy. *Archive for Our Times: Previously Uncollected and Unpublished Poems*. Ed. Dean J. Irvine. Vancouver: Arsenal, 1998. Print.

———. "Ballad of Me." *Collected Poems* 265–67.

———. *Collected Poems: The Two Seasons*. Toronto: McGraw, 1972. Print.

———. "Daddy's Girl/Jove's Daughter." 1979. TS. U of Manitoba Archives and Special Collections, Winnipeg.

———. *Day and Night*. Toronto: Ryerson, 1944. Print.
———. "Do Not Go Gentle: Poems Old and New." N.d. TS. U of Manitoba Archives and Special Collections, Winnipeg.
———. *Green Pitcher*. Toronto: Macmillan, 1928. Print.
———. "Inheritance." *Selected Poems* 57.
———. "An Interview with Dorothy Livesay." With Marsha Barber. *Room of One's Own* 5.1/2: 13–35. Print.
———. *Journey with My Selves: A Memoir, 1909–1963*. Vancouver: Douglas, 1991. Print.
———. "Jove's Daughter." *Archive* 242.
———. "Lament." *Selected Poems* 59–60.
———. "Look to the End." *Collected Poems* 347–48.
———. *New Poems*. Toronto: Emblem, 1955. Print.
———. "Of Mourners." *Collected Poems* 167.
———. *Phases of Love*. Toronto: Coach House, 1983. Print.
———. *Poems for People*. Toronto: Ryerson, 1947. Print.
———. *Right Hand, Left Hand: A True Life of the Thirties*. Victoria: Porcépic, 1977. Print.
———. *Selected Poems of Dorothy Livesay: 1926–1956*. Toronto: Ryerson, 1957. Print.
———. *The Self-Completing Tree: Selected Poems*. Victoria: Porcépic, 1986. Print.
———. "Self-Portrait." *Archive* 126.
———. "Signature." *Selected Poems* xxi–xxii.
———. *Signpost*. Toronto: Macmillan, 1932. Print.
———. "The Squire of Woodlot." N.d. TS. U of Manitoba Archives and Special Collections, Winnipeg.
———. "The Transplanted." N.d. TS. *Her Father's House*. U of Manitoba Archives and Special Collections, Winnipeg.
———. "Unwritten Letter." 1949. TS. U of Manitoba Archives and Special Collections, Winnipeg.
———. "Unwritten Letter." *The Self-Completing Tree: Selected Poems*. Victoria: Porcépic, 1986. 10. Print.
———. "West Coast." *Collected Poems* 140–45.
———. *A Winnipeg Childhood*. Winnipeg: Peguis, 1973. Print.
Macpherson, Jay. "Absence, Havoc." *Welcoming* 15.
———. "The Anagogic Man." *Boatman* 56.
———. "The Beauty of Job's Daughters." *Boatman and Other* 75.
———. *The Boatman*. Toronto: Oxford UP, 1957. Print.
———. *The Boatman and Other Poems*. Toronto: Oxford UP, 1968. Print.
———. "Conjuring the Dead." *Welcoming* 14.
———. "Discovery." *Welcoming* 43.
———. "The End." *Welcoming* 59.
———. "The Fisherman." *Boatman* 70.
———. "A Garden Shut." *Boatman and Other* 78–79.

———. "Karloff Poem." *Welcoming* 37.
———. "Lady Haunts Ghosts." *Welcoming* 23.
———. "Lost Books & Dead Letters." *Welcoming* 10.
———. "The Love-Song of Jenny Lear." *Boatman and Other* 85.
———. "Love-Song II of Jenny Lear." *Boatman and Other* 86.
———. "Masters & Servants." *Welcoming* 10.
———. "No Man's Nightingale." *Boatman* xi.
———. "Notes & Acknowledgements." *Welcoming* 63.
———. "Orion." *Welcoming* 39.
———. "Phoenix." *Boatman* 66.
———. "Poets & Muses." *Welcoming* 9.
———. "Playing." *Welcoming* 55.
———. *Poems Twice Told: The Boatman and Welcoming Disaster.* Toronto: Oxford UP, 1981. Print.
———. "Poor Child." *Boatman* 5.
———. "Some Ghosts & Some Ghouls." *Welcoming* 23.
———. *The Spirit of Solitude: Conventions and Continuities of Late Romance.* New Haven: Yale UP, 1982. Print.
———. "Still waiting for the spark from heaven." *Welcoming* 12.
———. "Substitutions." *Welcoming* 16–17.
———. "They Return." *Welcoming* 39.
———. Untitled article. *U of Toronto Quarterly* 61.3 (1992): 388. Print.
———. *Welcoming Disaster.* Toronto: Saannes, 1974. Print.
———. "The Well." *Welcoming* 38.
———. "What Falada Said." *Welcoming* 52.
———. "While Philomel's Unmeasured Grief." *Boatman* 30.
———. "A Winter." *Boatman and Other* 73.
———. "The Woods No More." *Boatman and Other* 80.
———. "A World of Glass." *Boatman and Other* 80.
Marlatt, Daphne. *Ana Historic.* Toronto: Anansi, 1997. Print.
———. "How Hug a Stone." 1983. *Ghost Works.* Edmonton: NeWest, 1993. 129–87. Print.
McNeilly, Kevin. "Five Fairly Short Talks on Anne Carson." *Canadian Literature* 176 (2003): 6–10. Print.
Mehuron, Kate. "Sentiment Recuperated: The Performative in Women's AIDS-Related Testimonies." *Feminist Interpretations of Jacques Derrida.* Ed. Nancy J. Holland. University Park: Pennsylvania UP, 1997. 165–92. Print.
Millay, Edna St. Vincent. "Elegy Before Death." *Second April.* New York: Kennerley, 1921. 21–22. Print.
Miller, Arthur. *Death of a Salesman: Text and Criticism.* Ed. Gerald Weales. New York: Penguin, 1967. Print.
Milton, John. "Il Penseroso." 1645. *Complete Poems and Major Prose.* Ed. Merritt Y. Hughes. Indianapolis: Odyssey, 1957. 72–75. Print.
———. "Lycidas." 1638. *Complete Poems and Major Prose.* 116–25. Print.

Miller, Nancy K. *Bequest and Betrayal: Memoirs of a Parent's Death*. New York: Oxford UP, 1996. Print.

Mouré, Erin. "Acknowledging the Red Spades: An Interview with Erin Mouré." With Dennis Denisoff. *West Coast Line* 27.2 (1993): 124–35. Print.

———. "The Acts 2." *Furious* 86.

———. "The Acts 3." *Furious* 87.

———. "The Acts 5." *Furious* 89.

———. "The Acts 7." *Furious* 91.

———. "The Acts 14." *Furious* 98.

———. "The Acts 15." *Furious* 99.

———. "The Anti-Anaesthetic." *Open Letter* 9.3 (1995): 13–24. Print.

———. "Betty." *Furious* 78–79.

———. "Breakneck Speed." *Furious* 65.

———. "Changes the Surface: A Conversation with Erin Mouré." *Waves* 14.4 (1986): 36–44. Print.

———. "Fifteen Years." *Furious* 25.

———. *Furious*. Toronto: Anansi, 1988. Print.

———. "Gorgeous." *Furious* 80–81.

———. "Hooked." *Furious* 46–47.

———. Interview by Peter O'Brien. *Rubicon* 3 (1984): 24–44. Rpt. in *So to Speak: Interviews with Contemporary Canadian Writers*. Ed. O'Brien. Montreal: Vehicule, 1987. 230–49. Print.

———. "Miss Chatelaine." *Furious* 54–55.

———. "my existence whenever I start to think." *Sounding Differences: Conversations with Seventeen Canadian Women Writers*. Ed. Janice Williamson. Toronto: U of Toronto P, 1993. 206–20. Print.

———. "Patron." *Furious* 63.

———. "Poetry, Memory and the Polis." *Language in Her Eye: Writing and Gender*. Ed. Libby Scheier, Sarah Sheard and Eleanor Wachtel. Toronto: Coach House, 1990. 201–8. Print.

———. "Pure Reason: Femininity." *Furious* 24.

———. "Pure Reason: Having." *Furious* 18.

———. "Pure Reason: Science." *Furious* 21.

———. "Salt: Condition." *Furious* 71–72.

———. "Speaking of Which." *Furious* 38–39.

———. "Surface." *Furious* 100–1.

———. "Thirteen Years." *Furious* 26.

———. "To Speak of These Things: A Letter." *Canadian Fiction* 57 (186): 132–35. Print.

———. "Wearing the Map of Africa." *Furious* 69–70.

———. "Whose." *Furious*. 15.

———. "With a Small Comb." *Furious* 32.

Namjoshi, Suniti. "Double Landscape." *Canadian Literature* 67 (1976): 21–30. Print.

———. "In the Whale's Belly: Jay Macpherson's Poetry." *Canadian Literature* 79 (1978): 54–59. Print.

Newlove, John. "And the Dead Rose Up From the Water." *Lies*. Toronto: McClelland, 1972. 9. Print.

Oliver, Kelly. *Subjectivity Without Subjects: From Abject Fathers to Desiring Mothers*. Lanham, MD: Rowman, 1998. Print.

Pacey, Desmond. "English-Canadian Poetry, 1944–1954." *Culture* 15.2 (1954). Rpt. in *The Making of Modern Poetry in Canada*. Ed. Louis Dudek and Michael Gnarowski. Toronto: Ryerson, 1967. 160–69. Print.

Page, P. K. "Afterword." *Wisdom From Nonsense Land*. By R. and L. Page. Victoria: Porcépic, 1991. N. pag. Print.

———. *Alphabetical*. Victoria: Reference West, 1998. Print.

———. *As Ten, As Twenty*. Toronto: Ryerson, 1946. Print.

———. "A Biographical Interview." *Malahat Review* 117 (1996): 33–54. Print.

———. "A Conversation with P.K. Page." *Canadian Poetry* 22 (1988): 68–77. Print.

———. *Cullen*. Duncan, BC: Outlaw, 2009. Print.

———. "Entranced: A Conversation with P.K. Page." *P.K. Page: Essays on Her Works*. Ed. Linda Rogers and Barbara Colebrook Peace. Toronto: Guernica, 2001. 110–28. Print.

———. *Evening Dance of the Grey Flies*. Toronto: Oxford UP, 1981. Print.

———. "Father: Melanie's Nite-Book." *The Hidden Room: Collected Poems*. Vol. 1. Erin, ON: Porcupine's Quill, 1997. 146–48. Print.

——— "The First Part." *Evening Dance* 70–74.

———. *The Glass Air*. Toronto: Oxford UP, 1985. Print.

———. *The Metal and the Flower*. Toronto: McClelland, 1954. Print.

———. "Now This Cold Man ..." *Cry Ararat!: Poems New and Selected*. Toronto: McClelland, 1967. 41. Print.

———. *Planet Earth: Poems Selected and New*. Ed. Eric Ormsby. Erin, ON: Porcupine's Quill, 2002. Print.

———. "Portrait of Marina." *The Metal and the Flower*. Toronto: McClelland, 1954. 47–49. Print.

———. "The Selves." *Evening Dance* 62–63.

———. "Spring." *As Ten, As Twenty*. Toronto: Ryerson, 1946. 23. Print.

———. "That's Me Firing Salvador: An Interview with P. K. Page." *West Coast Review* 22.2 (1987): 42–64. Print.

———. "This Cold Man." *The Hidden Room: Collected Poems*. Vol. 1. Ed. Stan Dragland. Erin, ON: Porcupine's Quill, 1991. 59. Print.

———. *Unit of Five: Louis Dudek, Ronald Hambleton, P. K. Page, Raymond Souster, James Wreford*. Ed. Ronald Hambleton. Toronto: Ryerson, 1944. Print.

———. "Voyager." *Evening Dance* 34–35.

———. "War Lord in the Early Evening." *The Glass Air: Poems Selected and New*. Toronto: Oxford UP, 1991. 80–81. Print.

Paul, Nancy. "'Redressing the Balance': Female and Male in the Early Poetry of P. K. Page." *Essays in Canadian Writing* 58 (1996): 115–35. Print.

Phillips, Adam. "Fickle Contracts: The Poetry of Anne Carson." *Raritan* 16.2 (1996): 112–19. Print.

Plath, Sylvia. "Daddy." *Ariel*. New York: Harper, 1961. 49–51. Print.

Potts, Abbie Findlay. *The Elegiac Mode: Poetic Form in Wordsworth and Other Elegists*. Ithaca, NY: Cornell UP, 1964. Print.

Press, Karen I. "Amen, She Said: The Language of Religion / The Religion of Language in Erin Mouré and Lola Lemire Tostevin." *West Coast Line* 32.1 (1998): 123–46. Print.

Pritchard, Allan. *West of the Great Divide: Man and Nature in the Literature of British Columbia. Canadian Literature* 102 (1984): 36–53. Print.

Rae, Ian. "'Dazzling Hybrids': The Poetry of Anne Carson." *Canadian Literature* 166: 17–41. Print.

———. *From Cohen to Carson: The Poet's Novel in Canada*. Montreal: McGill-Queen's UP, 2008. Print.

Ramazani, Jahan. *Poetry of Mourning: The Modern Elegy from Hardy to Heaney*. Chicago: U of Chicago P, 1994. Print.

Reaney, James. "The Third Eye: Jay Macpherson's *The Boatman*." *Canadian Literature* 3 (1960): 23–34. Print.

Rich, Adrienne. "Compulsory Heterosexuality and Lesbian Existence." *Blood, Bread, and Poetry: Selected Prose, 1979–1985*. New York: Norton, 1986. 23–75. Print.

———. "Diving into the Wreck." *Diving into the Wreck: Poems, 1971–1972*. New York: Norton, 1973. 23. Print.

———. "When We Dead Awaken: Writing as Revision." *On Lies, Secrets, and Silence: Selected Prose, 1966–1978*. New York: Norton, 1979. 33–49. Print.

Riegel, Christian. *Writing Grief: Margaret Laurence and the Work of Mourning*. Winnipeg: U of Manitoba P, 2003. Print.

Rooke, Constance. "P. K. Page: The Chameleon and the Centre." *Malahat Review* 45 (1978): 169–95. Print.

Rose, Gillian. *Mourning Becomes the Law: Philosophy and Representation*. Cambridge UP, 1996. Print.

Rossetti, Christina. *Goblin Market and Other Poems*. 1862. New York: Dover, 1994. Print.

Rothenberg, Jerome. *Technicians of the Sacred: A Range of Poetries from Africa, America, Asia, Europe and Oceania*. Berkeley: U of California P, 1968. Print.

Rubin, Gayle. "The Traffic in Women: Notes on the 'Political Economy' of Sex." *Toward an Anthropology of Women*. Ed. Rayna Reiter. New York: Monthly Review P, 1975. 157–210. Print.

Sacks, Peter. *The English Elegy: Studies in the Genre from Spenser to Yeats*. Baltimore: Johns Hopkins UP, 1985. Print.

Saul, John Ralston. *The Unconscious Civilization*. Concord, ON: Anansi, 1995. Print.

Scarry, Elaine. *The Body in Pain: The Making and Unmaking of the World*. New York: Oxford UP, 1985. Print.

Schenck, Celeste. "Feminism and Deconstruction: Re-constructing the Elegy." *Tulsa Studies in Women's Literature* 5.1 (1986): 13–27. Print.
Schiesari, Juliana. *The Gendering of Melancholia: Feminism, Psychoanalysis, and the Symbolics of Loss in Renaissance Literature.* Ithaca, NY: Cornell UP, 1992. Print.
Schleifer, Ronald. *Rhetoric and Death: The Language of Modernism and Postmodern Discourse Theory.* Champaign: U of Illinois P, 1990. Print.
Scobie, Stephen. *Ghosts: A Glossary of the Intertext.* Toronto: Wolsak, 1990. Print.
———. *Signature Event Cantext.* Edmonton: NeWest P, 1989. Print.
Scott, F. R. "The Canadian Authors Meet." *Overture.* Toronto: Ryerson, 1945. 37. Print.
Scott, Gail. "A Feminist at the Carnival." *Spaces Like Stairs.* Toronto: Women's P, 1989. 115–36. Print.
Shakespeare, William. *King Lear.* 1608. London: Oxford UP, 1914. Print.
Shaw, W. David. *Elegy and Paradox: Testing the Conventions.* Baltimore: Johns Hopkins UP, 1994. Print.
Shelley, Mary. *Frankenstein, or the Modern Prometheus.* 1831. Boston: Cornhill, 1922.
Shelley, Percy Bysshe. "Adonais: An Elegy on the Death of John Keats." 1821. *The Complete Poetical Works of Percy Bysshe Shelley.* Ed. Thomas Hutchinson. London: Oxford UP, 165. 430–44. Print.
Silverman, Kaja. *Male Subjectivity at the Margins.* New York: Routledge, 1992. Print.
Smart, Elizabeth. *By Grand Central Station I Sat Down and Wept.* 1946. London: Flamingo, 1992. Print.
Smith, A. J. M. *News of the Phoenix.* Toronto: Ryerson, 1943. Print.
———. "The Poetry of P. K. Page." *Canadian Literature* 50 (1971): 17–27. Print.
Smythe, Karen E. *Figuring Grief: Gallant, Munro and the Poetics of Elegy.* Montreal: McGill-Queen's UP, 1992. Print.
Solway, David. "The Trouble with Annie." *Books in Canada* 30.1: 24–26. Print.
Söderlind, Sylvia. "Ghost-National Arguments." *U of Toronto Quarterly* 75.2 (Spring 2006): 673–92. Print.
Sophocles. "Oedipus the King." *Three Theban Plays: Antigone, Oedipus the King, Oedipus at Colonus.* Trans. Howard Banks. New York: Oxford UP, 1956. 39–84. Print.
Stein, Gertrude. *Everybody's Autobiography.* New York: Random, 1937. Print.
Steiner, George. *Antigones.* Oxford: Clarendon P, 1984. Print.
Sullivan, Rosemary. "Macpherson, Jay." *The Oxford Companion to Canadian Literature.* Ed. Eugene Benson and William Toye. Toronto: Oxford UP, 1997. 715. Print.
———. *The Red Shoes: Margaret Atwood Starting Out.* Toronto: Harper, 1998. Print.
———. "A Size Larger Than Seeing: The Poetry of P. K. Page." *Canadian Literature* 79 (1978): 32–41. Print.
Swinburne, Algernon Charles. "Ave Atque Vale." 1868. *Collected Poetical Works.* Vol.1. London: Heinemann, 1924. 346–53. Print.

Szumigalski, Anne. *Voice*. Regina: Coteau, 1995. Print.

Tennyson, Alfred. "In Memoriam A. H. H." 1849. *The Poetical Works of Tennyson*. Ed. G. Robert Strange. Boston: Houghton, 1974. 163–98. Print.

Tostevin, Lola Lemire. "Breaking the Hold on the Story: The Feminine Economy of Language." *A Mazing Space: Writing Canadian Women Writing*. Ed. Smaro Kamboureli and Shirley C. Neuman: Edmonton: Longspoon, 1986. 385–91. Print.

———. "by the smallest possible margin." *'sophie*. Toronto: Coach House, 1988. 45–48. Print.

———. *Cartouches*. Vancouver: Talonbooks, 1995. Print.

———. "Distance Will Reveal Its Secrets: An Interview with Lola Lemire Tostevin." With Barbara Carey. *Paragraph* 14.1 (1992): 3–5. Print.

———. *Double Standards*. Edmonton: Longspoon, 1985. Print.

———. *Frog Moon*. Dunvegan, ON: Cormorant, 1994. Print.

———. "from Cartouches: hieroglyphs of a visit." *Inside the Poem: Essays and Poems in Honour of Donald Stephens*. Ed. W. H. New. Toronto: Oxford UP, 1992. 281–83. Print.

———. "Paternal Body as Outlaw." *Open Letter* 6 (1986): 77–80. Print.

———, and Smaro Kamboureli. "Women of Letters: Envois between Victoria and Toronto." *Tessera* 5 (1988): 13–26. Print.

Turner, Victor. *Drama, Fields, and Metaphors: Symbolic Action in Human Society*. Ithaca, NY: Cornell UP, 1974. Print.

Twain, Mark. *The Adventures of Huckleberry Finn*. London: Chatto, 1884. Print.

Uppal, Priscila. *We Are What We Mourn: The Contemporary English-Canadian Elegy*. Montreal: McGill-Queen's UP, 2008. Print.

Upton, Lee. *Defensive Measures: The Poetry of Niedecker, Bishop, Glück and Carson*. Lewisburg, PA: Bucknell UP, 2005.

Van Spanckeren, Kathryn. "Humanizing the Fox: Atwood's Poetic Tricksters and *Morning in the Burned House*." *Margaret Atwood's Textual Assassinations: Recent Poetry and Fiction*. Ed. Sharon Rose Wilson. Columbus: Ohio State UP, 2003. 102–20. Print.

Visser, Margaret. *Beyond Fate*. Toronto: Anansi, 2002. Print.

von Maltzahn, Nicholas. Rev. of *Morning in the Burned House*. *Journal of Canadian Poetry* 12 (1997): 5–11. Print.

Wah, Fred. *Waiting for Saskatchewan*. Winnipeg: Turnstone, 1985. Print.

Warland, Betsy. *Bloodroot: Tracing the Untelling of Motherloss*. Toronto: Second Story, 2000. Print.

Weir, Lorraine. "Jay Macpherson." *Canadian Writers and Their Works*. Ed. Robert Lecker, Jack David, and Ellen Quigley. Vol. 6. Toronto: ECW, 1989. 173–218. Print.

———. "Toward a Feminist Hermeneutics: Jay Macpherson's *Welcoming Disaster*." *Gynocritics/La Gynocritique: Feminist Approaches to Writing by Canadian and Québécoise Women*. Ed. Barbara Godard. Toronto: ECW, 1987. 59–70.

Williams, Raymond. *The Politics of Modernism: Against the New Conformists*. Ed. Tony Pinkney. London: Verso, 1989. Print.

Woodcock, George. "Level Best." Rev. of *Morning in the Burned House. Quill & Quire* Feb. 1985: 25. Print.

Woodward, Kathleen. *Aging and Its Discontents: Freud and Other Fictions.* Bloomington: Indiana UP, 1991. Print.

Woolf, Virginia. *On Being Ill.* London: Hogarth P, 1926. Print.

Yeager, Patricia. "The Father's Breasts." *Refiguring the Father: New Feminist Readings of Patriarchy.* Ed. Yeager and Beth Kowaleski-Wallace. Carbondale: Southern Illinois UP, 1989. 3–21. Print.

Yeats, W. B. "Easter 1916." 1921. *The Collected Poems of W. B. Yeats.* London: Macmillan, 1950. 202–5. Print.

York, Lorraine. *Literary Celebrity in Canada.* Toronto: U of Toronto P, 2007. Print.

Zeiger, Melissa F. *Beyond Consolation: Death, Sexuality and the Changing Shapes of Elegy.* Ithaca, NY: Cornell UP, 1997. Print.

Index